How to

for

WITH A HELPFUL SUPPLEMENT
ON BUDGET WINES AND SPIRITS

NEW REVISED EDITION
PREPARED AND EDITED BY JOSÉ WILSON

NEW YORK

EAT BETTER LESS MONEY

JAMES BEARD
and SAM AARON

SIMON AND SCHUSTER

CONTENTS

Why This Book Was Written

When *How to Eat Better for Less Money* was first published, in 1954, it was designed to fill what I felt to be a gap in the cookbook field—the need for a realistic, down-to-earth approach to the subject of eating well without straining the food budget. After a lapse of fifteen years, during which time the book went out of print, the subject has become even more timely, as the cost of living continues to climb. The letters I have recently been getting, asking me if it was possible to get hold of a copy of the original book, convinced me that now was the time to revise it and bring it up to date, adding new recipes and new material.

My special field of knowledge is good food and drink. In my work I travel constantly across the country, giving cooking demonstrations and advising large food companies, and I have the opportunity to see the possibilities that do exist for eating well on a sensible food budget. This book, then, is intended to stimulate the imagination and challenge the ingenuity of the person who enjoys cooking, but who might enjoy it more if only the results were more exciting. It is designed to suggest ways in which you, your family and your guests can eat well, often extremely well, at low cost. It is not a book for the small and special group who don't have to bother their heads about the cost of food (although if they love to eat, they too might benefit from it), but for you, the average American in the middle-income bracket. If your problem is how to eat well on a modest, fairly fixed budget, how to plan more interesting menus and how to make your guests feel that dinner at your house is an experience worth looking forward to, then this book is for you.

Let me begin by saying that I intend to stick to realities. Almost everybody likes a thick juicy steak accompanied by a good burgundy, but most of us can't afford such luxuries very often. However, there is no need to go to the penny-pinching extreme of serving meat loaf made with half a pound of hamburger and one cup of oatmeal, as some people do. Within the limitations of your budget you can set a table that has variety and distinction. You can serve gourmet food.

7

A much misunderstood and misinterpreted word "gourmet." It does not mean rich dishes from the *haute cuisine*. Actually, the word can be applied to the simplest of food—nothing more than a potato cooked to the point at which it bursts its tight skin and shows its snowy interior. It is not the basic cost of the food but the care with which it is selected and prepared that makes it gourmet rather than pedestrian.

The same is true of liquor and wine. You can serve excellent cocktails made from reasonably priced liquor, and you can take a tip from the thrifty French, who drink carafe wines daily at very little cost, and serve our own good jug wines. You can also cultivate the art of cooking with wine, which some people still tend to think of as an expensive practice indulged in by Continental chefs. Actually, it is a homely tradition that has been carried on for centuries in both rich and poor families all over Europe.

For the Wines and Spirits Section of this book, I have asked my close friend and co-author, Sam Aaron, to reveal to you the secrets he has acquired during his thirty-five years in the field. As president of Sherry-Lehmann, Inc., New York's leading wine and spirits merchants, president of the Wine and Spirits Guild of America and chief consultant for the *Wines and Spirits* book in Time-Life's Foods of the World series, Sam Aaron is eminently qualified to guide you through the complexities of getting the best buys for your money. His advice appears later in this book, and I strongly urge you to follow his suggestions if you wish to improve the drinks and wines you serve at cocktail and dinner parties and, at the same time, spend less than you may be doing now. Mr. Aaron's emphasis will not be on Château Lafite-Rothschild, Romanée-Conti, the rare expensive cognac, an exalted sixteen-year-old bourbon, the currently fashionable brand of gin or Scotch, but on how to extract the maximum pleasure from the world of wines and spirits for the minimum amount of money consistent with a policy of seeking excellence and integrity in what you buy.

How to Buy Wisely

Now to the logistics of eating better for the amount of money you can —or would like to—spend. Let me say at the start that there are ways of saving pennies which gain nothing, notably cutting down on quality. If you are going to have a roast, buying an inferior grade instead of prime or choice beef is false economy and a negation of good eating. Similarly, although you can save by substituting margarine for butter in sautéing or baking, there are other ways you can cut costs without depriving your family of the flavor that butter gives to a dish.

Waste is one of the great money drains. When our mothers told us, "Waste not, want not," they were right. It is obviously more economical to shop in quantity if you can, and to plan a week's menus around your major purchases, rather than rushing out at the last minute to get something for dinner and ending up with chops or a steak because you couldn't think of a way to cook any of the cheaper cuts quickly. If you shop for your big food items only once or twice a week, you can plan a series of meals around anything that happens to be a good buy and can be used in different ways—a large turkey, corned beef, or brisket and chicken for a Pot au Feu. However, although there is a lot to be said for continuity in meal planning, it can also be pretty dreary to find yourself doggedly eating up the remains of Sunday's pot roast for the rest of the week. That is where your ingenuity and your freezer come in. If you have a freezer or even a good-size freezing compartment in your refrigerator, you can freeze whole pieces of a roast or parts of a turkey, or use leftovers to make some unusual and tasty dish like moussaka or turkey divan. Look on your freezer as a food bank where you store against a rainy day. You can make up basics like beef ragout in quantity and freeze them—and save on utility bills at the same time by making a lot in one big pot. Then with something really good and filling already on hand, you are not so apt to overspend at the store when you want a meal in a hurry. Three or four made-up dishes, a stack of frozen crêpes and pie shells, frozen spaghetti sauces and frozen stocks will help you turn out a marvelous meal in minutes, and also inspire you to use up some of those leftovers that are hanging around in the refrigerator for crêpe or quiche fillings, soufflés and soups. Time is money, too, and you can make it work for you by cooking intelligently.

The next thing of importance is to shop wisely—and prudently. The smart shopper is a comparison shopper. Make the most of living in a competitive society. Don't always buy at the nearest market just because it is convenient or the manager is nice to you. You may find, if you look around, that the biggest chain supermarket in your neighborhood doesn't always have the best prices on everything—or the best quality. Certain items that you buy frequently may be lower in price at another store, or the produce may be fresher. If you have to walk a couple of extra blocks, it is worth it. The same thing applies to shopping in ethnic food markets or areas, if you are lucky enough to have them in your city or town. All right, so it does mean a bus or subway ride to an unfamiliar part of town, but you will discover the prices are generally much lower, the produce frequently fresher and the choice much more varied; these stores are apt to carry inexpensive foods you may never see in your neighborhood such as stewing fowls, rabbits, pig's feet and hocks, offbeat seafood like squid and eels. And if you like good bread, not the packaged cotton-floss variety, these neighborhoods usually have little bakeries where the bread is freshly baked, honest and good—just like the kind you rave about in Europe. Europeans shop for perishable foods—fresh vegetables, fruits, bread and fish—every day, and if you follow their example, you'll not only have a lot of fun seeking out new places but also find some real food bargains.

On canned goods, supermarkets can usually manage to cut costs because they do a volume business and often pack under their own labels. Watch for sales of canned goods and buy by the case if you have the storage space (but don't buy something you are not likely to use just because it is on sale—that's more false economy). You also save by buying staples such as rice in large packages (or, in markets where it is sold loose, by the pound) but always check the contents and weight of the jumbo package to be sure you are really saving money; so many of those big deals turn out to be a hollow illusion.

How to Cut Food Costs

As I point out in the meat chapter, it pays to buy meat from a butcher rather than packaged, because you can ask for the bones, trimmings and fat. The same thing applies at the fish store: ask for bones and heads for fish stock. If you are not sure of your butcher, check the weight of the meat he sells you at home on your own scales. Also check the cost per pound of boned meats and poultry against the amount of meat you get from a cut or a bird with the bone in. Remember, labor costs are figured into the price of boned meats and poultry, so you are better off doing your own boning. Check, too, ounce for ounce, as to how much it costs to make your own chicken stock or corned-beef hash as against the canned variety, or the price ratio between fresh and frozen vegetables. Fresh vegetables, generally speaking, are a better buy than frozen ones. Stringbeans, broccoli, cauliflower, zucchini and many other vegetables cost less fresh than frozen. Watch for seasonal gluts of fruits and vegetables and buy when they are most plentiful and cheapest. Even prices of fish, meat and poultry vary according to supply and demand. Turkey is cheaper around holiday times, and so is ham. There are certain times of year when inexpensive fish can be found in the fish stores; fresh herring is an example. Most of the catch is smoked or pickled, but you can often find it in the fish stores in winter.

If you are taking a weekend trip to the country in spring, summer or fall, make a point of buying eggs, vegetables and fruit at the roadside stands and farms. A bargain on a bushel basket of dead-ripe tomatoes can be turned into delicious fresh tomato soup or sauce and banked in the freezer. Country supermarkets often have a different variety of foods at better prices than city ones, and it is certainly well worthwhile taking advantage of any good buys and filling the trunk of the car after a weekend expedition. Make a habit of going to parts of your state or neighboring states with a rural area and farmer's markets; it is a fascinating way to spend a weekend for anyone interested in regional American food.

Imagination—the Priceless Ingredient

I am sure you know only too well what the inexpensive and the expensive foods are, so the recipes I have included in this book are based on what anyone can afford to buy. Our grocery stores and markets offer a choice of meats, vegetables and fruits unequaled in any other country in the world, so there is no reason why you cannot serve distinctive meals at all times. We have some great traditional dishes of our own and, given the imagination and the will to try, you can adapt the national cookery of other parts of the world to your needs.

My underlying purpose in this book is to help you develop imagination and interest in your cooking without straining your budget. There is a flavorful, rewarding approach to inexpensive eating, but you have to work at it. Some of the suggestions for meat and poultry dishes may take a little more time to prepare than the average American cook is used to spending, but the results are worth the extra time and effort.

I hope you will read this book thoroughly rather than just leaf through it for recipes. If you skim hurriedly, you may miss valuable ideas for saving money and planning your meals economically. Taken as a whole, it presents an approach to food and cooking that will give your meals individuality and zest at modest cost and also, I hope, help you find out for yourself that cooking, like all creative arts, can be the greatest of fun and the most satisfying means of self-expression.

JAMES A. BEARD

Picking the Right Equipment

Too few people, I have found, appreciate the fact that you can't be a good cook or a thrifty cook without using good equipment. Pans that are too thin will not distribute heat evenly; they burn and scorch food. Cheap knives that can't be sharpened properly are another kitchen bugaboo. They make even the simplest job of chopping or slicing a grim struggle. Just as there is no true economy in buying second-rate food, so you save nothing by buying cheap equipment. It does not perform properly and soon is unusable. Good pans of heavy metal and top-quality carbon steel knives (provided they are cared for and sharpened regularly) will last a lifetime. The initial investment may seem high, but amortized over fifteen or twenty years the cost amounts to no more than a dollar or two a month for a whole *batterie de cuisine*, surely a price well worth paying for properly cooked food. I feel the same way about electric appliances. The only blenders and mixers worth having are those with good motors, sturdily constructed. Personally, I consider the Kitchen Aid mixer, which I have used happily for many years, to be the best buy on the market—and most serious professional cooks agree with me. It *is* expensive, almost three times as costly as other mixers, but it stands up to constant hard wear and comes with a range of attachments for everything from mixing bread dough to freezing ice cream that makes it an auxiliary kitchen in itself.

I am not going to recommend any particular brand of cooking equipment, beyond saying that pans should be really heavy-duty and have tight-fitting lids. The finest material, in my opinion, is heavy copper with an alloy or stainless steel lining, followed by heavy cast aluminum and heavy stainless steel, cast iron (but don't use this for wine cookery, as it discolors the liquid) and enameled cast iron. For baking, stainless-steel pans are preferable to tin or aluminum; they won't warp and are easier to clean. When it comes to simplifying cleanup, I am a great advocate of aluminum-foil broiling pans that can be washed and used over and over again. Anything that saves time and work in the kitchen is to be encouraged and adopted. Another absolute essential, to me, is a good meat thermometer, the kind that registers from zero so that you can test the temperature of meat when it comes out of the refrigerator as well as during cooking. There is one such meat thermometer on the market, made by Taylor. Again, it is expensive, but well worth the price. The only way to get properly cooked meat is to use a meat thermometer. All other methods of determining cooking time are, at best, hit-or-miss.

While it may seem an extravagance, I also believe in keeping certain pans for just one cooking job—a pan for omelets, a crêpe pan, a heavy iron skillet for making sauté potatoes and Potatoes Anna, and an enamel or stainless-steel pan for cooking eggs (and sauces with wine).

A few final words on a most important aspect of cooking—the care of equipment. Your working tools should always be kept in mint condition—metal pans clean and polished, knives clean and sharp and stored in a slotted wood case or similar device that stops the edges from banging together, chopping boards and measures wiped off after every use. Good cooks are (or should be) meticulous about keeping their equipment in good shape.

Here is a list of what I consider essential for a kitchen stocked to meet basic requirements. I am not including the usual array of kitchen tools and utensils such as vegetable peelers and pancake turners, which I assume you have already, only the things you need to cook really well—pots and pans of the right sizes, a range of knives for all jobs, and some special pieces for certain dishes or types of cooking.

Pots, pans, baking and roasting equipment

(For pots and pans, select those made of any of the materials previously mentioned.)

1- or 1½-quart saucepan with lid.

2- or 2½-quart saucepan with lid. (One of the saucepans should be of stainless steel or enameled iron, for cooking eggs and sauces with wine.)

Fry pan, 10¼- or 11-inch diameter. Preferably with metal handle so it can go into the oven.

Sauté pan with straight sides, flat bottom, 10¼-inch diameter, with cover. (This pan, which has a capacity of about 3 quarts, can double for other types of cooking.)

Omelet pan, iron, Teflon-coated iron or cast aluminum, 9-inch diameter.

Braising pan or similar large pot with cover, round or oval, 7½- to 8-quart capacity.

Crêpe pan, iron, 6-inch diameter.

Small metal pan for melting butter, warming spirits for flambéing.

Open roasting pan, heavy-gauge stainless steel, approximately 18 inches by 12 inches and 2½ inches deep.

Roasting rack, stainless-steel, V-shaped self-locking type.

Meat thermometer that registers from 0°.

1½-quart china soufflé dish.

Baking dish, oval, about 17 inches by 11 inches, ovenproof porcelain or earthenware.

Tart pans, 10-inch diameter with removable bottoms, or 10-inch flan ring.

Jelly-roll pan, approximately 15 inches by 11 inches.

1- or 1½-quart terrine with cover, porcelain or earthenware, for pâtés.

OTHER COOKING EQUIPMENT

Fish cooker, 18 inches or 22 inches long.

Earthenware crock or bowl, large enough to marinate big pieces of meat.

Food mill, 2 screen, for puréeing and straining.

Mortar and pestle.

Mixing bowls, stainless steel and Pyrex.

"Mouli" triple drum mincer, grater, shredder.

Collapsible steam basket, stainless steel.

Stainless-steel piano-wire whisks, 10 inch and 12 inch.

Stainless-steel and Pyrex measuring cups.

Stainless-steel measuring spoons.

Stainless-steel basting spoon, 13 inches long.

Metal spatula with flexible 8-inch blade.

Metal slotted spatula, turner type.

Set of 3 boxwood spatulas.

Set of wooden spoons.

Large ladle, 6-ounce-capacity bowl.

Small ladle, 1-ounce-capacity bowl (for measuring crêpe batter).

Four-sided stainless-steel box grater.

Metal kitchen tongs.

Metal scoops.

Kitchen or poultry shears.

Larding needle (long, wood-handled type for interior larding).

Trussing needle.

Coarse-grind pepper mill.

Kitchen scales.

Wood chopping block or butcher's block.

Meat grinder, either manual type or attachment for electric mixer.

Kitchen Aid mixer, preferably with all attachments.

Electric blender.

KNIVES (preferably of high-carbon stainless steel)

Paring knife, 3½- to 4-inch blade.

Utility knife, 6-inch blade.

Cook's knife, 10-inch blade.
Slicing knife, 10-inch scalloped blade.
Slicing knife, 9-inch straight blade.
Boning knife.
Butcher's steel, for sharpening knives.
Heavy-duty cleaver, 6-inch blade, for cutting, flattening meat.

According to the types of cooking you do most, add to this list cake and pie pans; loaf pans; cooky sheets; muffin pans; pastry board, bags, tubes and brushes; rolling pins; pastry cutters; a selection of molds and small baking tins; cake racks; colanders and sieves; candy and deep-fat thermometers; a rotary beater; electric hand mixer; rubber spatulas and scrapers; slotted spoons and skimmers; gadgets such as vegetable peelers and melon-ballers, skewers for en-brochette cooking, and so on.

You may notice that I have not included on the basic list a large un-tinned copper bowl for beating egg whites. This is an expensive piece of equipment and, although it does a wonderful job of increasing the expansion of the egg whites for soufflés, I have had perfectly satisfactory results from beating the egg whites electrically in the Kitchen Aid mixer. To my mind, you are better off putting your money into a versatile piece of equipment rather than into one that has only a single use.

Shopping Sources for Equipment

The following stores sell cooking equipment by mail order. The first seven stores listed will send a catalogue without charge. La Cocina has an annual catalogue, for which the charge is $2.00. Jurgensen's has only an annual Christmas catalogue. No catalogue is supplied by A. L. Cahn.

Bazaar de la Cuisine
160 East 55th Street
New York, New York 10022

The Kitchen at Truc
40 Brattle Street
Cambridge, Massachusetts 02138

Hammacher Schlemmer
147 East 57th Street
New York, New York 10022

The Store Ltd.
The Village of Cross Keys
5100 Falls Road
Baltimore, Maryland 21210

Thomas E. Cara Ltd.
517 Pacific Avenue
San Francisco, California 94133

Williams-Sonoma
576 Sutter Street
San Francisco, California 94102

Northwest Gourmet Center
1718 Lake Avenue South
Renton, Washington 98055

La Cocina
5808 Kennett Pike
Wilmington, Delaware 19807

Jurgensen's Grocery Store
409 North Beverly Drive
Beverly Hills, California 90210
and
1071 Glendon Avenue
Westwood Village, California
90024

A. L. Cahn and Sons, Inc.
274 Park Avenue South
New York, New York 10010

Weights, Measurements and Equivalents

3 teaspoons equal 1 tablespoon or ½ ounce.

2 tablespoons equal ⅛ cup or 1 ounce or 1 jigger.

4 tablespoons equal ¼ cup or 2 ounces.

8 tablespoons equal ½ cup or 4 ounces.

16 tablespoons equal 1 cup or 8 ounces or ½ pint.

2 cups equal 1 pint or 16 ounces.

4 cups equal 1 quart or 32 ounces.

16 cups equal 4 quarts or 1 gallon.

When measuring liquids, use a glass measuring cup with graduated markings and hold at eye level.

Beans, dried

White: 1 pound or 2 cups, uncooked, equals 6 cups cooked.

Kidney: 1 pound or 2⅔ cups, uncooked, equals 6¼ cups cooked.

Lima: 1 pound or 3 cups, uncooked, equals 7 cups cooked.

Bread

1 slice dry bread equals ⅓ cup dry bread crumbs.

1 slice soft bread equals ¾ cup soft bread crumbs.

Butter

1 stick equals 4 ounces or 8 tablespoons or ½ cup.

Cheese

1 cup grated cheese equals 4 ounces.

1 cup cottage cheese equals 8 ounces.

Chocolate

1 square baking chocolate equals 1 ounce.

Cream

1 cup heavy cream equals ½ pint and makes 2 cups whipped cream.
1 cup sour cream equals ½ pint.

Eggs

5 medium eggs, shelled, equal 1 cup.
8 medium egg whites equal 1 cup.
12 to 14 egg yolks equal 1 cup.

Flour

Cake: 1 pound equals 4½ cups, sifted.
White: 1 pound equals 4 cups, sifted, or 3⅓ cups, unsifted.
Whole wheat: 1 pound equals 3½ cups.

Fruits, fresh

1 lemon equals 2 to 3 tablespoons juice.
1 medium orange equals 6 to 8 tablespoons juice and 2 to 3 teaspoons rind.

Fruits, dried

1 pound dates equals 2½ cups chopped.
1 pound seedless raisins equals 2¾ cups.

Gelatin

1 envelope equals 1 tablespoon.

Nuts

Almonds:
   1 cup chopped blanched almonds equals 4¼ ounces.
1 pound unshelled almonds equals 1½ cups nut meats.
1 pound blanched, slivered almonds equals 3¾ cups or 6⅔ cups grated.
Pecans:
   1 pound, unshelled, equals 2¼ cups nut meats.
Walnuts:
   1 pound, unshelled, equals 2 cups nut meats.
   1 cup, chopped, equals 4¼ ounces.

Pasta

Macaroni:
   ½ pound, uncooked, equals 4 cups cooked.
Noodles:
   ½ pound, uncooked, equals 4 to 5 cups cooked.
Spaghetti:
   ½ pound, uncooked, equals 4 to 5 cups cooked.

Rice

1 pound or 2 cups, uncooked, equals 6 cups cooked.

Seasonings

A pinch or dash equals 1/16 teaspoon.

Sugar

Brown:
   1 pound equals 2¼ cups, firmly packed.
Confectioner's:
   1 pound equals 2¾ cups.
Granulated:
   1 pound equals 2¼ cups.

SUBSTITUTIONS

For thickening:
  1 teaspoon arrowroot or potato flour or
  2 teaspoons cornstarch equal 1 tablespoon flour.

For seasoning:
  1 teaspoon crumbled dried herbs equals 1 tablespoon chopped fresh herbs.

For sweetening:
  1 cup honey equals ¾ cup sugar plus ¼ cup liquid.
For 1 cup whole milk substitute ½ cup evaporated milk and ½ cup water or ¼ cup dry milk crystals and 1 cup water.
For 1 cup sour milk or buttermilk substitute 1 cup whole milk plus 1 tablespoon lemon juice or vinegar.

When you are buying canned goods, it is helpful to know exactly how much, in terms of cup measurements, you can get from a can. Also, in some cookbooks you will find a No. 2 or No. 303 can listed. These were terms used by the canning industry and are no longer to be found on cans—the label now gives the approximate net weight or fluid measure. For your convenience, we include both descriptions.

Approximate net weight or fluid measure	Approximate number of cups	Industry term
8 oz.	1	8 oz.
10½ to 12 oz.	1¼	Picnic
12 oz.	1½	12 oz. (vacuum)
14 to 16 oz.	1¾	No. 300
16 to 17 oz.	2	No. 303
1 lb. 4 oz. or 1 pt. 2 fl. oz.	2½	No. 2
1 lb. 13 oz.	3½	No. 2½
3 lb. 3 oz. or 1 qt. 14 fl. oz.	5¾	No. 3 cyl. or 46 fl. oz.

The labels of cans or jars of identical size may show a net weight for one product that differs slightly from the net weight on the label of another product, due to the difference in the density of the food. An example would be pork and beans (1 lb.) and blueberries (14 oz.) in the same-size can. Meats, fish and seafood are almost entirely sold under weight terminology.

1

SOUPS

It is hard to understand why the soup kettle has almost become just a pleasant memory. To my way of thinking, a stock made in a large kettle filled with meat and bones is far better than anything put up in cans. If you want to save money and at the same time serve tastier meals, preparing old-fashioned soups is certainly one of the most important steps you can take. There is no truth in the notion that good soup requires a lot of time and effort. After the initial preparation, even the longest-cooking soup can be safely left to simmer by itself to a state of savory goodness, with an occasional check to see that it is not cooking too violently and the liquid reducing too much. Fish soups and cream vegetable soups take almost no time, and with the blender, now a standard piece of equipment in most kitchens, you can whip up a delicious cold soup in a matter of minutes.

A wise cook will always have a good supply of homemade beef and chicken broth on hand in the refrigerator or freezer and make it the basis for an endlessly varied supply of good nourishing soups—from a thick peasant soup to warm the cockles of the heart on a cold winter night to the delicate lightness of the Greek lemon-and-rice soup, Avgolemono, a perfect beginning for a dinner party.

The most wonderful of all soups is the classic French Pot au Feu, a whole meal in itself—in fact, a whole string of meals, for you can easily plan on serving the constituents of the dish three nights running: broth and vegetables one night, meat the next, chicken the third. A Pot au Feu is great food, gourmet food, because it is simple, honestly flavored and thoroughly delicious. If you are wise, you will have it once every week or so in winter and save part of the stock. Add to it the bones from chicken or any fowl that you may have, or chop bones, roast bones or other meat bones and water from cooked vegetables. Cook this down each time until you have a rich and flavorful base for soups, stews, or braising vegetables and meats. Store it in your refrigerator and boil it up once a day to keep it fresh. In the old days, before refrigeration, the stockpot stayed on the back of the wood stove and every day the housewife added a little bit of extra meat trimmings, broth or bones. If you can manage to keep a stock going all the time on your stove, by all means do so. It develops a fine flavor.

POT AU FEU

3 pounds brisket of beef
1 shinbone of beef
2 onions, each stuck with 2 cloves
6 carrots, peeled
3 small turnips, peeled
6 leeks, split and well rinsed
2 cloves garlic
1 bay leaf
A pinch of thyme
1½ tablespoons salt
A few sprigs parsley
1 small (about 3 pounds) fowl

Put the beef into a deep pot or kettle with the beef bone (extract the marrow first, and reserve), onions, carrots, turnips, leeks and garlic. Cover with water (about 4 quarts) and add the bay leaf, thyme and salt. Bring to a boil and boil hard for 5 minutes. Skim off the scum, add the parsley, reduce heat, cover and simmer gently for 1½ hours. Add chicken. Simmer till meat and chicken are tender.

Skim the fat from the surface of the broth. Strain off the broth and serve it first, with the marrow which has been poached for 3 minutes in a little salted water. Then serve the meat, chicken and vegetables, which will be somewhat mushy but flavorful (you can, if you like, add more whole onions and carrots during the last hour of cooking). Accompany the meats and vegetables with French bread or boiled potatoes, coarse salt, hot mustard, horseradish and homemade cucumber pickles. After this, all you need to complete a glorious meal is a salad and some cheese. Drink a red wine.

As I have pointed out, you can stretch the Pot au Feu over three meals by serving the broth, vegetables and marrow for one meal, the meat for another and the chicken for a third. Leftover broth makes a great base for soups.

Here is another way to make an excellent soup stock:

BEEF BROTH

2 pounds shin of beef with bone
1 beef bone or veal knuckle
1 small fowl
1 onion
1 leek
1 rib celery with leaves
1 carrot
1 turnip
A few sprigs parsley
A pinch of thyme or oregano
Salt

Put the beef into a deep pot or kettle with the beef bone or veal knuckle (the knuckle is full of gelatin and adds body to the stock), the chicken and the flavoring vegetables, parsley and thyme or oregano. Cover with water and bring to a boil. Skim off the scum, cover the pot, reduce the heat and simmer for 4 hours, adding about 1 tablespoon salt for each 6 cups liquid after it has simmered for 2 hours. During the cooking time, test the chicken and remove when it is tender. Take the meat from the bones, reserving it for other dishes (such as soups, hash, rissoles), and return the bones to the pot.

After 4 hours, take the pot off the heat and let the broth settle for ½ hour. Line a large colander with a cloth napkin and strain the broth through it. Cool before refrigerating. This will make about 2 quarts broth.

BEEF CONSOMME

2 quarts beef broth
1 pound chopped beef with no fat
Chicken bones (optional)
1 onion stuck with 3 cloves
1 bay leaf
A few celery leaves
1 egg white, slightly beaten
1 eggshell

Put the broth, chopped beef, chicken bones (if you have any left over), onion, bay leaf and celery leaves into a pot and bring to a boil. Reduce heat and simmer until reduced about ¼ in bulk. Strain through a cloth napkin or a tea towel, return liquid to the pan and clarify by adding the egg white and eggshell and beating well with a rotary beater while cooking over the heat for a few minutes. Strain through a fine towel which has been wrung out in cold water. Serve this Beef Consommé hot or use it jellied in the summer.

Jellied Beef Consommé: Add 1 envelope gelatin softened in ¼ cup cold water to each 2 cups boiling Beef Consommé. Stir until thoroughly dissolved, and chill. Or, to use as an aspic for cold meat dishes, stir the hot consommé-gelatin mixture over ice until it gets syrupy and thick, then brush or spoon over the meat and chill until set.

BEEF-STOCK SOUPS

The plain Beef Broth can be used as a base for all kinds of vegetable soups. Estimate 1 cup broth, plus other ingredients, for each serving.

VEGETABLE SOUP

2 quarts beef broth
2 carrots, finely diced
2 turnips, finely diced
3 large onions, finely diced
2 cloves garlic, finely minced
1 twenty-nine-ounce can tomatoes
1 cup peas
1 cup lima beans
¼ cup finely chopped parsley
1½ cups macaroni, broken into small pieces, or other small pasta (optional)
Grated Parmesan cheese

Put the broth, carrots, turnips, onions and garlic into a pot and simmer for 25 minutes. Add the tomatoes, peas, beans, parsley and pasta, if desired. Simmer for 15 minutes. Taste for seasoning.

Serve with grated Parmesan cheese and accompany with crisp buttered toast. This hearty soup may be served as a main course. Follow it with an equally hearty salad, to which you have added hard-cooked eggs and shredded cheese, then a good dessert and you will have a satisfying meal.

BEAN SOUP

1½ cups dried pinto beans, navy
   beans or marrowfat beans
2 quarts beef broth
2 cloves garlic, chopped
1 twenty-nine-ounce can tomatoes
1 cup finely chopped onion
A sprig of thyme
Crumbled bacon

Soak the beans overnight and cook them until just tender. Combine the broth, beans and their cooking water, garlic, tomatoes, onion and a good sprig of thyme in a pot and simmer for 25 minutes. Serve topped with crumbled bacon. Or add plenty of chopped parsley in place of the thyme and top with a dab of sour cream or yoghurt.

VEGETABLE AND CHEDDAR-CHEESE SOUP

4 cups beef broth
½ cup each finely chopped carrot,
   celery and onion
3 cups medium white sauce
1½ cups grated cheddar cheese
Worcestershire sauce

Simmer the broth and vegetables for 30 minutes. Add the white sauce and cheese and let it simmer for about 15 minutes, until well blended. Add a good dash of

Worcestershire sauce. Serve with plenty of crisp toast. This is a very heavy soup.

SPINACH AND CHICK-PEA SOUP

8 cups beef broth
2 cups canned drained chick-peas
1 cup each chopped carrot, onion,
   celery, turnip
1 cup coarsely chopped spinach
2 cups canned or stewed tomatoes

Simmer the broth, chick-peas, carrot, onion, celery and turnip for 30 minutes. Add the spinach and tomatoes and simmer a few minutes longer. Serve with grated Parmesan cheese.

POTATO–LEEK SOUP

6 cups beef broth
4 large potatoes, peeled and cut in
   small cubes
6 leeks, split and well cleaned

Simmer broth, potatoes and leeks for 45 minutes to 1 hour. Taste for seasoning. Serve hot, with a good dab of sour cream on each serving, or cold with a sprinkling of chopped parsley and dill.

CABBAGE SOUP

6 or more cups beef broth
4 carrots, thinly sliced
3 potatoes, peeled and diced
1 small head of cabbage, shredded

Simmer vegetables in broth for 1 hour, adding more broth if necessary. Add to soup small pieces of soup meat, if available, or leftover boiled beef. Serve with chopped parsley and float toasted French bread in the soup.

PEASANT SOUP

1 large head of cabbage, cut in eighths
6 carrots, peeled and quartered
3 or 4 turnips, peeled
Beef broth
Pieces of soup meat

Simmer the vegetables until tender in just enough broth to cook them. Serve in huge bowls, putting in each some of the broth, pieces of the soup meat, a piece of cabbage and some carrot and turnip. Pass large slices of toasted French or Italian bread and a bowl of grated Parmesan cheese with some chopped green onion or chives to sprinkle on the top. With the addition of a little extra boiled beef this soup, served from a tureen, makes a delicious Sunday supper for guests on a cold winter night. Follow it with a salad and a hot dessert, such as Apple Charlotte.

ONION SOUP

6 medium onions, peeled and sliced
Beef or bacon fat
6 cups beef broth
3 ounces dry sherry
6 slices crisply toasted French bread
Swiss or Parmesan cheese, grated

Sauté the onions in the fat until they are brown and soft. Add the broth and sherry and cook 15 minutes. Ladle into individual ovenproof casseroles or bowls, top with a slice of toast sprinkled with grated cheese and put into the oven until the cheese melts and a slight crust forms on top of the soup. This is a good late-evening snack for an after-theater or bridge supper. Have the casseroles all ready except for the toast and cheese topping; it will take just a few minutes to finish.

LEGUME SOUPS

If you have a ham or a piece of smoked pork or a smoked tongue to boil, save the stock and use it to make a good rich split-pea or lentil soup. A leftover ham bone also makes a tasty stock; simmer it in water to cover until you have a rich, flavorful broth. Taste the broth for seasoning.

LENTIL OR SPLIT-PEA SOUP

1½ cups lentils or green split peas
8 cups stock
1 large onion stuck with 2 cloves
1 bay leaf
2 cloves garlic
Salt, freshly ground pepper, to taste
Crisp fried croutons

Soak the lentils or split peas overnight, unless they are the quick-cooking variety. Wash them and add to the stock with the onion, bay leaf and garlic. Bring to a boil, skim off any scum, reduce the heat and simmer until the peas or lentils are thoroughly cooked. Remove the bay leaf and onion and taste for seasoning. Serve the soup as it is, or purée it. Top with the croutons.

VARIATIONS

1. Purée the soup and add slices of cooked frankfurters or knackwurst. Top with chopped parsley.
2. Top the Lentil Soup with sour cream and chopped onion.
3. Scrape bits of ham from the ham bone used for stock and add to the Split-Pea Soup. Serve with hot corn bread. This with a salad and hot apple pie is a big meal.
4. To 4 cups of Split-Pea Soup add 1 cup of tomato purée, ½ cup of finely chopped onion and 1 tablespoon chopped fresh basil or 1 teaspoon dried. Simmer until well blended.
5. To 4 cups of Split-Pea Soup add bits of ham and 2 to 3 tablespoons of curry powder. Serve with a small dab of cooked rice in each soup plate.

LENTIL–CHARD SOUP

1½ cups lentils
2½ pounds Swiss chard (spinach may be substituted)
½ cup olive oil
¾ cup chopped onion
3 to 4 cloves garlic, crushed with salt
1 rib celery, chopped
¾ cup lemon juice
1 teaspoon flour

Wash and pick over the lentils. Cover them with cold water and cook, covered, until tender. Wash the leaves of the Swiss chard or spinach and chop. Add to the lentils with 1 cup water and cook until the chard is done, adding more water if necessary.

Heat the oil in a skillet and sauté the chopped onion, garlic crushed with salt, and celery until vegetables are tender and flavors blended. Add to lentil mixture. Mix the lemon juice and flour and stir into the soup. Cook gently, stirring occasionally, until the soup is rather thick. Taste for seasoning. Cool slightly before serving in soup bowls. Pass crusty French or Italian bread to mop up the juices. Serves 6. This thick and hearty soup tastes delicious served cold the next day.

CHICKEN SOUPS

It is well worthwhile to make your own chicken broth. For a nominal cost you can keep on hand a supply of good tasty broth to use for soups or all kinds of cooked chicken dishes from pot pie to curry. Chicken necks, wings, backs and gizzards make an excellent stock. Or you can buy a whole fowl and use the meat for other dishes.

BASIC CHICKEN BROTH

One 4-pound fowl or 3 pounds necks, wings and backs and 2 gizzards
1 onion
1 rib celery
1 sprig parsley
Salt, peppercorns

Put the fowl or chicken necks,

wings, backs and gizzards into a deep pot with the onion, celery, parsley, salt to taste, and a few peppercorns and water—rather more than is needed to cover the chicken. Bring to a boil. Skim off any scum, reduce heat, cover and simmer for 2 hours. If you are using a whole fowl, remove it as soon as it is tender and cut the meat from the breast, thighs and drumsticks to reserve for salad or other dishes. Return the carcass to the pot and simmer for a further 45 minutes. Remove bones from the broth and strain it through cheesecloth or a linen napkin. Let it cool until any fat that is left rises to the top. Skim this off. To serve, reheat broth. Makes about 2½ quarts.

VARIATIONS

1. To the Basic Chicken Broth, add the chicken meat, cut in fine strips.
2. To the Basic Chicken Broth, add fine noodles cooked in boiling salted water until *al dente*.
3. Add a small amount of raw rice to the Basic Chicken Broth and cook until just done.
4. Combine Basic Chicken Broth with an equal amount of tomato juice. Add a slice of lemon and 1 small onion stuck with a clove. Simmer for 15 minutes, strain.

DOUBLE CHICKEN BROTH

To the Basic Chicken Broth, add another fowl. Bring to a boil, reduce heat, cover, and simmer gently for 3 hours. Remove the fowl, taste the broth for seasoning and add salt if necessary. Strain the broth through a linen napkin. Use the poached fowl for salad or any dishes calling for cold cooked chicken.

DOUBLE CHICKEN CONSOMME

Let the strained Double Chicken Broth cool and skim off all fat, then strain again through a fine linen towel. Add to the broth an egg white, beaten until frothy, and an eggshell. Return to the heat and cook a few minutes, beating well with a rotary beater. Strain once more through a fine towel which has been wrung out in cold water. The broth will now be perfectly clear and concentrated. Serve very hot in demitasse cups. This makes an elegant beginning for a special dinner.

AVGOLEMONO SOUP

8 *cups Double Chicken Broth*
½ *cup washed rice*
Salt
2 *whole eggs*
2 *egg yolks*
Juice of 2 lemons

Bring the chicken broth to a boil, add the rice and cook until tender. Taste for salt.

Beat the eggs and egg yolks until light and frothy, and slowly beat in the lemon juice. Add a little of the hot broth to the egg-lemon mixture, blending it in well so that the eggs do not curdle. Slowly add to the broth in the pan, stirring constantly. Heat through, but do not allow to boil. Serves 6.

CREAM VEGETABLE SOUPS

This is an economical way to use leftover cooked vegetables and to make the most of the seasonal crop, when prices are low, or your own vegetable patch. The basic mixture of purée and stock may be frozen, then defrosted when needed and the cream or milk and thickening added. Served hot in the winter or cold in the summer, cream vegetable soups are substantial enough to make a main luncheon course, with a hearty salad or toasted sandwiches. The Basic Chicken Broth is a wonderful base for cream soups.

BASIC CREAM SOUP

2 cups chicken broth, homemade or canned
1 cup finely cut vegetable (see suggestions below)
1 small onion, minced or grated
¼ cup chopped parsley
Salt, freshly ground pepper, to taste
1 cup cream, half-and-half or rich milk
1 or 2 teaspoons (or more) arrowroot

Put the broth into a pan, add the cut vegetables and simmer until tender. While they are cooking, add the onion and parsley (you may, if you like, sauté the onion lightly in a little butter first). Drain the vegetables, reserving the broth. Purée the vegetables by putting them through a sieve or food mill and return to the broth. Or purée the vegetables with the broth in an electric blender. Taste for seasoning, adding salt and pepper if necessary. Add the cream or milk, put over low heat and add the arrowroot, mixed with a little milk. Stir until soup comes to a boil and thickens. Garnish with chopped parsley, strips of pimiento, chopped chives or a dash of paprika. Serves 4.

These vegetables are suggested for cream soups:

1 cup finely cut asparagus
1 cup finely cut carrots
1 cup finely cut cauliflower
1 cup finely cut celery
1 cup finely cut fresh broccoli
1 cup finely chopped onion
1 cup fresh green peas
1 cup finely cut potatoes and onions or potatoes and leeks
1 cup chopped fresh spinach

Cream of Corn Soup: Follow the Basic Cream Soup recipe above, using 1 cup cooked corn kernels, but do not purée. Simply blend broth and corn kernels with cream and thicken.

Cream of Mushroom Soup: Sauté 1 cup (about ½ pound) sliced mushrooms in 3 tablespoons butter until soft. Proceed as for Cream of Corn Soup.

SEAFOOD SOUPS and BISQUES

There is a trick to making seafood soup which is both a shortcut and an economy measure. This soup, fragrant with an assortment of shellfish, is marvelously satisfying, yet the amount of seafood needed for six persons is fairly minimal.

SEAFOOD SOUP

6 cups milk, half-and-half or
  evaporated milk diluted
  with water
1 tablespoon grated onion
1 teaspoon salt
½ teaspoon freshly ground black
  pepper
¾ cup soft bread crumbs
1½ cups fresh, frozen or canned
  shrimp, crabmeat, lobster
  or cray-fish, coarsely cut up
Scotch whiskey or cognac

Put the milk, half-and-half or diluted evaporated milk into the top of a double boiler with the onion, salt, pepper and bread crumbs. Let the mixture heat through and thicken slightly. Add the selection of seafood and just heat it through. Add a good slug of Scotch or cognac, taste for seasoning and serve. The use of bread crumbs is a vast improvement over the sticky flour-paste thickening which so often ruins a good soup. Serves 6.

SEAFOOD BISQUE

If you are boiling shellfish, such as lobster or shrimp, for dinner, here is a way to make use of the leftover broth. Add to the cooking water 1 onion stuck with 2 cloves, a bay leaf, a sprig of parsley, salt, pepper, a touch of thyme and a dash of lemon juice. When you have taken the cooked meat from the shells, return the shells to the broth and cook the liquid down until it is full of flavor. Add about ½ cup raw rice to 6 cups of broth, and cook until mushy. Put through a sieve, forcing the rice through to act as a thickening agent. The stock can be stored in a screw-top jar in the refrigerator, or frozen in plastic containers. When you are ready to serve the soup, reheat the stock and add 1 cup cream or evaporated milk. Season with salt, freshly ground white pepper, a dash of Tabasco and a pinch of your favorite herb. This makes an excellent luncheon dish the day after a seafood dinner, and if there are any pieces of seafood left over they can be used to garnish the soup.

CLAM BISQUE

12 to 14 fresh clams, or 2 seven-
  ounce cans whole or
  minced clams
1 pint heavy cream
1 teaspoon salt
¼ teaspoon Tabasco
4 small pats butter
1 tablespoon finely chopped parsley
  mixed with a pinch of thyme
2 to 3 tablespoons cognac,
  if desired

Whirl the fresh clams with their liquor or the undrained canned clams in a blender until a smooth purée. Combine in the top of a double boiler with the cream, salt and Tabasco. Heat to the boiling point, stirring occasionally. Put a pat of butter in each of four heated soup cups and ladle the hot soup on top. Sprinkle each serving with parsley and thyme. If desired, add cognac before ladling soup into cups. Serves 4.

CHOWDERS

Chowders are among the most nourishing, satisfying and inexpensive of soups. The old-fashioned New England-style clam or fish chowder is never made with tomatoes, a heresy to Down East aficionados, but simply with a base of onion, salt pork, potatoes and milk or cream. Corn chowder, a vegetable variation, is equally hearty and has the additional advantage of being a quick, easy dish that can be put together in no time for unexpected guests.

NEW ENGLAND CLAM CHOWDER

You can use fresh clams, either hard-shell or soft-shell (razor) clams, or canned minced clams for this. To yield 1½ cups minced or chopped clams, buy 1 quart unshucked or 1 pint (2 cups) shucked clams, or 2 seven-ounce cans minced clams.

1½ cups minced or chopped clams
2 medium potatoes, peeled and diced

3 to 4 slices salt pork (or bacon), cut in small cubes
1 medium onion, peeled and chopped
Salt, freshly ground black pepper
2 cups light cream or evaporated milk
A pinch of thyme
Paprika

If you are using fresh clams, wash them well and chop them, or mince them by putting them through the coarse blade of a grinder, saving all the liquor.

Cook the potatoes in boiling salted water until just cooked but still firm. Drain, saving the liquid, and cook the potato liquid down a little.

Fry the salt pork or bacon in a skillet until brown, remove, and add the onion to the fat in the skillet. Sauté until golden and limp; do not allow to brown. Combine the salt pork or bacon, the onion, potatoes, potato water, clam liquor and chopped raw clams (if you are using minced canned clams, add just the liquor, reserving the clams). Bring to a boil, lower the heat and simmer gently for 5 to 10 minutes. Season to taste with salt and pepper and slowly add the cream or milk. If you are using canned clams, add them at this point with the cream. Gently heat the soup just to the boiling point; do not allow to boil. Stir in the thyme just before serving and sprinkle the top of each bowl of chowder with a little paprika. Serves 4.

CORN CHOWDER

Follow the directions for New England Clam Chowder, but substitute 1½ cups cooked corn kernels, canned corn kernels or canned cream-style corn for the clams, adding them and the corn liquid at the last minute, with the cream.

NEW ENGLAND FISH CHOWDER

Follow the directions for New England Clam Chowder, but substitute 1½ to 2 cups of any cooked, flaked fish for the clams, adding it at the last minute, with the cream.

COLD SOUPS

Cold soups are a wonderful basis for hot-weather meals. Cold split-pea soup or chilled borscht can be a meal in itself, while a more delicate chilled cucumber or avocado soup, teamed with a fairly substantial salad, is fine enough fare for a summer luncheon party.

VICHYSSOISE

8 to 10 leeks, well cleaned
3 tablespoons chicken fat
4 medium potatoes, peeled and diced
2½ cups chicken broth
Salt, freshly ground pepper, nutmeg
Sour cream
Chopped chives

Wash the leeks well, being careful to remove all the grit between the layers. Trim leeks of roots and green part and slice the white part. Melt chicken fat in a pan and gently sauté the white part of the leeks. Meanwhile boil the diced potatoes in salted water until soft.

Add 1 cup chicken broth to the leeks and let them simmer gently while the potatoes finish cooking. Drain and add the potatoes and 1 cup chicken broth. Break the potatoes up with a fork so that they blend in thoroughly. Season with salt and pepper to taste and a little nutmeg.

Put the soup through a fine sieve or food mill and add enough of the remaining ½ cup broth to thin it down to a proper consistency. Chill for 24 hours. Serve icy cold with a little sour cream added to each serving, and top with chives. Serves 4.

CHILLED CUCUMBER SOUP

2 cups chicken broth
2 cucumbers, peeled, seeded and cut into strips
1 tablespoon finely chopped onion
Salt, freshly ground pepper
1 teaspoon either fresh dill or dill weed
2 cups yoghurt
Paper-thin slices of cucumber, fresh chopped dill

Combine broth, cucumbers and onion and cook over low heat until cucumbers are just tender. Whirl in blender with salt and pepper to taste and the dill or dill weed. Cool. Combine with the yoghurt and correct the seasoning. Chill. Serve in chilled cups, garnished with cucumber slices and chopped dill. Serves 4.

COLD SPLIT-PEA SOUP

Prepare Split-pea Soup according to the recipe on page 23. Or, for a quicker version, cook 1½ cups of quick-cooking split peas in 6 cups water with 3 bouillon cubes until tender, season with salt and pepper and put through a fine sieve. Add 3 tablespoons grated onion and chill for 24 hours. Serve in any of the following ways.

1. Add cream or evaporated milk and top with chopped chives or green onion.
2. Add well-chilled tomato sauce and a dash of curry powder. Top with chopped almonds.
3. Add cream or evaporated milk and serve with chopped hard-cooked egg and thinly sliced cucumber.

CHILLED BORSCHT

6 to 8 young beets, peeled and coarsely grated
1 small head cabbage, cut in eighths
1 small onion, grated
1 bay leaf
1½ teaspoons salt
1 lemon, cut in thin slices
Beef Broth or canned consommé
Sour cream, thinly sliced cucumber, chopped hard-cooked egg

Put the grated beets in a deep kettle with the cabbage, onion, bay leaf, salt, lemon, and enough broth or canned consommé to cover. Bring to a boil, cover with lid, and reduce heat. Simmer for 1 hour. Purée the vegetables, return them to the broth and chill thoroughly. Serve cold, topped with sour cream, cucumber slices and chopped egg. Serves 4 to 6.

QUICK ICED TOMATO SOUP

1 10½-ounce can condensed tomato soup
1½ cups sour cream
1 teaspoon fresh chopped basil or dried basil
1 tablespoon grated onion
½ teaspoon salt
½ teaspoon freshly ground black pepper
Ice cubes

Just before you are ready to serve, combine all ingredients, including ice cubes, in a large cocktail shaker and shake vigorously until well blended and chilled. Pour into 4 chilled cups and garnish with chopped parsley or chopped hard-cooked egg.

BLENDER GAZPACHO

A 29-ounce can (3½ cups) Italian plum tomatoes
1 cup tomato juice
2 cloves garlic, minced
3 to 4 sprigs parsley
A few celery leaves
½ cup fresh basil leaves or 1½ teaspoons dried basil
1½ teaspoons salt
Freshly ground black pepper, to taste

1 to 2 red Italian onions, coarsely
cut up
1 bunch green onions, coarsely cut
up
3 large tomatoes, peeled, seeded
and coarsely cut up
2 medium green peppers, seeded
and coarsely cut up
2 cucumbers, peeled, seeded and
coarsely cut up
4 stalks celery, coarsely cut up
1 tablespoon wine vinegar
2 tablespoons olive oil
¼ cup dry sherry

Put the canned tomatoes, tomato
juice, garlic, parsley, celery leaves,
basil, salt and pepper in a large
skillet. Cover and cook gently for
about 1 hour, or until the flavors
are well blended. Remove and put
through a food mill or force
through a strainer. Reserve.

Chop the cut-up vegetables in
the blender (separate them into 2
or 3 batches, as the blender container should be no more than two-
thirds full) until fairly fine.

Combine the chopped vegetables
with the strained tomato mixture,
adding a little more tomato juice if
necessary. Mix in the vinegar, oil
and sherry, and taste for seasoning.

Chill. Serve very cold. Serves 6
to 8.

This version of Gazpacho, made
with rich chicken broth, is also delicious:

POTAGE ESPAGNOL

8 to 10 ripe tomatoes, peeled,
seeded and chopped
3 cucumbers, peeled, seeded and
finely chopped
6 green onions, finely chopped
3 cups Double Chicken Broth,
chilled
2 teaspoons salt
1 to 2 teaspoons dry mustard
2 tablespoons chopped fresh basil
or 1½ teaspoons dried basil
Garnish: garlic croutons, chopped
green pepper, chopped parsley,
finely chopped hard-cooked egg

Combine the tomatoes, cucumber,
green onions and Double Chicken
Broth. Season with salt, mustard
to taste, and the fresh or dried
basil. Chill for 10 to 12 hours.
Serve with croutons (small bread
cubes browned in garlic-flavored
olive oil), pepper, parsley and egg,
to be sprinkled on top as a garnish.
Serves 6.

2

APPETIZERS

and

FIRST COURSES

The appetizer course plays a very definite and essential part in the structure of a fine meal. Far from being an expendable extravagance, it serves a twofold purpose—it stimulates the taste buds for what is to come and, at the same time, takes the sharp edge off appetite, so that the ensuing courses are savored more slowly, sparingly and appreciatively. If you are trying to cut down on substantial and expensive foods like steak and roasts, a slice of pâté or stuffed shellfish or vegetables at the beginning of the meal can be followed by poached fish or a soufflé without anyone feeling deprived or disappointed. Furthermore, when you are entertaining, the wide range of choices in first courses enables you to balance your menus properly—playing off a light and piquant food against a rich one, an unusual and exotic dish against something simple and basic. Beware, though, of serving foods that are too near together in texture and taste—seafood with mayonnaise before a dish with a cream sauce, for instance. The element of contrast has to be present at all times.

When it comes to cocktail parties, good appetizers are equally important. Today, no hostess plans on just a few potato chips to appease her guests' hunger; she knows she must feed them well. Years of experience have proved to me that substantial and straightforward foods are much more popular, and certainly more economical, than lots of little canapés and fussy, dainty sandwiches. You don't have to provide more than three or four kinds of food, provided they are varied and filling enough. You might have a pâté with French bread, a platter of raw vegetables and a spicy dunk, one or two cheeses or a cream-cheese mixture, and a tray of small appetizers that can be passed around, such as tiny hot Baby Reuben Sandwiches or Stuffed Puffs. Or, if you want to keep it really simple, have hot corned or roast beef or a ham with breads and a choice of mustards (leftovers can be the basis for weekday meals, as suggested in Chapter 4). I have found that the heartier the food, the more the guests tend to concentrate on it rather than on the drinks. It is usually at parties where the fare is sparse that the alcoholic consumption rises sharply.

MEAT APPETIZERS

One of the best foods for a cocktail party is a big mound of Steak Tartare. I have found that most people, especially men, prefer something exceptionally good that they can help themselves to—something that really satisfies. This is perfect cocktail food—hearty but delicate in flavor and seasoned enough to whet the thirst.

STEAK TARTARE

2 pounds raw top round, without fat, finely ground twice
2 medium onions, finely chopped
½ cup capers
¼ cup chopped parsley
2 teaspoons (or more, to taste) Dijon mustard
1½ teaspoons salt
1 teaspoon freshly ground black pepper
Dash of Tabasco
Dash of Worcestershire sauce
½ cup cognac

Combine the chopped steak with the remaining ingredients, mixing well. Mound in a large bowl and serve sprinkled with additional chopped parsley, and with anchovies, a jar of Dijon mustard and toast fingers, rye bread or pumpernickel on the side.

You may, if you prefer, roll the meat mixture into small balls, and then roll the balls in finely chopped nuts or chopped parsley. Spear on toothpicks. Makes about 4 dozen balls.

Here is another hearty meat appetizer, great for outdoor parties. It is a specialty of Elena Zelayeta, the famous Mexican cook and author.

CARNITAS

Cut 1½ pounds lean boneless pork into 1½-inch cubes. Sprinkle with salt and pepper and bake in a 300° oven for about 1½ hours, stirring and draining off the fat a few times. Stick each nugget of meat on a bamboo skewer and finish cooking over charcoal until brown and crispy. Serve the carnitas with *mantequilla de pobre*, or poor man's butter, made by mashing an avocado with chopped tomato and seasoning it with a tart French dressing, and tostados—fresh or canned tortillas, quartered and fried until crisp.

SAVORY MOUTHFULS

For cocktail parties and holiday entertaining, it is always good to have in your repertoire some really original hot or cold sandwiches. You can make a reputation with just a few simple but tasty things. One little sandwich of which I have made literally thousands depends for its success on the subtle blend of flavors—onion and brioche, the French egg bread. These are always a great hit.

BRIOCHE SANDWICHES

Cut Brioche Bread into thin slices and cut these into rounds with a cutter. Peel and thinly slice about 6 or 8 small white onions and chop a large bunch of parsley. Spread the brioche rounds with mayonnaise, top half of them with slices of onion, and salt well. Put a round on top of each and press together firmly. Roll the edges first in mayonnaise and then in the chopped parsley. Chill in the refrigerator several hours before serving.

BRIOCHE BREAD

(a quick version for sandwiches)

2 packages dry yeast
¼ cup warm water
1¼ cups buttermilk, at room
    temperature
2 eggs
¾ cup butter, softened
⅓ cup sugar
2 teaspoons baking powder
1 tablespoon salt
5 to 5½ cups all-purpose flour

Soften the yeast in the warm water in a large mixer bowl. Add the buttermilk, eggs, butter, sugar, baking powder, salt and 2½ cups of the flour. Blend at low speed, then beat 2 minutes at medium speed. Stir in the remaining flour by hand. Turn out onto a lightly floured surface and knead until smooth, about 3 to 5 minutes.

Shape the dough into round loaves and place in greased large brioche molds or 1-pound coffee cans. Cover and allow to rise in a warm place until light, about 45 minutes. Bake in a 350° oven until golden brown and done, about 45 minutes. Remove from pans and brush tops with butter.

Something else that I serve with great success at cocktail parties is a huge platter of small hot biscuits (you can make these with a biscuit mix), split, buttered and filled with any of the following.

1. Slices of chicken or turkey with a little mustard.
2. Fresh, frozen or canned crabmeat (there are several grades of canned crabmeat, and the least expensive will do very well) heated with butter, chopped onion and parsley.
3. Small pork sausages or frankfurters and mustard.
4. Either of the Quick Liver Pâté recipes.

Or you might serve hot corn bread (made from a mix or your own favorite recipe and baked in a flat sheet), cut in squares, split, buttered and sandwiched with small slices of country-cured or Virginia ham. You'll need plenty of these.

Another simple but sensationally effective little hot sandwich is the Baby Reuben, a creation of "Yours Truly," a catering service in Portland, Oregon.

BABY REUBEN SANDWICHES

Put thin slices of corned beef, sauerkraut and Swiss cheese between slices of cocktail rye bread. Brush the outsides of these tiny sandwiches with melted butter and toast on a griddle until the bread is lightly browned on both sides and the cheese melted. Serve piping hot.

For a summer cocktail party, vary the menu by passing little stuffed puffs made as for cream-puff shells.

STUFFED PUFFS

1 cup hot water
½ cup butter
¼ teaspoon salt
¼ teaspoon sugar
1 cup flour
4 eggs (approximately)

Combine the water, butter, salt and sugar in a saucepan and heat until the butter is melted. Add the flour and stir vigorously with a wooden spoon until the dough forms a firm ball and comes away from the sides of the pan. Remove from the pan to a bowl and beat in the eggs, one at a time. If they are very large, you may not need four; if they are small, you may need more. Use enough to make the dough firm, smooth and waxy.

Butter a baking sheet and drop the dough onto it by small spoonfuls, or force the dough through the plain tube of a pastry bag, making small mounds. Bake in a 375° oven until they become dry, puffy shells, about 45 minutes. Split the shells open with a sharp, thin-bladed paring knife and stuff with any of the following mixtures.

1. Finely chopped cooked chicken blended with mayonnaise, chopped toasted almonds, chopped parsley and a touch of tarragon.

2. Finely flaked crab, shrimp, tuna or salmon blended with mayonnaise, a touch of lemon juice and Dijon mustard, a few drops of Tabasco and a little scraped onion.
3. Deviled ham blended with a little mayonnaise and chopped pickle —sweet, sour or dill.
4. Any good liver pâté mixture, such as those below and on pages 36–37.
5. Any piquant cheese mixture such as grated or shredded aged cheddar moistened with cream and spiced with a few grains of cayenne.
6. Guacamole (avocado mashed with a little grated garlic, finely chopped onion and hot chili pepper, seasoned to taste with salt and a little lemon juice).

PATES

Pâtés are one of the best foods for first courses or cocktail parties, for only a small amount of their rich goodness is sufficient to make your guests feel superbly well-fed.

PORK LIVER PATE

This is one of the simplest forms of pâté and very easy to prepare. It may be used for hors d'oeuvre and sandwiches or snacks, and the difference in cost and flavor between this and the pâté sold in shops is quite noticeable.

2½ pounds pork liver
3½ pounds fresh pork with fat
2 medium onions, finely chopped
3 cloves garlic, finely chopped
1 teaspoon thyme

1½ tablespoons salt
2 teaspoons freshly ground black
 pepper
½ cup cognac
4 eggs
½ cup flour
Thin slices fresh pork siding

Grind the pork liver and meat with a good deal of the fat, using the medium to fine blade of the meat grinder. Mix in the onions, garlic, seasonings and cognac, blending well. Beat in the eggs, one at a time, then stir in the flour; this part of the mixing may be done with an electric mixer. Line about 5 or 6 small 2-cup casseroles with pork siding (this is the same cut as bacon, but has not been salted or smoked). Almost fill the casseroles with the pork mixture, leaving room for expansion at the top. Top with more slices of pork siding. Cover the casseroles with their lids or with several layers of aluminum foil, tied on tightly. Stand the casseroles in a baking pan or dish deep enough to allow boiling water to be poured in to reach halfway up the casseroles. Bake in a 350° oven for 2 hours. Remove from the pan and cool for 15 minutes. Remove lids or foil. Put pieces of foil on top of the casseroles and weight each pâté down with a plate and a weight that rest directly on the foil, until thoroughly cooled and firm. Allow casseroles to stand in a dish or pan while cooling. The weighting may result in an overflow of fat.

Another form of pâté, very rich and flavorful, is the French Ril-lettes, made from fresh pork and leaf lard. This can be served in the same way as the Pork Liver Pâté and is especially good at cocktail time or as a first course. Either one keeps for several weeks if properly made, sealed with a layer of fat, and refrigerated.

RILLETTES DE TOURS

3 pounds leaf lard (kidney fat)
3 pounds fresh pork (shoulder, loin
 or leg), cut in small pieces
1 cup water
Salt, freshly ground black pepper

Render the leaf lard in a large pot. When it is melted, add the pork and water. Cover and cook slowly on top of the stove or in a 250° to 300° oven until the meat is so tender that it almost falls apart; this will take about 4 hours.

Remove the meat from the fat and shred it with two forks. Season to taste with salt and pepper. Spoon the shredded pork into small pots with some of the fat, mashing so that the pork absorbs the fat. Ladle enough fat on top to make an airtight cover over the Rillettes. To serve as an hors d'oeuvre, spread on toast.

CHICKEN LIVER PATE

½ pound chicken livers
4 tablespoons butter
2 eggs
½ cup cognac or bourbon
1 onion, chopped
2 cloves garlic, finely chopped
½ teaspoon allspice
1 tablespoon salt

1 teaspoon rosemary
½ teaspoon freshly ground black pepper
1 pound ground pork (sausage meat may be used)
¼ cup flour
Salt-pork strips

Sauté the chicken livers lightly in the butter until they are just firm enough to handle. Trim them and whirl in a blender with the eggs, cognac, onion, garlic, and seasonings.

Blend this mixture with the pork and the flour. Pour into a bread tin or pâté mold lined with salt pork strips, and cover with a lid or with foil. Bake in a 350° oven 1½–2 hours, or until the liquid in the pan and the fat are clear. Cool for 15 minutes. Weight and cool thoroughly.

COUNTRY PATE

2 pounds lean pork
1 pound fresh side pork with fat, diced small
2 pounds ground veal
1 tablespoon basil
1¼ tablespoon salt
1 teaspoon freshly ground black pepper
½ teaspoon Spice Parisienne
1 pound pork liver
6 cloves garlic
2 eggs
⅓ cup cognac
Salt pork strips
2 to 3 strips bacon

Cut half the lean pork into ½-inch dice and grind the rest. Blend with the diced pork fat, veal, basil, salt, pepper, and spice. Divide the pork

liver in half and whirl one half in the blender with the garlic and the eggs, the other half with the cognac, adding a trifle more cognac if the mixture doesn't completely cover the blender blades.

Mix all together thoroughly with your hands or with a heavy wooden spatula. Line a large round earthenware dish with strips of salt pork. Mound the mixture in it, top with bacon strips and bake in a 350° oven, uncovered, 1½ to 2 hours, or until the fat runs clear. Cool and chill.

QUICK LIVER PATE

½ pound Braunschweiger (smoked liverwurst)
½ cup butter
2 teaspoons scraped onion
2 tablespoons chives, finely chopped
2 tablespoons parsley, finely chopped
2 tablespoons cognac or kirsch

Have the liverwurst and butter at room temperature. Combine all ingredients and blend thoroughly with a fork or with an electric mixer. Serve as a spread. The mixture can also be shaped into a long roll or a ball and dipped in chopped toasted nuts or chopped parsley.

MOLDED TUNA PATE WITH COGNAC

A 3- or 4-ounce can chopped mushrooms
1 envelope unflavored gelatin

1 tablespoon cognac
2 6½- or 7-ounce cans tuna
¼ teaspoon Tabasco
½ cup Green Goddess Salad
   Dressing or Homemade
   Mayonnaise (below)
¼ cup parsley leaves

Drain the liquid from the mushrooms into a blender container.
Sprinkle gelatin over the liquid
and allow to soften. Heat ½ cup
water to boiling and add to the
blender. Blend at low speed until
the gelatin is dissolved. Add the
mushrooms and remaining ingredients. Blend at high speed until
thoroughly smooth. Pour into a
4-cup mold. Chill until firm. Unmold and serve with melba toast or
crisp crackers.

GREEN GODDESS
SALAD DRESSING

Thoroughly mix 1 cup mayonnaise,
2 tablespoons each chopped fresh
parsley, chives and tarragon (or 1
teaspoon dried tarragon), 2 teaspoons chopped capers, and 2
tablespoons chopped anchovy fillets. Correct the seasoning.

HOMEMADE MAYONNAISE

2 egg yolks
1 teaspoon salt
½ teaspoon dry mustard
1 pint olive oil
Lemon juice or wine vinegar

Have all the ingredients at room
temperature. Beat the egg yolks,
salt and mustard together in a
bowl, using an egg beater, wire
whisk or electric mixer. Start adding the oil, a few drops at a time,
beating it in thoroughly after each
addition. Continue adding oil until
the mixture is thick, stiff and pale
yellow. Thin with lemon juice or
vinegar. This makes about 2 cups
mayonnaise.

VARIATIONS

Mustard Mayonnaise: Add 1 tablespoon Dijon mustard to 1 cup mayonnaise.

Curry Mayonnaise: Add 1½ teaspoons curry powder to 1 cup mayonnaise, or more, to taste.

Green Mayonnaise: Add ½ cup
mixed chopped green herbs— parsley, chives, tarragon, watercress and
spinach—to 1 cup mayonnaise.

Tartar Sauce: Add 2 tablespoons
finely chopped onion, 2 tablespoons
chopped dill pickle, 2 tablespoons
chopped parsley and lemon juice to
taste to 1 cup mayonnaise.

Rémoulade Sauce: Add 3 finely
chopped shallots or 1 large clove
garlic, chopped, 1 tablespoon capers, 1 tablespoon finely chopped
parsley, 1 teaspoon Dijon mustard,
1 tablespoon chopped fresh tarragon (or 1 teaspoon dried tarragon)
and 1 finely chopped hard-cooked
egg to 1 cup mayonnaise. Taste for
seasoning—the sauce may need a
touch of salt or some lemon juice
or vinegar. Let the sauce stand for
an hour or so to mellow before using.

SEAFOOD APPETIZERS

Fresh, frozen or canned seafood can be prepared and served in innumerable ways to give you a great variety of inexpensive first courses and appetizers. Canned fish also belongs on the tray of *hors-d'oeuvre variés*, served French style with Vegetables Vinaigrette or Vegetables à la Grecque, pâtés, salads and cold sliced meats. With little more than a can of tuna, sardines or anchovies you can always depend on having a tasty, appetizing start to a meal.

SHRIMPS REMOULADE

Peel and devein 1½ pounds shrimp, leaving the tails on. Drop them into boiling salted water, let the water return to a boil, reduce heat to a simmer and cook 4 minutes. Remove and chill thoroughly. For each serving, arrange several shrimp around a small sherbet glass or stemmed glass so that the tails hang down outside. Fill the glasses with lettuce and Rémoulade Sauce for dipping the shrimp. Serves 6.

CLAMS AU GRATIN

½ cup finely chopped mushrooms
½ cup finely chopped shallot or onion
Butter
2 tablespoons finely chopped parsley
2 tablespoons finely chopped tomato
Salt, freshly ground black pepper
36 small clams on the half shell
⅓ to ½ cup dry bread crumbs

Sauté the mushrooms and shallot or onion in 6 tablespoons butter for 3 minutes. Add the parsley, tomato, and salt and pepper to taste. Spoon mixture over the clams. Sprinkle with crumbs, dot with butter and bake in a 400° oven for 5 to 8 minutes, or until clams are just heated through. Serves 6.

CLAMS CASINO

24 clams on the half shell
½ cup butter
⅓ cup chopped shallots or onions
¼ cup chopped parsley
¼ cup chopped green pepper
Lemon juice
Bacon slices, partially cooked

Arrange the clams on beds of rock salt. Blend together the butter, shallots, parsley and green pepper. Spoon over clams and add a squeeze of lemon juice to each one. Cut the bacon into pieces just big enough to cover the top of each clam, and top mixture with bacon. Bake in a 450° oven until bacon is browned and clams are cooked through. Serves 4.

ANCHOVIES

Shop for the large 1-pound or 2-pound tins of fillets in pure oil, packed in Spain, Portugal or Italy. They vary a good deal in quality, from firm to mushy, so it is wise to search out the best brands. If properly wrapped, the opened tins will keep in the refrigerator for 2 weeks.

ANCHOVIES WITH TOMATOES

12 large ripe tomatoes, peeled, seeded and chopped
6 tablespoons olive oil
2 teaspoons finely chopped fresh basil or 1 teaspoon dried basil
2 cloves garlic, finely chopped
1 teaspoon freshly ground black pepper
Salt to taste
Anchovy fillets
Capers
Black olives
Chopped parsley

Cook the tomatoes slowly in the oil with the basil, garlic, pepper and salt. (Be sparing with the salt, as the anchovies will be salty.) When the tomato mixture is thickened (more a fondue than a purée), taste for seasoning. Allow to cool, and spoon into a serving dish. Top with anchovy fillets, capers, and black olives. Add olive oil if needed. Garnish with chopped parsley.

ANCHOVIES NIÇOISE

For this, use a large tin of anchovy fillets. One large tin is equal to 6 to 8 of the small ones. Remove anchovies from the tin and arrange one third of them in a layer in a serving dish. Cover with a layer of chopped shallots or onions, a layer of chopped pimientos and then another layer of anchovies. Top this layer with a layer of chopped ripe olives, a layer of shredded green pepper and a layer of thinly sliced red onion. Top with remaining anchovies and cover lavishly with chopped parsley. Pour over all a mixture of ½ cup olive oil, ¼ cup dry white wine, ¼ cup wine vinegar and a sprinkling of oregano. Marinate for 2 hours. Serves 6 to 8 as a first course.

ANCHOVY SALAD

6 tomatoes, peeled and quartered
3 green peppers, seeded and shredded
20 small green onions, finely chopped
1 large cucumber, peeled, seeded and sliced
2 small cans flat anchovy fillets, drained and separated
½ cup olive oil
Juice of 2 lemons
2 cloves garlic, grated
3 hard-cooked eggs, sliced

Combine all the vegetables and the anchovies and toss lightly with a dressing made by combining the oil, lemon juice and garlic. Serve in a large glass dish garnished with hard-cooked-egg slices. Serve with bread sticks or crackers. Serves 6.

Note: The salad is better if made about 3 hours in advance and allowed to stand in a cool place to mellow. Add the eggs when ready to serve.

SARDINES

Sardines are not a species of fish, but simply the young of a herring-like fish. There are so many different sizes, flavors, and styles of packing of sardines that it is difficult to choose among them. This, however, is how I have come to rate them over the years, in order of excellence:

1. The plain French sardines.
2. Fine Portuguese sardines, especially those packed in olive oil.
3. Spiced sardines, usually French, packed with a lemon slice, bay leaf and herbs.
4. Small French sardines packed in an oval tin with thin slices of truffle and remarkably fine olive oil.
5. Maine sardines packed in olive oil. (These are very much improved and can hold their own with most of the imported brands.)
6. Exceedingly small Norwegian sardines packed in olive oil. (These are quite good, but they do not have the distinction of the others.)

In addition, you can find sardines from nearly every country that has a fishing industry, and they are one of the cheapest of all canned fish. They come in large or medium sizes, boneless or bone-in, skinless or unskinned. Although boneless and skinless sardines are considered to be more delicate, I find they lack the richness of those left intact. Some people like to store their sardines for several years in a cool cellar, turning the tins twice a year, which is supposed to mellow the flavor of the fish and enrich the texture.

To serve sardines, remove them from the tin to a serving dish and garnish with a little chopped parsley and with lemon wedges. They may also be served surrounded with hard-cooked-egg halves and topped with onion rings.

SCANDINAVIAN SPECIAL

This is a dish that has become almost a tradition for some of the great holidays in the northern countries. This particular recipe makes a large amount, but it will keep well in the refrigerator in glass jars or a mold. If you are going to keep it, omit the onion juice.

4 to 5 cans sardines
Salt
1 teaspoon paprika
1 pound (or more) cream cheese
2 tablespoons lemon juice
½ cup chopped parsley
Onion juice

Mash the sardines very fine and season with ½ teaspoon salt and the paprika. Blend the cream cheese with the lemon juice, chopped parsley and a little onion juice. Season to taste with salt. Mix the sardines and the cream-cheese mixture, whipping it up really well until light and well blended. You may need to add a little more lemon juice. Put into a decorative mold or jars. If you use a mold, oil it slightly first. Unmold onto a platter or plate for serving and garnish with watercress. Serve with crackers as a first course or a cocktail spread.

BROILED SARDINES

Carefully transfer the contents of a can of sardines onto a baking sheet and broil for about 5 minutes 4 inches from the heat, basting with a mixture of oil, lemon juice and chopped parsley. Serve on crisp buttered toast as a first course or a cocktail appetizer.

VARIATIONS

1. Sprinkle the sardines with a little curry powder and baste with oil and vinegar mixed with additional curry powder.
2. Baste with a mixture of oil and tomato catsup seasoned with salt and a touch of cayenne. Serve on fried toast.
3. Baste with a mixture of equal parts of oil and dry sherry. Serve on fried toast.

GRILLED SARDINE TOASTS

2 cans sardines
2 tablespoons chopped onion
1 tablespoon lemon juice
½ cup grated Switzerland Swiss or cheddar cheese

Mash the sardines and mix with the onion, lemon juice and cheese. Spread on pieces of bread that have been toasted on one side only (spread sardine mixture on untoasted side) and put under the broiler just long enough for the cheese to melt. These make good cocktail canapés or snacks.

VARIATION

Add a little curry powder and mayonnaise to the mixture.

TUNA

Tuna is a classic part of the hors-d'oeuvre tray. Best for the *hors d'oeuvres variés* are the brands packed in oil and imported from Europe. These contain either solid-pack meat or sliced fillets. If imported tuna is not available, use tuna packed in brine or a solid-pack white meat, draining it well and anointing it with good olive oil ahead of time so that it absorbs some of the oil flavor. Serve tuna with nothing more than capers or parsley for a garnish.

VARIATIONS

1. Serve with artichoke hearts, anchovy fillets and black olives.
2. Surround with hard-cooked egg halves, capers, and anchovy fillets.
3. Serve garnished with alternating slices of hard-cooked egg and tomato. Garnish with capers and black Niçoise olives.
4. Scoop out the seeds and pulp from small ripe tomatoes. Fill with flaked tuna that has been dressed with olive oil and tossed with finely chopped garlic, capers, and parsley. Garnish with black olives and anchovy fillets.
5. Split rather small cucumbers (peeled if waxed), remove seeds, and stuff with flaked tuna fish blended with a mustard mayonnaise. Top with capers and black olives.
6. Place tuna with the oil from the can in a serving dish and cover with finely chopped scallions, chopped

parsley and extra oil if needed. Serve with wedges of lemon.

MUSHROOMS WITH GARLIC BUTTER

4 slices bread
Oil
3 cloves garlic
16 large mushroom caps
Lemon juice
4 tablespoons butter
4 tablespoons finely chopped parsley
Paprika, chopped parsley, for garnish

Fry the bread in oil flavored with 1 garlic clove, until crisp and browned on both sides. Remove and keep hot. Add a little more oil to the pan and sauté the mushroom caps, sprinkling with a little lemon juice, until just cooked through but still firm. Remove to a hot dish. Knead together the butter, 4 tablespoons parsley and remaining 2 cloves garlic, crushed. When well blended and soft, spread the butter on the fried toast and arrange 4 mushrooms on each slice. Dot each mushroom with a little more of the garlic butter, sprinkle liberally with more chopped parsley, and dust with paprika. Put under the broiler for just a minute before serving. Serves 4.

STUFFED MUSHROOMS

3 dozen medium-sized mushrooms
2 cloves garlic, finely chopped
1 cup toasted bread crumbs
½ cup grated Parmesan cheese
1 egg, well beaten
Salt, freshly ground black pepper
2 tablespoons olive oil
Chopped parsley (about 6 tablespoons)
2 ounces butter
1 cup dry white wine

Wipe the mushrooms well with damp paper towels to remove any dirt. Dry well. Remove the stems and chop them finely. Combine with the garlic, bread crumbs, cheese, egg, salt and pepper to taste, and olive oil. Stuff mushroom caps with the mixture, sprinkle with parsley, dot with butter and arrange in a baking pan. Pour in the white wine and bake in a 400° oven for 15 minutes. Serve on buttered toast with a sprinkling of Parmesan cheese, as a first course. Serves 6.

VEGETABLES A LA GRECQUE

Vegetables à la Grecque are poached in a highly flavored sauce until tender but crisp, and are then left to cool in the sauce. Here is a list of vegetables that lend themselves to this type of preparation:

Artichokes (small French variety), whole
Artichoke bottoms
Jerusalem artichokes
Asparagus
Green beans
Brussels sprouts
Carrots

Cauliflower (divided into flowerets)
Eggplant (in cubes or whole small ones)
Leeks
Mushrooms
Small white onions
Zucchini

Sauce a la Grecque

2 cups water
½ cup olive oil
½ cup wine vinegar or
2 tablespoons lemon juice,
plus 1 or 2 lemon slices
1 teaspoon salt, or more to taste
1 teaspoon crushed coriander seeds
1 teaspoon thyme
1 bay leaf
1 or 2 garlic cloves (optional)
½ teaspoon freshly ground black pepper

Combine all ingredients in saucepan or skillet large enough to accommodate vegetable to be cooked. Add vegetables, bring sauce to a boil, then reduce heat and simmer uncovered until tender. By no means allow the vegetables to become soft and mushy.

Variations

1. Substitute white wine for water.
2. For white onions: Add a good pinch of saffron, 1 tablespoon tomato paste and ½ cup small white raisins for the last few moments of cooking.
3. For mushrooms: Reduce the water to 1 cup and increase the oil to ¾ cup.
4. Add herbs to taste. Tarragon, dill, rosemary and basil are most commonly used for this sauce.

VEGETABLES VINAIGRETTE

Any of the vegetables listed above may be poached in broth or salted water, then drained and dressed with a well-seasoned vinaigrette.

Vinaigrette Sauce

Make this in proportions of 3 or 4 parts olive oil to 1 part wine vinegar, with salt, freshly ground pepper to taste, herbs of your choice, and a generous portion of chopped parsley. Garlic is optional.

RAW VEGETABLES WITH DIPS AND DUNKS

If you are having a large cocktail party, you can save yourself a great deal of trouble and expense by serving a variety of raw vegetables (the French call this les crudités) with two or three good dips or dunks. Even the calorie-conscious can enjoy raw vegetables with a clear conscience, and for them you might provide small dishes of coarse salt, one or two of the seasoned salts and a pepper grinder, in case they prefer to skip the sauces. Wedges of lemon to squeeze on the unsauced vegetables are a good idea, too.

Select the best and crispest vegetables your market has to offer. Here are some suggestions for crudités:

Raw carrots, peeled and cut into
fine strips
Radishes—the   red   and   the
white icicle
Celery strips
Green pepper strips or rings
Cauliflower flowerets
Cherry tomatoes
Little green onions
Raw asparagus
Cucumber strips or slices
Fennel slices
Zucchini slices or strips
Raw snow peas
Broccoli buds
Turnips, thinly sliced
Fresh fava beans (to be dipped
in coarse salt)

As a dip for the vegetables, serve
Mustard Mayonnaise, or mayonnaise flavored with crushed garlic
and finely chopped anchovies, or
with any desired combination of
any of the following seasonings:
Worcestershire sauce, chili sauce,
curry   powder,   grated   onion,
chopped chives, chopped parsley,
mashed sardines, capers, chopped
pickles, chopped olives; and with
lemon juice, freshly ground black
pepper or a few grains of cayenne
to taste.

You can also make an excellent
dunk by mixing 1 pint sour cream
with 4 tablespoons grated horseradish, 3 cloves grated or finely
chopped garlic and 1 teaspoon
freshly ground black pepper. Vary
this by adding a touch of curry
powder. Or use a mixture of half
mayonnaise, half sour cream, and
season to taste.

A spicy dunking sauce, which
might be offered as an alternate to
a flavored mayonnaise, comes from
Provence, where it is also used to
sauce eggs. This sauce can be stored
in the refrigerator for days. Recipes
vary, but they all call for anchovies
and black olives.

TAPENADE

18 anchovy fillets with their oil
20 to 24 soft black Italian olives,
    pitted
3 to 4 cloves garlic
¼ cup olive oil
A 4-ounce can tuna in oil
28 capers
1 tablespoon Dijon mustard
¼ cup cognac
Dash of lemon juice

Put the anchovies, olives and garlic
in a blender with some extra oil and
blend until smooth. Add and blend
the remaining ingredients, again
with extra oil if needed. Taste for
seasoning.

VARIATION

Chop ⅓ pound soft black olives
very fine and blend with 1 teaspoon
Dijon mustard. Add 16 to 18
chopped or crushed anchovy fillets,
½ cup capers, ½ cup olive oil, a
touch each of ground cloves and
ground ginger, a dash of cognac and
freshly ground pepper to taste. Beat
well until thoroughly blended.

Two unusual appetizers of dried
legumes make a great hit at cocktail parties. One, from Cuba, is
made with black-eyed peas; the
other, from the Middle East, with

chick-peas. Both cost practically nothing.

CUBAN PUFFS

1 pound black-eyed peas
4 cloves garlic
4 small hot chili peppers, seeded
1 teaspoon salt
Fat for deep-frying

Soak the peas overnight. Next morning, rub the peas between your hands until all the husks are loosened, then put them in water and the husks will rise to the top. Grind the peas with the garlic and chili peppers. Add the salt and beat in an electric mixer or by hand until the mixture is creamy (this takes a long time by hand), adding a little water if necessary. Drop the mixture by teaspoonfuls into deep fat heated to 370° and cook until lightly browned and puffed. Drain on absorbent paper and serve hot.

HUMMUS BI TAHINI

2 cups chick-peas
1 cup tahini (see note)
1½ cups lemon juice
3 cloves garlic, crushed
Salt
Chopped parsley

Soak the chick-peas overnight in water to cover. The next day, drain, pick them over and wash. Cover with fresh water and cook until tender. Drain thoroughly and press through a sieve or food mill.

Beat the tahini and lemon juice alternately into the chick-pea purée, a little at a time. Add the crushed garlic and salt to taste and blend thoroughly. (You can do all the mixing in a blender if you have one; it is much simpler.) Taste for seasoning, adding more lemon juice if necessary. The mixture should be creamy and of a thick dipping consistency. Refrigerate for a few hours or until ready to use. To serve, heap the chick-pea mixture in a bowl and top with a liberal sprinkling of chopped parsley. If the flat loaves of Syrian bread are available in your locality, serve them, split in two and torn into small pieces, as scoops with which to dip into the purée. You may also toast the bread lightly if you wish. Otherwise, serve with very thin slices of French bread.

Note: You may also make this with canned chick-peas. Tahini is a sesame paste sold in Middle East stores.

3
FISH
and
SHELLFISH

It is one of the sadnesses of our American civilization that fish, the incomparable bounty of our oceans, lakes and rivers, is given such short shrift. To many people the frozen, anonymous fillet sold in supermarkets across the land *is* fish. All too few have tasted fish in its perfect state, fresh from the water with all the flavor and texture intact. It may be that this is one reason why it is so hard to buy any but the commonest fish in this country and those at a price that is out of all proportion to their abundance. And when it comes to shellfish, the narrowing down of choice is even greater. Probably the most popular forms of seafood in the United States are lobster, shrimp and the so-called "filet of sole," all of which one must rate among the more expensive foods. However, there are many more shellfish and fish available, not to mention the invaluable salt codfish and smoked haddock, or finnan haddie, and their lack of general popularity often means that they are more reasonably priced. Actually, if you compare the price of fish with that of meat, pound for pound, it is often the better buy, and certainly fish, as a food high in protein, ought to be included in everyone's diet at least once a week.

Like other foods, fresh fish and shellfish have their seasons. At certain times of year they are more plentiful and, therefore, better and cheaper. As seasons vary from area to area, coast to coast, and fish to fish, it is often hard to know what the best buy is at any given season. The best person to give you this information is your local fish dealer or, if you like to do your own research at home, you might study the market report put out by the U.S. Department of the Interior's Bureau of Commercial Fisheries, which lists the catches and receipts in different ports of all fish and shellfish in states across the country, and also the imports of frozen fish.*

* *This annual report is available without charge from the United States Department of the Interior, Bureau of Commercial Fisheries, 201 Varick Street, Room 951, New York, N.Y. 10014.*

Shop Around for Fish

When it comes to buying fish, do a little comparison shopping. Investigate the fish stores and stalls in the foreign food markets in your town or city—the areas where fish-eating people shop—and you will find not only that the choice is greater but also that the prices are apt to be much lower than at your supermarket or local fish store. Demand has a great deal to do with it, also overheads. I have seen fresh shrimp selling at 98 cents a pound in a Puerto Rican produce market when it was half as much again in the midtown areas.

If you live in an area where it is next to impossible to get fresh fish, it is certainly worthwhile to buy frozen fillets or whole small fish, such as rainbow trout. Always keep frozen fish, in its package, in the freezer until you are ready to use it and cook it frozen or immediately after it has thawed, or a lot of the flavor and juices will be lost.

When buying fish, estimate ⅓ to ½ pound edible fish (that is, without head, tail or bones) per serving. If you are buying fish with the bone in, increase the amount to 1 pound per serving.

Finally, a word on cooking fish. In its natural state, fish is tender enough to eat raw, as the Japanese do, but few of us like to eat raw fish. When you cook it, remember that the shortest time possible is best, as long cooking tends to remove the juices and makes the flesh ragged and dry. I have found that an excellent rule of thumb is to give it 10 minutes for each inch of measured thickness, a much better guide than minutes per pound. This applies to any form of cooking—poaching, baking, broiling or sautéing. Then, of course, there is the flaking test: if the fish flakes when tested with a fork or a toothpick, it is done.

As it is not possible (or necessary) to give a detailed course on fish cookery in this book, I have selected two basic methods that can be used for fish fillets and whole fish. The first is cooking en papillote, or in a paper case (this was originally cooking parchment, but now we use aluminum foil), a method that keeps all the juices in fish and permits many flavor variations. The second is the baking of stuffed fish—a good way not only to stretch what you buy at the store, but also to treat the whole fish that are frequently caught during vacations at the seashore or the lake. In addition, I have included some ways to treat less costly shellfish and inexpensive salted or smoked fish, and a good curry recipe that can be made with any selection of seafood available. I hope they will inspire you to give fish a more prominent place on your menu.

FILLETS OF FISH EN PAPILLOTE

Fillets of any white fleshed fish such as cod, haddock, ocean perch, sole or flounder may be cooked in this manner. It is also an excellent way of treating frozen fillets. Thaw them first at room temperature or in the refrigerator until they can be separated easily.

For each fillet, tear off a piece of heavy-duty aluminum foil large enough to encase the fillet completely. Brush one side of the foil with oil or melted butter and place the fillet in the center. Season to taste with salt and a freshly ground pepper and add a squeeze of lemon juice. Add any of these flavorings: 1. 1 teaspoon grated raw onion and 1 tablespoon finely chopped parsley; 2. 1 tablespoon cream and a little grated Parmesan cheese; 3. 1 or 2 teaspoons Duxelles.

Dot fillets with butter and bring both sides of the foil up over the top of the fillet. Make a double fold to seal, and turn up the ends of the foil so that the juices will not run out. Arrange packages on a baking sheet and bake in a 425° oven for 18 minutes. Open one package and test for doneness with a fork or toothpick. If the fish flakes easily, it is done. If not, rewrap and cook a few more minutes. If you like a browned finish on your fish, open the top of the foil and bend it back to expose the fish. Put under the broiler for a minute, or until just lightly browned.

You can also cook small trout, such as the frozen rainbow trout, en papillote.

TROUT EN PAPILLOTE

Season the inside of rainbow trout with salt and pepper and put in a sprig of parsley. Brush the fish with butter, season it with salt and pepper and top with a slice of lemon. Wrap the fish in foil as described above for Fillets of Fish en Papillote and bake in a 400° oven for 10 minutes, then open the foil at the top, turn it back a little and continue baking until the trout flakes easily when tested—this will take only a few minutes. If you wish extra flavorings, top the trout with sliced mushrooms and a teaspoon of chopped chives, or with 1 teaspoon grated onion, a pinch of basil and 2 tablespoons tomato paste. Allow 1 rainbow trout per serving.

If you are dealing with a whole fish or fish steaks, you can make them go farther and taste more interesting by stuffing them. Here is the basic way of cooking a stuffed fish:

BAKED STUFFED FISH

A whole fish weighing from 4 to 6 pounds will serve 4 easily. Have the head and tail removed, if you like, although we feel the fish looks better and certainly stays moister and juicier during cooking if they are left on. Good choices for baking, among the less expensive fish, are young cod and haddock.

More costly, but delicious baked, are mackerel, sea bass and red snapper. Wash the fish well, then stuff it with any of the stuffings given below. Fasten the fish with small skewers or toothpicks. Line a baking pan with heavy foil, allowing it to overlap at the ends (this will help you to lift out the baked fish) and brush it with oil or melted butter. Lay the fish on the foil, rub it with butter and cover with strips of bacon. Bake in a 450° oven, allowing 10 minutes per inch of measured thickness and basting with melted butter. Test for doneness with a fork; the flesh should flake easily. Remove to a hot platter and serve with lemon butter.

VARIATION

Baked Stuffed Fish Steaks: Instead of a whole fish, use 2 large fish steaks, putting the stuffing in between them, sandwich style. Bake as directed above.

BREAD STUFFING

2 large onions, sliced
4 tablespoons butter
1 cup bread crumbs
¼ cup chopped parsley
2 tablespoons chopped celery
   leaves
½ teaspoon thyme
1 teaspoon salt
1 egg, well beaten

Sauté the onion in the butter until soft. Combine with remaining ingredients and mix thoroughly.

VARIATIONS

1. Add sautéed chopped mushrooms.
2. Omit the celery leaves and thyme. Add 2 tablespoons chopped toasted almonds.

CLAM STUFFING

½ cup chopped onion
¼ cup butter
2 cups buttered crumbs
¼ cup chopped parsley
1 seven-ounce can minced clams
   with liquid
Salt, pepper, nutmeg
2 eggs, well beaten

Sauté the onion in the butter. Combine with the crumbs, parsley, clams and their liquid, salt, pepper and nutmeg to taste, and the beaten eggs. Mix well.

VEGETABLE STUFFING

2 onions, thinly sliced
1 clove garlic, chopped
2 tablespoons butter
1 green pepper, seeded and
   chopped
4 ripe tomatoes, peeled, seeded and
   chopped
2 tablespoons chopped parsley
Salt, freshly ground black pepper

Sauté the onion and garlic in the butter until just soft. Add the green pepper, tomato, parsley, and salt and pepper to taste. Mix well.

Mussels are a much neglected form of shellfish. If you can buy mussels cheaply in your neighborhood, here are some good ways to prepare them.

MOULES MARINIERE

1 large onion, peeled and chopped
2 cloves garlic, peeled and chopped
3 to 4 sprigs parsley
2 quarts mussels, bearded and well scrubbed
7 tablespoons butter
Freshly ground pepper, salt
1 cup white wine
2 tablespoons chopped parsley

Put the onion, garlic and parsley sprigs into a heavy enameled cast-iron or stainless-steel pan. Add the mussels, 4 tablespoons of the butter and a few grindings of pepper. Pour the white wine over them, cover the pan tightly and steam over low heat just until the mussels open.

Remove the top shells (or leave them on if you prefer), and arrange the mussels in the lower shells in a hot serving dish. Strain the broth through a cloth and combine it with the remaining 3 tablespoons of butter and the chopped parsley. Heat thoroughly. Taste the broth for salt, and add if necessary (it will probably not need it, as the mussel liquor is salty itself). Pour the broth over the mussels. Serve with plenty of French bread for mopping up the juices and a good brisk white wine. Serves 4.

VARIATIONS

Mussels with Cream: Add 1½ cups of heavy cream to the strained mussel broth and cook down for 3 minutes over brisk heat. Thicken with Beurre Manié (tiny balls of butter and flour kneaded together).

Mussels Gratinéed with Spinach: Shell the cooked mussels and combine them with 1½ cups cooked chopped spinach. Season to taste with salt and pepper. Cook the strained broth with 1½ cups heavy cream and thicken, as for mussels with cream. Blend this sauce with the mussels and spinach and pour into a baking dish. Top with buttered crumbs and ½ cup grated Swiss cheese. Bake in a 425° oven until the cheese melts and the crumbs are slightly browned.

Mussels Poulette: Combine the strained mussel broth with 1½ cups of heavy white sauce and stir over low heat until thoroughly blended and thickened. Stir in the juice of 1 lemon and pour the sauce over the mussels on the half shell.

Clams are usually a good buy. We have given you some appetizer recipes in Chapter 2. Now here are two main dishes, the second of which may be made with canned minced clams if you wish.

CLAM PIE

1 carrot, peeled and cut in thin
julienne strips
1 onion, peeled and cut in thin
julienne strips
1 bay leaf
Salt, pepper
2 cups white wine
2 quarts clams in shell, well
scrubbed
2 cups Sauce Velouté
1 pound mushrooms, sliced
5 tablespoons butter
3 tablespoons sherry or Madeira
Rough Puff Paste (see below)
1 egg, beaten with a little water

Combine the carrot, onion, bay leaf, 1 teaspoon pepper and white wine in a large kettle. Add the clams. Cover and steam over medium heat until the clam shells open. Remove the clams from the shells and strain the broth through a linen cloth. Using some of the clam broth for liquid, make a Sauce Velouté.

Sauté the mushrooms in the butter. Season to taste with salt and pepper. Mix the mushrooms and clams with the sauce and flavor with sherry or Madeira. Taste for seasoning. Pour into a baking dish or pie dish and cool. Place a support in the center of the dish to hold up the crust, and top the pie with rolled-out puff paste. Brush with egg mixture and bake in a 450° oven for 10 minutes. Reduce the heat to 350° and continue baking until the crust is nicely browned. With this pie, drink ice-cold beer or a well-chilled white wine such as Liebfraumilch. Serves 6 to 8.

ROUGH PUFF PASTE

This dough is not as delicate as French puff pastry, but it is exceedingly good.

2¼ cups flour
¼ teaspoon salt
¾ cup lard or butter
Dash of lemon juice
Ice water

Sift the flour and salt and add the lard or butter, cut into pieces the size of large cherries. Mix and blend well. Make a well in the center and add the lemon juice and just enough ice water to make an elastic dough. Press into a ball and chill for 15 minutes.

Place on a floured board and roll into a long strip. Fold away from yourself into three folds. Seal the edges with the rolling pin and turn the pastry halfway around so that the folded edges are to your right and left. Roll again and fold. Chill for 15 minutes. Repeat the process and chill another 15 minutes. Then repeat once more and chill the dough until needed.

SCALLOPED CLAMS

¾ cup (6 ounces) butter
½ cup toasted bread crumbs
1 cup cracker crumbs
Salt, pepper, paprika
2 cups minced clams
2 tablespoons finely minced onion
2 tablespoons finely minced parsley
⅓ cup cream

Melt ½ cup butter and mix with the bread and cracker crumbs. Season with salt and pepper to taste and a dash of paprika. Reserve a third of the crumb mixture and mix the rest with the clams, onion and parsley. Pour into a buttered baking dish and top with reserved crumb mixture. Dot with butter and pour cream over all. Bake in a 375° oven for 20 to 25 minutes. Serves 4.

One of the cheapest and most versatile of fish products is salt codfish, a favored food in many European countries such as Portugal, France and Italy as well as in New England. Here are some of my favorite dishes:

CREAMED CODFISH AND POTATOES

1½ pounds salt codfish
5 or 6 medium-size potatoes, peeled and halved
1½ cups Béchamel Sauce made with half milk, half clam broth
Salt, freshly ground pepper to taste
½ teaspoon ground ginger or ¼ teaspoon grated fresh ginger root
2 hard-cooked eggs

Soak the codfish overnight or for several hours, changing the water once. Drain the codfish (next morning) and put into a saucepan with the potatoes and water just to cover. Bring to a boil, reduce the heat and simmer until the potatoes are tender and the fish flakes easily. Drain and return to the heat to dry out slightly.

Meanwhile, prepare the Béchamel Sauce, using a mixture of milk and clam broth for the liquid. Season with salt, pepper and ginger. Combine with the cod and potatoes and heat through. Chop the eggs and use them to garnish the dish.

VARIATION

Instead of Béchamel Sauce, add heavy cream to the cod and potatoes with 2 tablespoons butter and let it cook down. Season with plenty of freshly ground pepper.

CODFISH WITH AIOLI

2 pounds filleted salt codfish
6 to 8 potatoes
12 carrots
1 pound snap beans
6 hard-cooked eggs
Sauce Aioli (see page 57)

Soak the codfish overnight, changing the water once. Drain and poach in hot water until just tender and flaky. Peel the potatoes and boil in salted water until tender. Cook the carrots whole until tender. Cook the beans until just crisply tender. Arrange the fish and vegetables on a large platter and garnish with hard-cooked eggs, sliced. Serve with Sauce Aioli, plenty of French bread and a brisk white wine or a Tavel rosé. Serves 6.

CODFISH CAKES

1 pound salt codfish
5 medium potatoes, peeled and quartered

3 tablespoons butter
⅓ cup cream or evaporated milk
1 teaspoon ground ginger
1 teaspoon freshly ground black
    pepper
2 eggs
Butter or bacon fat for sautéing

Soak the codfish overnight in cold
water. In the morning, drain, cover
with fresh cold water, bring to a
boil and simmer for 10 minutes.
Remove, cool, and flake the fish
very fine. Meanwhile, boil the potatoes in salted water until just tender. Mash the potatoes with the
butter and cream or evaporated
milk, and season with the ginger
and pepper (do not add salt, as the
codfish will be salty). Add the
flaked fish and the eggs and whip
the mixture until light and well
blended. Form into cakes and sauté
in butter or bacon fat, turning
once, until nicely browned on both
sides. Serve with crisp bacon.
Serves 4.

Another inexpensive fish with great
flavor is finnan haddie.

FINNAN HADDIE DELMONICO

1 pound filleted finnan haddie
Milk
4 tablespoons butter
4 tablespoons flour
1½ cups light cream
Freshly ground black pepper,
    paprika, salt
½ cup grated cheese
Buttered bread crumbs

Poach the finnan haddie in milk
to cover for 15 minutes. Drain and
flake fish. Melt the butter in a
saucepan and blend in the flour.
Gradually mix in the cream (you
may use half cream and half milk
in which the fish was poached, if
you prefer). Season to taste with
pepper, paprika and a little salt if
the fish is not too salty itself. Stir
over medium heat until thickened
and then combine with the flaked
fish. Mix in the ½ cup grated
cheese and pour into a buttered
casserole. Top with buttered
crumbs and more grated cheese.
Bake in a 375° oven for 20 to 25
minutes, or until brown and crusty
on the top. Serve with toast. Serves
4. This makes an excellent brunch
dish.

FINNAN HADDIE REMOULADE

Poach 4 pounds filleted finnan
haddie in water to which you have
added 3 crushed garlic cloves, 2
sliced onions, 1 cup white wine,
1 tablespoon chopped parsley, 1
bay leaf, 1 teaspoon mustard and
½ cup olive oil. Let fish cool in the
bouillon. Drain and serve on a platter with greens with Rémoulade
Sauce.

A wonderfully easy dish that
uses up leftover fish is Kedgeree.
It is also delicious when made with
poached finnan haddie or barbecued sturgeon, even canned salmon
or tuna.

KEDGEREE

Combine in the top of a double boiler over hot water 2 cups flaked cooked fish, 2 cups cooked rice, ½ cup milk, 4 chopped hard-cooked eggs, plenty of chopped parsley and salt and pepper to taste (you can also add a dash of curry powder or paprika if you like). Heat through, mixing well together, and serve at once.

With a hot vegetable, such as buttered carrots, a green salad and dessert, this makes an extremely satisfying meal. Alone, it is an excellent brunch dish. Serves 4.

Next, a party curry that is basically economical because it can be based on the best fish and shellfish buys in your local markets. You can use a selection of any of the fish and shellfish mentioned.

CURRIED SEAFOOD

3 medium onions, finely chopped
2 cloves garlic, finely chopped
4 to 5 tablespoons butter or oil
2 cooking apples
2½ tablespoons curry powder
½ cup white wine
2½ cups fresh or canned clam juice
1 teaspoon ground or grated fresh ginger
½ teaspoon freshly ground black pepper
3 pounds assorted fresh, frozen or canned shellfish and fresh or frozen fish (crab, shrimp, mussels, scallops, lobster tails, lobster, conch, abalone, cod, halibut, haddock, carp, sea bass, flounder, etc.)
Beurre Manié
Salt to taste

Sauté the onion and garlic in the butter or oil until delicately colored and limp. Peel one apple and leave the peel on the other. Core and chop them both and add to the onion mixture. Cook until the apples are tender. Mix in the curry powder and cook 5 minutes. Add the white wine and clam juice and stir in the ginger and pepper. Simmer sauce for 15 minutes or so. Cut the raw fish in strips and add. Simmer gently for 5 minutes. Add the seafood (if large, like lobster tails, cut in pieces) and cook 5 minutes longer. Thicken the sauce with Beurre Manié (small balls of butter and flour kneaded together), stirring until smooth. Salt to taste and add more curry, if you like. Serves 8. Serve from a hot casserole with rice, cooked and colored with saffron and mixed with seedless raisins, puffed in hot water and added during the last 10 minutes of cooking, and a few toasted almonds. If you like, you may press the rice into a buttered mold and unmold it on a hot platter. Top with crisp French-fried onions. Also serve the following accompaniments, in separate little dishes.

Firm bananas, thinly sliced and flavored with a dash of salt and lemon juice.
Thinly sliced cucumbers, sprinkled with oil and lemon juice.
Grated fresh coconut.
Finely chopped hard-cooked eggs.
Chutney; or green tomato pickles.
Crisp, crumbled bacon.
Chopped peanuts.

And finally, one of my favorite recipes for a fish mousse, a wonderful luncheon or buffet dish. You can make this with any white-fleshed fish such as sole, flounder, halibut, haddock or pike or, if you can afford it, with salmon. I happen to like the delicacy and richness of a butter sauce with fish mousse, rather than a white sauce. Sauce Mousseline and Sauce Aurore are both good with this.

FISH MOUSSE

1 pound halibut, trimmed and bones removed, or 1 pound fillets of lemon sole or flounder
3 egg whites
1 cup heavy cream
1 teaspoon salt
½ teaspoon white pepper
Pinch of nutmeg
¼ teaspoon Tabasco
1½ tablespoons finely chopped fresh dill (if available)

Grind the fish twice with the fine blade or cut into small pieces and pound in a mortar. Or you may work it well over a bowl of ice with a wooden spatula. Continue working with the spatula and gradually work in the egg whites over ice. Gradually add cream and flavorings until all the liquid is absorbed. Chill for an hour. Work it again briefly and pour into a buttered 1½-quart fish mold. Cover the mold with buttered waxed paper or brown paper and place in a pan with about 1½ inches hot water. Bake in a 350° oven for 25 to 30 minutes, or until the mousse is firm. Serve with either Sauce Mousseline or Sauce Aurore, both of

which are variations on Hollandaise Sauce. Serves 4.

Blender method for Fish Mousse: Blend the fish with the egg whites, the seasonings and cream. It is best, in my opinion, to divide it into two parts. Blend one part and then the other and combine the two. Chill in a bowl of ice or in the refrigerator for an hour. Proceed as above.

HOLLANDAISE SAUCE

Melt ¼ pound butter in the top of a double boiler over hot water. (If you don't have a double boiler, you can improvise one by setting a heatproof glass bowl in a saucepan, with the rim of the bowl resting on the rim of the pan so that it does not touch the bottom. Add hot water to the pan to just below the level of the bottom of the bowl.) Place double boiler over low heat.

Beat 3 egg yolks, 2 teaspoons lemon juice and ½ teaspoon salt together lightly. Add them to the melted butter, beating constantly, and continue to beat until the sauce is thickened and hot. The water must on no account be allowed to boil or the egg yolks will curdle, so keep the heat low and add cool water to the pan if the water becomes too hot. If the sauce does start to curdle, beat in a spoonful or so of hot water. If the sauce seems too thin, beat another egg yolk, add the hot sauce and then beat over hot water until thickened. Serve sauce at once. If you have to hold it, remove pan from the heat and cool the water to lukewarm by adding cold water. Let the sauce stand over the lukewarm water, covered tightly with plastic wrap so that it does not form a skin.

You may, if you wish, add ¼ teaspoon dry mustard to the sauce, for Mustard Hollandaise, or substitute tarragon vinegar for the lemon juice.

VARIATIONS

Sauce Mousseline: Whip heavy cream and blend in an equal amount of Hollandaise.

Sauce Aurore: Blend 1 tablespoon tomato paste into the Hollandaise.

Sauce Béarnaise: Cook 1 teaspoon dried tarragon, 2 teaspoons finely chopped green onion, 2 teaspoons chopped parsley in 3 tablespoons

tarragon vinegar and 1 tablespoon water with salt and pepper to taste until the mixture almost forms a glaze. Beat this glaze into the egg-yolk mixture for Hollandaise Sauce, then beat into the butter as directed.

SAUCE AIOLI
4 cloves garlic, peeled
2 eggs
1 tablespoon lemon juice
½ teaspoon salt
1½ cups (approximately) olive oil

Place garlic in the blender with the eggs, lemon juice and salt. Blend. Slowly add the oil, blending it in, until the mixture thickens to the consistency of mayonnaise. Taste for seasoning and add more lemon juice, if necessary.

4

MEAT

Meat is our most popular food and, unfortunately, at this time increasingly expensive. It is the basis of most people's diet, an important source of protein, and for many it is essential to good eating. There is no getting around the fact that man is a carnivore—a meat eater.

We do not agree with those who say that half a pound of meat mixed with cereals and flavorings will satisfy your family's need for meat. Nor do we agree with the other extreme view that one has to eat steak, chops or roasts every day. As in everything, there is a middle course that offers many ways to save a dollar here and there on your meat bills.

Know Your Meat Cuts

First of all, if you are going to eat both economically and well, you need to know something about meat cuts. We have found few precut and packaged meats that give the same satisfaction as cuts ordered directly from the butcher. First, when buying packaged meats you sacrifice the use of any bones and trimmings that may have come off the cut. These are an invaluable addition to your stockpot. Secondly, meat that has stood in a paper or plastic package tends to lose juices and flavor. Third, certain stores have a practice of putting the best pieces of meat on top and inferior ones underneath, unsuspected until unwrapped. As the cost per pound is the same whether you buy packaged or freshly cut meat, it is obviously a wise practice to have your meat cut to order, and also to learn something about the cuts—which ones have the least bone and the least connective tissue, for instance. There is no saving in buying a cheaper cut of meat if most of it is waste. We have found that one of the main reasons people buy packaged meat is their ignorance of meat cuts and their dislike of showing that ignorance. The answer to that is to know your butcher and consult him about what you want to make and the cut of meat you should buy. If he is reliable, and most butchers are, he will tell you which are the best buys and how to use them. Always ask him to give you the bits of bones and trimmings that he cuts from your roasts or pieces of meat to add to your stockpot. The first time you go to a butcher, watch the scales carefully to be sure you are getting fair weight. Also check to see how much he trims the cuts before he weighs them. Some butchers will charge you for much more waste meat than others.

Best Buys in Supermarkets

Today, when the neighborhood butcher, like so many small, personal businesses, is disappearing, it is heartening to find that the supermarkets, where most Americans shop, are improving the quality and range of the meat they carry. This is not true of all supermarkets everywhere, but in my travels around the country I have found many chains that show great vision and buying acumen. Among them I would list A&P, Safeway, Bohack's, Gristede's, D'Agostino's and Waldbaum's in the East, Loblaw's in the East and Canada, Kroger's in the Middle West, Jurgensen's in California and Arizona and the Safeway International Markets in the West. By checking the supermarkets in your own and neighboring areas (local branches cater to local tastes and budgets, so cuts and quality differ considerably), you will soon know where to find the best buys in meat. Watch for specials and weekend sales. Many supermarkets feature "loss leaders," a popular cut such as a prime rib roast sold at a loss to attract trade to the store. Some stores (Jurgensen's among them) have sales two or three times a year at which you can buy, at a rock-bottom price per pound, a side or a quarter of top-grade beef, or a whole lamb or pig, and have it cut to your order. You will also find meat outlets that run special sales on meat—sides or quarters of beef cut into roasts, steaks and ground for hamburger. If you don't have a freezer that will take a large quantity of meat, look in the Yellow Pages for plants where you can rent a cold-storage locker.

Shopping Around for Meat

You definitely save money by shopping around for meat, watching for sales and buying in quantity. If you live in a town or city with ethnic markets, you should also investigate the butcher shops. German areas have excellent pork butchers, Italian markets specialize in veal and pork. Local preferences dictate the type and quality of the product. For instance, in New York City, where more roast lamb is eaten than in other parts of the country, some supermarkets have begun to carry the excellent, high-quality frozen legs and racks of lamb from New Zealand, a treat to anyone who likes the delicate flesh of this animal because the cuts are younger and smaller than the domestic version. Country butchers and supermarkets, also geared to local demand and tastes, are other good sources. A friend of mine is lucky enough to have a country butcher who will age steaks for him without charge. This kind of service depends entirely on the butcher and your relationship with him—most stores that sell aged meat charge a premium price for it.

Know Your Grades

It is still possible to find in supermarkets a head butcher who is understanding and knowledgeable. However, there are too many butchers these days who are little more than purveyors of packaged meat, so it pays to familiarize yourself with a few basic facts about meat, such as the various gradings. This too can help you to be economical in your purchasing. Most butchers nowadays carry only two or, at the most, three grades. These, in order of quality and cost, are:

Prime. Look for this purple stamp on the fat. It signifies the best quality. In beef, this is the fattest, heaviest and tenderest and not too easy to find, as most of the nation's prime beef goes to fine restaurants. If you can find it, you will pay for its superior texture and flavor. In lamb, "prime" signifies the young animal, with medium-red flesh, creamy fat, and bones with pink streaks in them. You can tell prime veal by its fine-textured pale, almost white flesh, lightly tinged with pink. Unfortunately, this type of veal is exceedingly hard to get in the United States. Most of the veal sold in our markets is really baby beef. When veal is not slaughtered young enough, it can be tough and tasteless. The best place to look for good veal is in an Italian market—Italians know and demand good veal. Prime pork is well fatted and grayish pink in color.

Choice. Not quite so fancy as prime, but a good honest grade of meat in all categories—the grade that most of us eat practically all of the time. Choice beef is tender, well marbled meat with practically the same qualities as prime. When it is properly aged, few people can distinguish it from prime, and it is almost as costly.

Good. Just what it says—good. It is not choice meat and is not always as tender and flavorful as the better grades, but it is acceptable in most cases as a standard grade of meat. In fact, a beef filet of this grade can be an excellent buy. Other beef cuts, however, will require long cooking or tenderizing.

Utility. Seldom found in the average market, this less desirable grade can be used only for slow-cooking dishes and needs ample flavoring and lubrication to make it palatable. Occasionally, the packers kill a large shipment of cattle just received from the range and sell it off as utility beef. Or there will be an oversupply of sheep and they will be killed off before they have fattened. Such meat is often retailed at sales, and you may be misled by the advertising and think you are buying your usual grade at a reduced price. In the long run it is more economical—that is, less wasteful—to buy the top grade you can afford, unless you have found a butcher who can supply you with unusually fine cuts in the cheaper grades.

When you buy meat, watch carefully and estimate the weight in actual meat apart from the waste and bone. It is no saving to pay $1.20 a pound for a cut and find that you average five ounces of bone per pound. You are better off paying $1.55 a pound for a boneless cut.

The Odd Cuts

Most Americans divide meat into two classes: the choice cuts, such as steaks, roasts and chops, and the thrifty family cuts so beloved by women's magazines and by supermarket advertisers. Most of the others are mysteries, and because of the lack of public demand, odd cuts are often very reasonably priced. Many of the little-known parts of the animal are considered choice morsels by true connoisseurs, and a bit of education on their use will help you bring greater variety to your table and enable you to serve genuinely epicurean meals at a low cost. So in this chapter we include recipes for such things as veal and lamb shanks, tripe and oxtail, calf's head and pig's feet.

Among the most valuable aids to good eating at low cost that we have encountered are a California-made meat tenderizer and an "instant" meat marinade, both containing the papaya enzyme that tenderizes protein. (Natives in tropical islands have long used papaya leaves and fruit with their meat dishes for this reason.) Over the years we have done many interesting kitchen tests and experiments with Adolph's tenderizer and Adolph's marinade and come to the conclusion that their properties are truly amazing. They really do have the power to turn a tough or poor-quality cut of meat into one that can be broiled like a better cut. If you don't believe this really works, cook two pieces of meat at the same time, one tenderized and one not, and check the difference. We have included meat-tenderizer recipes for less choice steak cuts and also for a rump roast.

Finally, although everyone knows that stuffing meat cuts or combining them with other ingredients in stews and casseroles makes them go farther, not everyone realizes the vast repertoire of such dishes that can be developed, many of them definitely to be rated as fine cuisine. In this chapter we have included many of our favorites and hope they will become yours.

MONEY-SAVING TIPS

Save beef and pork fats. They are most useful for cooking. Here are ways in which you may use them:

Beef fat. Beef drippings can be used for sautéing potatoes and onions, for browning meat for stews and braised dishes, for flavoring soups and vegetables. Rendered beef fat may be used to deep-fat-fry potatoes and onions. It is excellent for the crusts of meat pies and vegetable pies and can be used in making hot biscuits.

Pork fat. One of the finest, with many kitchen uses. The rendered kidney fat, called "leaf lard," is one of the most delicate you can find. Fry with pork fat and use it in baking, as you would margarine or vegetable fats.

Bacon fat. Rendered bacon fat is excellent for frying or sautéing chicken, potatoes, onions, and such vegetables as snap beans, spinach and parsnips. It may also be used in biscuits or muffins.

Keep fat in small pots or jars and add to them from time to time. If you cultivate this habit, you can save yourself many dollars a year and improve the flavor of your cooking.

BEEF

Beef is America's favorite meat, and those who know their beef like to buy it aged for roasting and broiling. Although the cost is higher, the beef is tenderer and more flavorful and there is less shrinkage in cooking, as much of the fluids have been lost in the aging process. While we leave it up to your purse and discretion as to how often you serve a good prime rib roast, this is not so spendthrift as it may seem, for not only will you get one good meal from it, but you can also use the leftovers, even the bones, as a basis for successive meals.

Roast Beef

In roasting beef it is important to remember that slow cooking not only keeps the meat from drying out but also saves you money, as there is less shrinkage than with high-temperature roasting.

RIB ROAST OF BEEF

When you buy a rib roast, try to get the first three or four ribs and be sure that the meat is prime or choice. It should be well marbled and have a covering of pinky-white fat. Have the chine bone removed and the roast cut short (ask the butcher to give you the short ribs he trims off) and then tied well with twine so that it stands up. Get a little extra suet with the roast for cooking potatoes. (If you have a good butcher, order your roast a fortnight or so ahead of time so that it may hang longer.)

To prepare the roast, score the fat and rub it well with freshly ground black pepper. Also rub some pepper into the flesh and the bone side. Arrange on a rack, rib side down, and roast at any of the following low temperatures, without basting:

200°—approximately 30 to 35 minutes per pound.
300°—approximately 15 to 18 minutes per pound.
325°—approximately 13 to 15 minutes per pound.

When you think the meat is almost done, insert a meat thermometer into the thickest part of the beef, without touching the bone. For rare beef, the temperature should register 120° to 125°. If you like your beef better done, roast until the thermometer registers 130° for medium rare or 140° for medium. If you don't use a thermometer, cut next to the bone with a sharp knife to test if done.

Salt the meat during the last 15 minutes of cooking.

After removing the roast from the oven, allow it to rest on a platter on its broader flesh side for 12 to 15 minutes before carving. Serve with the pan juices and a dish of potatoes that have been cooked in suet: chop fine the suet you bought, and melt in a skillet; add potatoes, peeled and cut in rounds, and fry until they are nicely browned and the little pieces of suet are crisp. Potatoes Anna are a rather more elegant accompaniment for roast beef if you are serving it for a dinner party.

Leftover roast beef is good as is. Or slice any cold roast beef rather thick for

DEVILED BEEF SLICES

Beat 2 eggs until light. Dip the beef slices into the beaten egg, then into fine dry bread crumbs. Melt beef drippings in a skillet and cook the beef slices until the meat is heated through and the coating is brown and crusty. Serve with Sauce Diable.

SAUCE DIABLE

2 ten-ounce cans beef consommé
3 shallots or green onions, chopped
2 ounces butter
1 tablespoon flour
2 teaspoons Worcestershire sauce
Dash of Tabasco
Juice of 1 lemon
2 teaspoons Dijon mustard

Cook the consommé until reduced to 1 cup. Meanwhile sauté the shallots or green onions in the butter until wilted. Mix in the flour, Worcestershire and Tabasco sauces, lemon juice and mustard. Mix in the reduced consommé and heat through. This sauce is also excellent with grilled kidneys, liver and other meats.

Use the bones of the Rib Roast for

DEVILED BEEF BONES

Carve the bones completely away from the roast, leaving plenty of meat on them. Separate into ribs and dip in ¼ cup melted butter mixed with 2 tablespoons tarragon vinegar. Roll in sifted dry bread crumbs and broil from 10 to 20 minutes, turning occasionally, until the crumbs are brown. Serve with Sauce Diable.

Cold roast beef also makes delicious hash. Follow the recipe for Corned Beef Hash, substituting roast for corned beef.

A less expensive roast but with excellent flavor and texture is the rump. (Sirloin tip and eye of round serve in the same way.) Sprinkled with meat tenderizer, it slices beautifully.

RUMP ROAST OF BEEF

Wipe the rump roast with a damp cloth and sprinkle meat tenderizer evenly over all the surfaces, using about ½ teaspoon per pound. Jab the meat with a fork at ½-inch intervals to allow the tenderizer to penetrate. Leave at room temperature for about 4 hours. Pepper the meat well and rub with a little salt. (If you used a seasoned meat tenderizer, omit the salt.)
Roast on a rack in a 325° oven until the meat reaches an internal temperature of 125° for rare beef. (See Rib Roast of Beef for other timings.) Season with salt and allow to stand for 15 minutes before carving. Jacket potatoes and a good salad go well with this.

Steak

If you want to eat steak but cannot afford the finest quality, buy arm or blade steak, chuck steak, round steak, rump steak or flank steak and sprinkle the surface with meat tenderizer. Let it stand ½ hour for each ½-inch thickness of meat. This is especially good for a steak you are going to serve as London Broil, sliced thin against the grain.

LONDON BROIL I

Buy a thick piece of rump or hip steak and tenderize as described above, jabbing some of the powder down into the meat by stabbing it with a large fork. Let the meat stand at room temperature for 2 hours. Broil to the desired state of doneness, then cut the meat in thin diagonal slices against the grain. Serve on toast or on a bed of potatoes or onions, or serve plain with the pan juices.

You can also make London Broil with thin flank steak or skirt steak.

LONDON BROIL II

Sprinkle the flank or skirt steak well with tenderizer and let it stand at room temperature for 1 hour. Pan-broil it in butter until well browned on the outside but still rare inside. Transfer to a board and carve in thin slices at a 45° angle.

The packaged instant meat marinade can turn broiled chuck or round steak into a tender, juicy delight.

MARINATED STEAK

1 package instant meat marinade
½ cup soy sauce
2 tablespoons finely chopped fresh or candied ginger
2 cloves garlic, finely chopped
⅓ cup oil
1 tablespoon grated orange rind
2 teaspoons chili powder
5 to 6 pounds chuck or eye of round, cut as for steak

Follow the directions for instant marinade given on the package, adding the soy sauce, ginger, garlic, oil, orange rind and chili powder to it. Marinate the meat according to directions on the package. Broil meat, turning it several times and brushing with the marinade, until it has reached the desired state of doneness. Serve with fried rice and a generous salad. Serves 6.

A final word on the subject of steak. There is a cut of rump steak known to good butchers that is as tender and delicious a morsel as you can find in the whole animal. This piece of meat should be quite a bit less expensive than choice porterhouse or sirloin. It has less waste and a great deal of flavor. Try cook-

ing it with rosemary—the matchless taste of the meat and the herb make a wonderful combination.

RUMP STEAK WITH ROSEMARY

Choose a fine thick steak of 3 to 4 pounds. With the heel of your hand, press dried or fresh rosemary into it on both sides. Grill as you would any other steak, and salt to taste when cooked—no pepper or other condiments, please.

Boiled Beef and Corned Beef

Fresh beef brisket, plate and short ribs have a fine flavor and are excellent for boiled beef dishes, such as Pot au Feu and Pressed Beef, and also for such national stews as the Spanish Cocido and the Brazilian Feijoada. Corned beef brisket is particularly fine, economical eating.

PRESSED BEEF

5 pounds short ribs
1 beef shinbone or calf's foot
2 onions, each stuck with 2 cloves
1 rib celery with leaves
1½ tablespoons salt
3 or 4 cloves garlic
1 bay leaf
Worcestershire sauce
1 or 2 small red chili peppers
1 egg white, beaten until stiff
1 eggshell

Have the butcher tie the short ribs with string, or tie them yourself.

Place them in a deep kettle with the shinbone or calf's foot, onions, celery, salt, garlic, bay leaf, a hearty dash of Worcestershire sauce and the peppers. Cover with water, bring to a boil, skim off the scum, reduce the heat and simmer for about 3½ hours, or until tender. Remove beef from kettle and cook the broth down very quickly until reduced about two thirds. Strain and clarify the broth with the egg white and eggshell according to the directions for Beef Consommé. Remove the string and bones from the beef and pack the meat in a deep bowl or mold. Pour the clarified broth over the meat, cover it with a plate or tray that fits within the bowl and weight it down so that it rests on the meat and pushes out the fat and excess juice. Chill overnight, unmold and serve sliced, with horseradish sauce and a potato salad. Nothing in the world is better. A bottle of rosé wine is excellent with this.

If you are giving a buffet party, use this pressed beef for a dish that has great distinction and is seldom served in America.

SALADE DE BOEUF PARISIENNE

Cut the cold pressed beef into thin slices and arrange in a long overlapping row on a large attractive serving platter. Garnish with slices of cold potato that have been marinated in garlic-flavored oil and vinegar, mounds of cold string beans, sliced tomatoes, sliced cucumbers, quarters of Boston lettuce and quarters of hard-cooked egg. Cover the beef with thin rings of sliced raw red onion and chopped parsley. Make a sauce by blending 1 cup olive or peanut oil, ¼ cup wine vinegar and ¼ cup each finely chopped onion, finely chopped pickle, finely chopped peeled and seeded tomato, finely chopped hard-cooked egg, and capers. Pour the sauce over the salad and refrigerate until ready to serve.

There are as many variations of the Spanish Cocido as there are of the French Pot au Feu. In some areas, a chicken is added, which gives a delicious and different flavor and stretches the dish even farther.

COCIDO

2½ pounds fresh beef brisket
4 carrots, peeled
4 leeks, trimmed and well washed
2 pounds salt pork
2 pounds chorizo (Spanish sausage)
2 twenty-nine-ounce cans chick-peas, drained
1 teaspoon salt
1 teaspoon rosemary
½ teaspoon freshly ground black pepper
1 good-sized head cabbage, cut in 8 wedges

Place the brisket in a large pot with the carrots, leeks, salt pork, chorizo, chick-peas and seasonings. Add enough water to slightly more than cover the meat and vegetables. Bring to a boil, reduce the heat, cover and simmer gently for 2½ to 3 hours. Add the cabbage and continue cooking until cabbage is just tender. Taste for seasoning.

Serve the broth in individual bowls. Slice the meats and arrange them on a platter with the carrots, leeks, cabbage and chick-peas. Surround with boiled potatoes and serve with coarse salt and a variety of mustards and crisp hot bread. Serves 6 to 8.

Another unusual, inexpensive entrée with enough flair for a party is a quick version of the Brazilian national dish:

FEIJOADA

[This freezes well.]

3 cups black beans
Salt
2 pounds fresh beef brisket, cut into large squares
2 pounds smoked beef tongue, peeled and cut into large squares
½ pound dried Portuguese, Spanish or Italian sausage, sliced 1 inch thick
1 pound salt pork, diced
1 bay leaf
3 cloves garlic, finely chopped
1 tablespoon butter
2 oranges, peeled and sliced

Wash the beans and soak them overnight in water to cover. Next morning, drain the beans and put them in a large kettle with water to cover. Bring to a boil. Add about 1 tablespoon salt, the meats, sausage and salt pork, and the bay leaf. Cover and simmer on low heat for about 2 hours, or until the beans and meats are thoroughly tender. Brown the garlic in the butter.

Take 1 cup beans from the kettle and mash them with the garlic, blending well. Stir into the beans and meat. Correct seasoning.

To serve, place the beans in the center of a large platter and surround them with the pieces of meat. Serve with the orange slices and with collard or mustard greens. Serves 6 to 8.

Traditionally, this is served with braised loin of pork, but the pork may be òmitted.

CORNED BEEF

A 4- to 5-pound piece of corned brisket
1 clove garlic, slivered
2 tablespoons freshly ground black pepper
2 onions, each stuck with 2 cloves
3 carrots, peeled
3 ribs celery
1 turnip
1 head cabbage, coarsely sliced
Bacon fat

Prepare the corned beef for cooking by soaking it in cold water for 3 hours. Remove and wash well in cold water. Pierce the meat in several places with the point of a small sharp knife and insert the garlic slivers, then rub all over with the pepper. Place in a deep kettle with the onions, carrots, celery, turnip and water to cover. Bring to a boil and boil for 5 minutes, then skim off the scum from the top, reduce the heat and simmer for about 4 hours, or until tender. Watch it carefully and test with a sharp knife or a fork. When the meat is almost done, braise the cabbage in the bacon fat until nicely browned but still on the crisp side. Drain the corned beef and serve it on a platter surrounded by the braised cabbage. Potatoes cooked in their jackets, and yellow turnips cooked until tender and mashed with plenty of butter, are good accompaniments. This is a hearty dish for a cold night when you have a few friends in. It calls for beer as a drink and a light dessert such as a slice of fresh pineapple or a few cubes of frozen pineapple with a good slug of rum poured over them.

A couple of nights after you have had a corned-beef dinner, you can feast on a supper of Corned Beef Hash.

CORNED BEEF HASH

[This freezes well.]

2 to 3 pounds cooked corned beef
4 good-sized potatoes
1 large onion, finely chopped
Salt, nutmeg, freshly ground black pepper to taste
Beef fat or butter

Chop the beef coarsely. Boil the potatoes in their skins until they can be pierced with a fork. Drain, cool, remove skins and chop. Chop the beef with the potatoes and onion until blended, but do not chop too fine. Season with salt, if necessary, a little ground nutmeg and freshly ground black pepper.

Melt the beef fat or butter in a skillet, add the hash and press it down firmly. Cook until brown on the bottom, then dot with butter and put under the broiler for a few minutes to brown the top. Serve from the skillet, with Horseradish Applesauce.

Note: The old Maine method was to melt ¼ cup fat or butter in a skillet, add ¾ cup boiling water and then the hash, which was cooked until the water evaporated and left a crust on the bottom, then folded over onto a hot platter.

Or, for a more elegant version, bake the hash with cream in a ring mold.

CORNED BEEF HASH RING

1 medium to large onion, finely chopped
1 to 2 tablespoons butter
1½ cups finely chopped corned beef
3 cups finely chopped, steamed or baked potato
Salt, freshly ground black pepper
¼ to ½ cup cream
Creamed hard-boiled eggs or succotash

Sauté the chopped onion in the butter until golden. Mix with chopped meat and potatoes and season to taste with salt and pepper. Add enough cream to barely moisten the mixture. Pack into a well-greased 1½-quart ring mold. Bake in a 350° oven for about 45 minutes. Allow to stand for a few minutes after removing from the oven, loosen around the edges and turn onto a hot platter. Fill the center with creamed hard-cooked eggs or creamed succotash. Serves 4.

Pot-Roasted, Braised and Stewed Beef

Top round, bottom round and rump are cuts that, while seldom tender enough for roasting, are excellent for longer, slower cooking with added moisture. Chuck, shoulder, shin and brisket are also suitable for this type of cooking. Recently, while experimenting with foil cookery, I came up with a variation on the pot roast which I think has many advantages over the old version. It is done completely in the oven at a low temperature.

FOILED POT ROAST

Take a 4-pound piece of boneless rump, round or chuck and put it on a large piece of heavy-duty foil. Sprinkle with 1 package onion soup mix or mushroom brown gravy mix and put a few slices of tomato on the top. Pull the foil up around the meat and seal loosely with a double fold, turning up the ends to keep the juices in. Cook in a 250° oven for 5 to 6 hours (the length of time will depend on the tenderness of the cut), by which time the meat will be deliciously flavored and tender, in a rich sauce made from the mix and its own juices. You may shorten the cooking time by putting the foiled pot roast in a 375° oven for 1 hour, then reducing the heat to 250° and cooking it for 2 to 2½ hours more, or until tender. It can remain in the turned-off oven until ready to serve and then reheated.

VARIATIONS

1. For an Italian version, sprinkle with Italian-style spaghetti sauce mix. Serve with the pan juices and cooked macaroni.
2. For a Mexican version, sprinkle with chili seasoning mix. Serve with rice.

One of the most delicious dishes you can make with boneless rump or round is the classic French Boeuf à la Mode.

BOEUF À LA MODE

[This freezes well.]

6 to 8 strips larding pork
½ cup whiskey or brandy
4 pounds boneless rump or round
1 pint red wine
Salt, pepper, nutmeg
Bouquet garni (1 bay leaf, 1 leek, 2 sprigs parsley tied together)
3 carrots
Beef fat
2 pigs' feet, split

Cut the larding pork into strips and soak in the whiskey or brandy for 1 hour. Lard the beef with the pork. Combine the whiskey or brandy, wine, salt, pepper and nutmeg to taste, bouquet garni and carrots. Marinate larded beef in this mixture in a large glass, pottery or enameled bowl for 8 to 12 hours, turning several times.

In a heavy casserole or Dutch oven, try out enough beef fat to make 3 to 4 tablespoons. Drain meat and brown on all sides in the hot fat. Season with salt and grind a little pepper over it. Heat the marinade and pour over the beef. Add the pigs' feet. Cover and simmer about 2 to 3 hours or until the beef is just tender but not mushy. Skim fat from the stock and strain it, discarding feet, carrots and bouquet garni. Serve the meat hot with boiled potatoes, buttered carrots and a sauce made from the marinade. Serves 6 to 8.

Boeuf à la Mode en Gelée: Place the cooked meat in a terrine or deep bowl. Skim and strain the stock—there should be 2 or 3 cups —and heat. Soften 1 tablespoon gelatin in 2 tablespoons cold water, stir into the hot stock until dissolved and pour over the meat. (If you did not use the pigs' feet, which contain natural gelatin, you will need to add more gelatin.) Cover terrine or bowl with foil. Put a plate on top and weight with something heavy, such as canned goods. Cool and chill until set. Turn out onto a platter, slice and serve with Hot Potato Salad and marinated cooked vegetables.

LEFTOVER POT ROAST OR BOEUF A LA MODE

[This freezes well.]

For a delicious way to turn leftover beef into a new and unusual dish, slice it and bake in a casserole with Ratatouille (see Chapter 6). Arrange a layer of ratatouille in the casserole, top with cold sliced pot roast, then another layer of ratatouille. Cover and heat in a 350° oven for 35 minutes, or until the meat is heated through and the ratatouille bubbling. You may sprinkle the top with grated Gruyère cheese during the last 10 minutes if you like. Serve from the casserole, with rice as an accompaniment.

For a hurry-up version of the famous German sauerbraten, which usually needs at least 3 days to marinate, sprinkle the meat first with tenderizer.

QUICK SAUERBRATEN

3 to 4 pounds top or bottom round
Seasoned instant meat tenderizer
2½ to 3 cups buttermilk
1 large onion, sliced
½ lemon, sliced (optional)
4 whole allspice
4 cloves
1 bay leaf
4 to 6 peppercorns
3 tablespoons oil or beef fat
14 gingersnaps crushed and mixed with 4 teaspoons cornstarch
1 teaspoon meat extract
1 tablespoon brown sugar or molasses
2 teaspoons Worcestershire sauce
2½ tablespoons or more Kitchen Bouquet
Freshly ground black pepper to taste

Thoroughly moisten all surfaces of the meat with water. Pat it on with your fingers or use a pastry brush. Sprinkle instant meat tenderizer evenly, like salt, over all surfaces of the meat, using about ½ teaspoon per pound. Use no salt with the seasoned tenderizer. Jab the meat deeply with a kitchen fork at ½-inch intervals.

Combine 2 cups of the buttermilk with the onion, lemon if used, and seasonings, and marinate the meat in this mixture in a cool place or the refrigerator for at least 4 hours. It is even better if soaked overnight. Turn several times.

Remove the meat from the marinade and strain the marinade, reserving the onion slices and liquid. Heat oil or fat in a heavy pot and brown the meat and onion slices. Add the strained marinade, cover the pot and simmer gently for 1½ to 2 hours, or until tender.

Remove the meat to a hot platter. Add to the pan juices enough extra buttermilk to make 2½ cups liquid and heat over a medium flame. Add the gingersnap-cornstarch mixture and then the remaining ingredients, increasing the amount of Kitchen Bouquet if you want a darker sauce. Cook slowly, stirring, until thickened. Serve hot over the meat. Serves 6.

The delectable combination of flavors in this Provençal stew makes it an excellent choice for buffet suppers or company dinners. Traditionally, it is cooked slowly for hours in a daubière—a round covered pot with an indentation in the cover to hold water—over a charcoal fire or on a special metal disk set in the fireplace. A good heavy braising pot gives equally good results.

DAUBE AIXOISE

[This freezes well.]

⅓ cup olive oil
3 slices thickly cut bacon, cut into small cubes
5 onions, peeled and quartered
2 or 3 carrots, scraped and cut into 3-inch slices
5 cloves garlic
1 leek, well washed
Peel of ¼ orange
2 cloves
1 bay leaf
1 teaspoon thyme or rosemary, or half and half
1 tablespoon salt
1 teaspoon freshly ground black pepper
2 tablespoons concentrated tomato paste
3 pounds of beef—shin or round —cut into large pieces
1 calf's foot or 1 pig's foot
Red wine
Cooked macaroni

Put the oil and bacon in the bottom of the pot and add the vegetables, seasonings and tomato paste. Place the beef and calf's foot or pig's foot on top and cover with red wine. Place a lid on the pot and cook gently over the lowest-possible heat or in a 200° oven for 4 to 4½ hours.

When the meat is tender, remove it to a hot platter. Skim the fat from the juices and strain. Pour this sauce over cooked macaroni and toss well. Serve with the beef. This daube is a dish that improves with reheating, even as many as two or three times. Serves 6.

We have often found that after a Saturday cocktail party, some people stay on and on and it becomes necessary to provide something substantial for the late-stayers as well as for yourself. The wise host or hostess will have something heating in the oven or something that can be hotted up quickly. We favor a big pot of Chili con Carne served with green salad and a lot of corn bread (made with a mix) or French bread. You can make the chili a day or two before, for it is one of those dishes that improves with keeping.

CHILI CON CARNE

[This freezes well.]

2 large onions, chopped
4 tablespoons beef fat
½ pound beef suet, finely chopped
3 pounds top round or rump, cut into small dice
2 cloves garlic
1 tablespoon salt
3 tablespoons chili powder
1 tablespoon cumin seeds
Dash of Tabasco
Beef stock (or water and bouillon cubes), heated to boiling

Sauté the onions in the beef fat until soft. Add the beef suet and cook very slowly until the suet is completely rendered and the onion practically melted into the fat. Add the meat, garlic and salt and let the meat cubes brown well on all sides and blend with the fat and onion. Mix in the chili powder, cumin and Tabasco and cover with boiling stock. Simmer over low heat, covered, for 2½ hours, stirring occasionally. Taste for seasoning and add more salt and chili powder if you like. This is an authentic chili recipe—it never contains beans. However, you can serve this with mashed kidney beans if you like. Serves 6 to 8.

Flank steak is delicious when broiled, and it is also useful for braising. In fact, this is a thrifty addition to the cooking repertoire, for the stuffing both stretches and makes a delicious accompaniment to the meat.

BRAISED STUFFED FLANK STEAK

[This freezes well.]

A 2-pound flank steak
4 tablespoons butter
2 tablespoons oil
1 onion, finely chopped
2 cloves garlic, finely chopped
1 teaspoon salt
½ teaspoon freshly ground black pepper
1 teaspoon thyme
2 tablespoons chopped parsley
1½ cups fresh bread crumbs
2 hard-cooked eggs, finely chopped
¼ cup Madeira or sherry
Bacon strips
Butter and oil
1 cup stock or water

Have the butcher score the flank steak or do it yourself, making rather full strokes across the steak diagonal to the grain of the meat with a sharp-pointed knife. Heat the butter and oil in a skillet and sauté the onion and garlic until golden. Mix in the seasonings, bread crumbs and eggs. Blend in the wine. Spread the stuffing on the unscored side of the steak and roll up. Cover with strips of bacon and tie securely with twine. Brown the roll in a small amount of butter and oil in a deep pan or casserole. Add the stock or water, cover and simmer for 1½ to 2 hours, or until just tender, adding additional liquid if necessary. Serve sliced, either hot or cold, with a Tomato Sauce or a Sauce Béarnaise. Serves 4.

Sometime when you wish to make a special impression on your family or on guests, try serving Oiseaux sans Têtes (birds without heads), made with inexpensive chuck.

OISEAUX SANS TETES

[This freezes well.]

1 pound ground pork, mainly lean
2 onions, finely chopped
1 clove garlic, crushed
½ pound mushrooms, chopped
Pinch of rosemary
1 teaspoon salt
1 teaspoon freshly ground black pepper
½ cup soft bread crumbs
8 pieces boneless chuck steak, cut about 4 by 6 inches and ½ inch thick
8 thin slices salt pork
Flour
Pork or bacon fat
2 or 3 carrots, peeled
2 onions, each stuck with 2 cloves
1 bay leaf
Stock or red wine
½ cup heavy cream
Beurre Manié

Combine the ground pork, onion, garlic, mushrooms, seasonings and bread crumbs to make a filling, blending well. Put a small amount on each beef slice and roll up tightly. Wrap each roll in a salt-pork slice and tie securely at either end with string. Roll the beef birds in flour and brown them on all sides in pork or bacon fat. Arrange in a pan with the carrots, onions and bay leaf. Cover with stock or red wine. Cover the pan and simmer for 1½ hours, or until tender. Remove the strings and arrange the birds on a hot serving platter. Keep warm. Strain and reduce the cooking liquid a little and skim excess fat from the top. Mix in the cream and thicken with Beurre Manié, if desired. Serve the birds with rice baked in tomato juice, and with young carrots steamed in butter and lightly glazed.

You can make the birds the day before and reheat them in the sauce—they are even better that way. Or make up a batch of them when beef prices are low and freeze them in the sauce for future use. This is a dish that can be found on the menus of really fine Paris restaurants, yet it is one of the simplest and least expensive you can make.

Other Parts of the Animal (Beef)

One of the most neglected variety meats is fresh beef tongue, which is scarcely ever served in America (though cured tongue is fairly common). Here are two ways to serve it:

FRESH BEEF TONGUE WITH WINE SAUCE*

[This freezes well.]

1 fresh beef tongue
1 onion stuck with 2 cloves
1 carrot
1 clove garlic
1 teaspoon thyme
1 bay leaf
1 tablespoon salt
1 teaspoon freshly ground black pepper
2 tablespoons butter
2 tablespoons flour
1 cup broth from tongue
½ cup currant jelly
½ cup sherry or Madeira
⅓ cup finely chopped almonds
⅓ cup raisins
1 tablespoon grated orange rind

Combine the tongue, onion, carrot, garlic, thyme, bay leaf, salt and pepper in a deep kettle with water to cover. Bring to a boil and boil for 5 minutes, skimming off any scum that rises to the surface. Reduce heat, cover and simmer the tongue until tender, about 2½ to 3 hours. Remove from the broth and, when cool enough to handle, trim and skin it. Strain broth.

Melt the butter in a skillet or saucepan, stir in the flour and brown lightly. Stir in 1 cup strained broth from the tongue and stir until lightly thickened. Stir in the remaining ingredients and simmer for 3 to 4 minutes. Add the tongue and reheat in the sauce over medium heat. Serve the tongue sliced with the sauce and accompany it with chopped spinach and buttered noodles. Serves 8.

Tripe, the stomach lining of the steer, is a much misunderstood and virtually ignored food that can be delectable.

TRIPE A LA MODE DE CAEN

[This freezes well.]

2 pounds large onions, sliced
5 pounds tripe, cut into 2-inch squares
2 calf's feet, split, or 2 pig's feet
1 pound beef suet, diced
Bouquet garni (2 leeks, 1 sprig thyme, 1 bay leaf, 1 onion stuck with 2 cloves tied in cheesecloth)
2 teaspoons salt
1 teaspoon pepper
¼ cup applejack or Calvados
1 cup cider (dry, not sweet) or dry white wine
2 cups flour mixed with water to make a stiff paste

This quantity requires a very large casserole, a 6- to 8-quart size, or the classic tripotière. The recipe can, of course, be halved.

Arrange a layer of sliced onions in the bottom of the casserole and follow with a layer of one third of the tripe. Next add the calf's or pig's feet and half the suet and then another layer each of onions and tripe. Now add the bouquet garni and the remaining tripe. Top with the rest of the suet, and add the salt and pepper, applejack or Calvados, cider, and enough water to cover. Place lid on the casserole and then seal the edges with the stiff flour-and-water paste.

Cook in a 250° to 275° oven for

12 hours. Remove from the oven, discard the paste seal, and uncover. Skim off the excess fat. Remove the bouquet garni and the calf's or pig's feet. Strip the meat from the feet and return it to the casserole. Taste for seasoning. Serve very hot with boiled potatoes. Serves 10.

Baby beef liver is another neglected delicacy. It is excellent sautéed in butter and served in a wine sauce.

BEEF LIVER BOURGUIGNONNE

4 good-sized slices young beef liver
Seasoned flour
12 tablespoons butter
6 slices bacon or salt pork, diced
4 medium onions, sliced
Red wine
3 cloves garlic, finely chopped
8 small bread croutons
Chopped parsley and chives

Dredge the liver slices with seasoned flour. Melt 6 tablespoons butter in a skillet and sauté the liver until nicely browned on both sides but still rare and juicy in the center. Remove liver to a hot plate and keep warm.

Add the bacon or salt pork and the onions to the skillet and sauté until onion is soft. Add just enough red wine to cover and simmer gently for 5 minutes.

Meanwhile, melt remaining butter in another skillet and lightly sauté the garlic. Add the bread croutons and cook, turning frequently, until browned and crisp.

Put the liver slices in the sauce and just heat through. Arrange liver on a hot platter and spoon some of the sauce over it. Top with croutons and garnish with chopped parsley and chives. Potatoes Anna (see Chapter 6) go well with this dish. Serve remaining sauce separately. Serves 4.

And so we come to the last bit of the steer—the *tail*. Bony but tasty, this thrifty cut makes a wonderful hearty ragout.

OXTAIL RAGOUT

[This freezes well.]

2 or 3 oxtails
Salt, freshly ground black pepper
Flour
2 ounces brandy
2 carrots, peeled and cut in pieces
1 onion stuck with 2 cloves
1 teaspoon thyme
1 sprig parsley
1 bay leaf
Water and broth or red wine

Have the butcher disjoint the oxtails—that is, cut them through at the joints, not hack into pieces. Place them in a flat baking dish, season with salt and pepper and sprinkle lightly with flour. Roast in a 450° oven for 30 minutes, shaking the pan from time to time and basting the meat with its own juices.

Remove pan from oven, pour off the fat and flame the oxtails with the warmed brandy. Transfer them to a deep casserole and add the carrots, onion, thyme, parsley, bay leaf and enough water and broth or water and wine to cover. Cook in a 350° oven, covered, for 3 hours, then reduce the heat to 250° and cook 3 hours more. Serve in deep bowls, with plenty of the rich broth. Boiled potatoes and braised cabbage sprinkled with poppy seeds go well with the ragout. Serves 4

to 6.

Note: The ragout is even better if made the day before, cooled, skimmed of fat and reheated.

For Chopped Beef and Hamburger see Ground Meat, pages 97–100.

VEAL

As we mentioned before, good veal is hard to find in U.S. markets. The tenderer, more expensive cuts are suitable for roasting and sautéing. However, there are other cuts, notably the neck and breast, that are less costly and just as delicious when properly prepared.

POITRINE DE VEAU FARCIE

1 good-sized breast of veal
1 pound ground lean pork, with a little fat, or ground leftover pork or ham
2 medium onions, finely chopped
1 cup soft bread crumbs
1 teaspoon tarragon
1 teaspoon salt
1 teaspoon freshly ground black pepper
5 tablespoons soft butter
½ cup chopped parsley
2 eggs
1 tablespoon olive oil
1½ cups white wine

Have the butcher cut a pocket in the veal breast. Combine the pork, onion, bread crumbs, tarragon, salt, pepper, 1 tablespoon butter, parsley and eggs, mixing well with your hands. Stuff the pocket with this mixture and place foil in the opening to prevent it from oozing out. Skewer or sew up securely. Melt the remaining butter and the oil in a pan and brown the veal well on both sides. When it is nicely browned, add the wine. Cover and simmer for about 3 hours, or until tender, or bake, covered, in a 325° oven for the same length of time. Remove to a hot platter, skim excess fat from the pan juices and boil them up quickly. Correct seasoning and serve separately. Buttered noodles or Risotto go well with this. Serves 6 to 8.

BLANQUETTE DE VEAU

[This freezes well.]

3 pounds veal shoulder, cut in serving-size pieces
1 onion, stuck with 2 cloves
2 carrots, peeled
Sprig of parsley
1 bay leaf
Salt, freshly ground black pepper
24 small white onions
12 mushroom caps
9 tablespoons butter
1 to 2 teaspoons sugar
4 tablespoons flour
1 cup heavy cream

2 egg yolks
1 teaspoon lemon juice
Steamed Rice

2 egg yolks
1 teaspoon lemon juice
Steamed Rice

Put the veal in a large saucepan and cover with cold water. Bring to a boil and boil 5 minutes, then skim off all scum. Add the onion stuck with cloves, carrots, parsley and bay leaf, cover and simmer for 30 minutes. Add 1½ teaspoons salt and continue simmering for 1¼ hours, or until tender.

Meanwhile, peel the onions and wipe the mushroom caps with a damp cloth. Cook the onions in 3 tablespoons butter until lightly browned. Cover and steam until tender. Add the sugar and shake the pan until they caramelize a little. Cook the mushroom caps in 3 tablespoons butter and season to taste with salt and pepper.

Remove the cooked veal from the pan and keep it warm. Strain the broth. Measure 2 cups broth for the sauce.

Melt the remaining 3 tablespoons butter in a saucepan and blend in the flour. Slowly stir in the 2 cups broth, stirring constantly until well thickened. Mix the cream with the egg yolks and stir a little of the hot sauce into the mixture. Add this to the sauce in the pan, stirring constantly over low heat. Stir until thickened, but do not let it boil. Season to taste and add the lemon juice. Arrange a mound of rice in the center of a large platter and put the veal around it. Pour the sauce over the veal and garnish with the onions and mushroom caps. Serves 6.

Other Parts of the Animal (Veal)

Calf's head is one of the rarely used parts of the calf, although it makes a superb dish. If you can find a butcher to provide you with a calf's head (easier in large cities), you can prepare Calf's Head Vinaigrette and gain a reputation for your *spécialité de la maison*.

CALF'S HEAD VINAIGRETTE

Have the butcher bone the calf's head or split it for you. Remove the brains and the tongue. Soak the head and tongue in cold water for 2 hours. Clean the brain by removing the membrane and any blood clots and soak for 2 hours in water acidulated with lemon juice.

Cook the tongue and head separately; the tongue will take a little longer. Put each in a deep kettle with an onion stuck with 2 cloves, a carrot, 1 tablespoon salt, and water to cover.

Bring the tongue to a boil, reduce heat, cover and simmer until tender, about 1½ hours. Remove from the broth and, when cool enough to handle, skin and trim it and slice thinly. Keep warm.

Bring the head to a boil and boil for 5 minutes. Skim off scum, reduce the heat, cover and simmer 1 hour, or until tender. Remove the pieces and cut them into serving portions. Or, with a sharp knife, remove the meat from the split head and cut it up. The entire meaty portion—ears, cheeks and muzzle—is edible and delicious. Return the meat to the broth to keep warm.

Poach the brains for 15 minutes in salted water flavored with a bay leaf, a few peppercorns and the juice of 1 lemon. Drain.

To serve, arrange the pieces of head on a platter around the sliced tongue and brains. Surround with plain boiled potatoes. Serve with a Vinaigrette Sauce. Serves 6.

While calf's liver is too expensive to be included here, veal kidneys are much more economical and are some of the most toothsome morsels in the realm of gastronomy. You can merely slice the kidneys thinly with their fat and grill or sauté them in butter with a dash of mustard, or you can prepare something as dramatic and rich as the following dish, which is ideal for brunch and can be made at the table in a chafing dish if you like.

VEAL KIDNEYS FLAMBE

4 veal kidneys
4 tablespoons butter
3 tablespoons oil
½ cup Armagnac or brandy
Salt, freshly ground black pepper to taste
1½ teaspoons Dijon mustard
1 tablespoon Worcestershire sauce
¼ teaspoon Tabasco
1½ cups heavy cream
Beurre Manié
Chopped parsley

Clean the veal kidneys and remove the tubes. Cut in medium-thin slices. Combine butter and oil in a large skillet or in the blazer pan of a chafing dish and heat until bub-

bling hot. Add the kidneys and brown very quickly over fairly brisk heat, shaking the pan and turning the kidney slices several times. Warm the Armagnac or brandy, pour over the kidneys, and flambé. Add salt and pepper, mustard, Worcestershire sauce, and Tabasco, and stir in the cream. Add small bits of Beurre Manié and stir until the sauce is just lightly thickened. Do not overcook or the kidneys will become tough. Correct the seasoning. Add chopped parsley and serve with fried toast or rice. Serves 4.

LAMB

Roast Lamb

Lamb is, generally speaking, an expensive meat, but there are many parts of the animal well worth considering, notably the shoulder, shanks, breast and neck. Although the leg is a fairly expensive cut, there are times, in some localities, when it is a bargain or on sale at a lower price because of an increased seasonal supply. That is the time to make an unusual party dish that gives lamb a special quality. We call it Mock Venison. This used to be a lengthy affair, as the lamb had to marinate for four days. By making it with the instant meat marinade, you can cut the time to 15 minutes.

MOCK VENISON
(Roast marinated leg of lamb)

[This freezes well.]

1½ cups red wine
Juice of 1 lemon

2 envelopes instant meat marinade
6 to 8 peppercorns, crushed
A 5- to 7-pound leg of lamb
3 cloves garlic, slivered

Combine wine, lemon juice, instant marinade and peppercorns. Make incisions in the leg and insert the garlic, then run a fork through the meat according to the directions on the package of marinade. Marinate leg for 15 minutes, turning so the marinade penetrates all sides.

Place leg on a rack in a roasting pan. Heat the marinade. Roast the lamb in a 400° oven, basting every 20 minutes or so with some of the heated marinade. Allow about 12 minutes per pound for rare lamb. When the internal temperature registers 140° to 145° when tested with a meat thermometer, transfer the lamb to a heated platter and allow to rest for 10 minutes before carving. Combine the pan juices with the remaining marinade and cook down until reduced by one third. Strain, correct the seasoning and serve with the lamb. Also serve potatoes that have been peeled, sliced and sautéed in beef fat or butter until nicely browned and crisp at the edges, and braised or puréed turnips. Serves 8.

Here is another unusual way to treat a leg of lamb. It is boned, flattened and then broiled like a very thick steak.

BUTTERFLY LEG OF LAMB

Have a leg of lamb boned and then opened out so that it lies flat. Spread it on a board and rub it well with garlic, thyme and either bay leaf or rosemary. Arrange on a rack and broil 4 to 5 inches from the heat for 40 to 50 minutes, depending on the state of rareness you prefer. Brush occasionally with melted butter or oil flavored with a little of the seasoning herb. Salt and pepper to taste. The lamb should be turned once or twice during the cooking. To serve, slice on a diagonal in thickish slices. Serves 6 to 8.

Many people consider the flavor of the shoulder meat to be superior to that of the leg—and certainly the difference in price is worth considering. The shoulder is a good buy for both roasting and braising.

BRAISED SHOULDER OF LAMB BONNE FEMME

1 shoulder of lamb, boned but not tied
2 cups finely grated fresh bread crumbs
½ cup chopped parsley
1½ cups finely chopped onion, sautéed in butter
2 tablespoons soft butter
Salt, pepper, rosemary
1 pound white pea beans
1½ cups finely diced carrots
2 cloves garlic

Mix the bread crumbs, parsley, ½ cup sautéed onion, and soft butter. Season with salt, pepper and a little rosemary, and mix well. Stuff the shoulder with this mixture and tie it well.

Roast in a large casserole in a

325° oven for 1 hour. Meanwhile, cook the pea beans (soaked in water overnight unless they are the processed, quick-cooking type) in water to cover with salt, pepper and a clove of garlic until almost done. Add to the casserole the beans, carrots, remaining sautéed onion and garlic. Cover. Continue cooking until the beans are tender and the meat done. Serve from the casserole. Serves 6.

LEFTOVER ROAST LAMB

Cold lamb is a delicious treat. Use it for sandwiches or to make dishes like Moussaka, stuffed eggplant or an unusual hash.

MOUSSAKA

2 medium eggplants
Olive oil
1 large onion, chopped
4 tablespoons butter
2 pounds cold lamb, ground or chopped very fine
½ pound mushrooms, finely chopped
4 or 5 tablespoons bread crumbs
1 clove garlic, finely chopped
2 tablespoons chopped parsley
3 eggs, slightly beaten
Salt, pepper, nutmeg
¾ cup tomato purée

Carefully peel skin from eggplants in large strips. Set aside. Cut 10 slices of eggplant, about ½ inch thick, and chop the rest. Brown chopped eggplant in oil and sauté slices in oil in another skillet.
Sauté onion in butter, then combine with the lamb, mushrooms, eggplant cubes, bread crumbs, garlic, parsley, eggs, salt and pepper to taste and a dash of nutmeg. Mix in the tomato purée.

Line a deep round oiled baking dish or mold or ovenproof glass casserole with the eggplant skin, purple side down, draping it around the inside and over the edge of the mold. Put in a layer of the meat mixture, then a layer of eggplant slices, and continue until mold is filled. Fold any overhanging edges of eggplant skin over it, cover top with more skin and stand the mold in a pan of hot water. Bake in a 350° oven for 1 to 1¼ hours, or until set. Remove from the oven and let it rest for a few moments and then unmold on a hot platter. Serve with Tomato Sauce and, if you wish, Rice Pilaf. Serves 6.

EGGPLANT STUFFED WITH LAMB

4 medium eggplants
3 tablespoons butter
2 tablespoons oil
1 large onion, finely chopped
2 cloves garlic, finely chopped
1 cup cooked rice
1½ to 2 cups finely ground cold lamb
4 tablespoons chopped parsley
½ cup chopped walnuts
2 tablespoons tomato paste or catsup
Salt, freshly ground black pepper
2 eggs, well beaten
Olive oil
Fine dry bread crumbs

Halve the eggplant lengthwise and remove the pulp with a sharp knife, leaving a thin layer inside each shell. Chop the removed pulp and set aside.

Heat the butter and oil in a heavy skillet, add the onion and garlic and sauté until just limp. Add the eggplant pulp and sauté for 4 minutes. Stir in the rice, lamb, parsley, walnuts, tomato paste and salt and pepper to taste. Blend well. Stir in the beaten eggs and cook for 2 minutes. Taste for seasoning. Fill the eggplant shells with the mixture, spoon a little olive oil over each one and sprinkle with crumbs. Arrange stuffed shells in a 2-inch-deep baking pan or dish and add about ½ inch of water and a few spoonfuls of oil. Bake in a preheated 350° oven for about 40 minutes, basting occasionally with a little oil or melted butter. Serve as a first course for dinner, or as a main dish for luncheon. Serves 8 as a first course, 4 as a main course.

LAMB HASH WITH ONIONS AND APPLES

[This freezes well.]

3 tablespoons oil
1 medium onion, cut in rings
3 cooking apples, diced
1½ to 2 cups diced cold lamb
Salt, freshly ground black pepper
1 tablespoon tomato sauce or catsup
½ cup lamb gravy, brown sauce or canned beef gravy

Heat the oil in a heavy skillet, add the onion and cook until just limp. Add the apples and toss well with the onion. Cook for about 3 minutes, or until blended. Add the

lamb and mix well. Add salt to taste, ½ teaspoon pepper and the tomato sauce or catsup. Cover and simmer for 5 minutes. Remove lid, add the sauce or gravy and heat through thoroughly. Correct the seasoning and serve over steamed rice with a garnish of chopped parsley. Serves 4.

VARIATION

Add 1 tablespoon curry powder to the onion-apple mixture. Serve the hash with some warm chutney.

Breast of Lamb

Breast of lamb is good many ways—braised, broiled, barbecued or made into stews. There is little meat on this cut, but the flavor is good, and it is most economical provided it is not too fatty. Buy the leanest you can find and allow about 1 pound per person, because of the bones.

BREAST OF LAMB DIABLE

4 pounds lamb breast
1 onion, stuck with 2 cloves
1 clove garlic
1 bay leaf
1 sprig parsley
1 rib celery
1 carrot
1½ teaspoons salt
Beaten eggs
Dry bread crumbs
Butter

Put the meat into a deep pot with the onion, garlic, bay leaf, parsley, celery, carrot and water to cover. Bring to a boil. Boil 5 minutes, then skim off scum. Reduce heat, add salt, cover and simmer until tender, about 1 hour. Transfer the meat to a large plate or platter and remove the little rib bones. Cover with another plate and weight down while cooling, to give a firm consistency. Strain and reserve lamb broth for soup stock or stews. Cut the cooled meat into serving-size pieces, dip them in beaten egg and then in dry bread crumbs. Sauté in butter until crisp and brown on all sides. Serve with Sauce Diable. Serves 4.

VARIATIONS

1. Instead of Sauce Diable, serve with a Sauce Soubise, a cream sauce mixed with finely chopped onions that have been steamed in butter, shredded Gruyère and grated Parmesan cheese, seasoned to taste with salt and pepper.
2. Sauté the coated lamb pieces in olive oil flavored with a little garlic instead of in butter. Serve with Tomato Sauce.
3. Instead of coating the lamb with egg and bread crumbs, brush the pieces with French mustard, salt and pepper and then roll them in bread crumbs. Broil, basting with butter and turning frequently to brown them evenly. Serve with Sauce Diable.

Lamb Stews and Casseroles

Breast of lamb can be used for a blanquette of young lamb. Or, if you prefer, use boned lamb shoulder. Both are good economical cuts.

BLANQUETTE OF YOUNG LAMB

[This freezes well.]

4 pounds lamb breast or boned shoulder, cut into 1½-inch cubes or pieces
8 tablespoons butter
Salt, freshly ground black pepper
1 pound small white onions, peeled
½ pound mushrooms, sliced
¼ cup dry sherry or white wine
1 cup medium cream sauce
½ cup heavy cream
Small fried croutons

Brown the lamb on all sides in 4 tablespoons hot butter. Salt and pepper to taste and cook about 20 minutes, then reduce the heat to low and cook for 15 minutes more.

Meanwhile, melt the remaining butter in a pan and sauté the onions until they are tender and lightly browned, but still on the crisp side. Add the mushrooms and cook with the onions about 5 minutes. Add the lamb. Rinse with the sherry or white wine the saucepan in which the lamb cooked, and pour over the lamb. Add the cream sauce and heavy cream. Cover the pan and simmer about 35 minutes. Serve with the croutons. Serves 6 to 8.

Note: This may be made the day before or in the morning and reheated just before serving time.

Here are two other ways to use thrifty lamb shoulder: a delicate lemon-flavored stew and a bean-and-lamb casserole.

LAMB WITH LEMON SAUCE

4 tablespoons olive oil
4 tablespoons butter
1 bunch green onions, chopped
1 head lettuce, shredded
2 large onions, peeled and chopped
3 pounds shoulder of lamb, cubed
Salt, freshly ground black pepper
1 teaspoon dill
White wine, stock or water
Arrowroot
Juice of 1 lemon
Rind of 1 lemon, finely chopped
3 egg yolks

Heat the oil in a large skillet with the butter. Add the green onions, lettuce and chopped onion and cook gently until wilted and soft. Add the lamb and cook, turning frequently, until colored, but not browned, on all sides. Season with salt and pepper to taste and add the dill. Barely cover with wine, stock or water and simmer gently until the lamb is tender. Taste for seasoning.

Mix a little arrowroot with the lemon juice and rind and stir slowly into the lamb stew. Cook, stirring constantly, until well blended and slightly thickened. Remove from the heat.

Beat the egg yolks slightly and mix in a little of the hot sauce. Slowly add to the stew, stirring it in carefully, a little at a time, so that the eggs do not curdle. Cook until thickened, stirring over very low heat, but do not let it boil. Serves 6 to 8.

HARICOT OF LAMB

[This freezes well.]

1 pound pinto beans or white pea beans
Salt, freshly ground black pepper
1 onion stuck with 2 cloves
1 bay leaf
3 cloves garlic
2½ pounds lamb shoulder, cut into 1½-inch cubes
Flour
4 to 6 tablespoons olive oil
3 leeks, washed and sliced
1 teaspoon thyme
Broth or red wine
Buttered crumbs

Soak the beans overnight in water to cover. Next day, drain them and put them in a kettle with 1 teaspoon salt, the onion, bay leaf and 1 clove garlic. Add water to slightly more than cover. Bring to a boil, lower the heat, and simmer gently until the beans are just tender.

Meanwhile, dust the lamb cubes with flour seasoned with salt and pepper. Brown them on all sides in the hot oil. Add the remaining garlic cloves, finely chopped, the leeks, thyme and enough broth or wine just to cover. Bring to a boil, reduce the heat and simmer, covered, until the lamb is just tender. Combine the lamb mixture with the cooked, drained beans and put in a baking dish. Bake uncovered in a 350° oven for 45 to 60 minutes, basting from time to time with a little more broth or wine. Sprinkle the top with buttered crumbs and bake 15 to 20 minutes more—it should be moist and mellow, neither too dry nor too juicy. Serves 6.

Lamb Shanks

Properly prepared, economical lamb shanks can be tasty, chewy morsels. This is my favorite method. Allow 1 lamb shank per person and get the meatiest you can find.

BRAISED LAMB SHANKS WITH RATATOUILLE

6 lamb shanks
Flour
Salt, freshly ground black pepper
4 tablespoons butter
2 tablespoons oil
2 cloves garlic, finely chopped
2 bay leaves
1 teaspoon oregano or tarragon
1 cup stock
Ratatouille (page 140)

Trim any excess fat from the lamb shanks and dust them in flour seasoned with salt and pepper. Sear them well in the hot butter and oil. When nicely browned all over, add the garlic, 1 bay leaf, oregano or tarragon, and stock. Cover and simmer for 1 hour.

Meanwhile, prepare Ratatouille. Transfer the Ratatouille to a baking dish. Top with lamb shanks. Pour pan juices over all. Bake, covered, in a 350° oven for 20 minutes, then remove the cover and bake 15 to 20 minutes longer or until the shanks are browned and tender. Serves 6.

Other Parts of the Animal (Lamb)

LAMB'S LIVER

The liver of the lamb is just as good as calf's liver, but less well known and therefore usually a good buy. Slice it paper-thin, dip it in flour and sauté in olive oil and butter with a few green onions and chopped parsley, turning once. It should cook in about 1½ minutes. Serve with boiled potatoes and crisp bacon.

LAMB'S BRAINS

These take the same treatment as calf's brains. Soak them in cold water and remove the membrane. Then poach them in a little water with lemon juice, slice them and combine with scrambled eggs.

Or sauté them lightly in plenty of butter and serve with beurre noir (butter that has been browned and mixed with a dash of wine vinegar or lemon juice).

Or chill the poached brains and serve them with a Vinaigrette Sauce.

LAMB TONGUES

These delicate little morsels can be served in various ways after they have been cooked and skinned. They may be served hot with a Vinaigrette or Gribiche Sauce, or with a Sauce Poulette. Or they may be pickled and eaten cold with potato or rice salad.

PICKLED LAMB TONGUES

8 to 12 lamb tongues
1 onion stuck with 2 cloves
2 cloves garlic
1 bay leaf

3 teaspoons tarragon
Salt, freshly ground black pepper
6 to 8 peppercorns
½ teaspoon mace
White wine vinegar or a delicate
apple cider vinegar

Clean the tongues and put into a
heavy saucepan with the onion,
garlic, bay leaf, 1 teaspoon tarragon, 1 tablespoon or more salt, 1
teaspoon freshly ground pepper and
water to cover. Bring to a boil, reduce heat, cover and simmer for 1
hour, or until tongues are just

tender. Drain. When cool enough
to handle, trim and skin the
tongues and cut them in half
lengthwise. Place them in a crock
or jar and pour over them a pickle
made with the remaining tarragon,
peppercorns, mace, vinegar to cover
and salt to taste. Allow to stand for
several days or a week before using.
These are delicious as a first course,
sliced and served with a Rémoulade
Sauce or a Tomato Sauce, or combined with ham and cheese for
sandwiches.

PORK

Pork is one of the most versatile, economical and underestimated of meats,
with an affinity for an extraordinary number of flavorings. I can't think of
any part of the pig that isn't good when prepared in one fashion or another.

There has been a trend in the last few calorie-conscious years toward
producing pork that is leaner, with less marbling of fat, which has the effect
of making the meat rather less tender. However, this seems to have made
little difference, as the meat when roasted is usually cooked at a temperature of 325°, and its own covering of fat makes it pretty well self-basting.
Also, as it has been proved that there is no danger of trichinosis after the
meat reaches an internal temperature of 160°, pork is now roasted for a
shorter time than formerly, when it was believed that the internal temperature had to be 180° to 185°. The American Meat Institute has recommended a 170° temperature, and certainly pork that is roasted to this mark
is much less likely to dry out. Remember, too, that the internal temperature
of roast pork, like that of other meats, increases after it is taken from the
oven, so if you want really juicy pork, remove it when the thermometer
reaches 165°.

The three recommended cuts of pork for roasting are the loin, the
shoulder, and the leg, or fresh ham. The most commonly used is the loin.
Pork loin is equally good hot or cold, so don't worry if you have leftovers.

Loin of Pork

The loin has a great deal of bone,
so when buying estimate about 1
pound per person. Have the chine

bone removed to make carving
easier, the bones cracked and the
loin tied securely. The loin constitutes the entire rack and is usually
sold in one piece (the whole loin)

or divided into the rib end and the loin end. If you are serving only 2, buy either the loin end with the filet or the smaller rib end. For a large dinner party, you will want the whole loin.

As pork is less expensive than other meats, you will find that the low price per pound of a whole loin gives you an advantage over buying just part of one. This makes a most spectacular crown roast.

CROWN ROAST OF PORK

Ask your butcher to tie the whole loin into a crown, and to scrape the bones. (Keep the scraps and use them for stock.) Wrap the ends of the rib bones with foil to prevent them from charring, and rub the meat well with salt, freshly ground black pepper and a bit of sage and rosemary. Fill the center of the roast with foil, place it on a rack in a roasting pan and roast in a 325° oven, allowing about 25 minutes per pound, until the interior temperature registers 165°. Baste from time to time with white wine.

Remove the meat from the oven when cooked and take the foil from the center and the bones. (You may cap the bones with paper frills if you like.) Fill the center with any of the following:

Sauerkraut cooked in white wine with a few juniper berries.

Buttered noodles mixed with sautéed sliced mushrooms.

Rice mixed with peas and parsley. Cut the roast into individual chops and serve one or two to a person.

PRUNE-STUFFED PORK LOIN

2 pounds large prunes
1 cup sherry
A 5- to 6-pound pork loin
Salt, freshly ground black pepper
12 small peeled potatoes or 6 large potatoes, halved or quartered
12 small white onions
2 tablespoons flour
1 cup cream

Soak the prunes in the sherry for 12 hours before stuffing the roast.

Have the chine bone removed and the roast trimmed. Make 2 long incisions in the fleshiest part of the meat, cutting it almost to the bone. Remove the prunes from the sherry and pit them. Fill the incisions in the roast with the pitted prunes, pressing them in tightly. Press the roast back into shape and tie securely with string in several places. Rub lightly with salt. Place on a rack in a roasting pan. Roast in a 325° oven, allowing about 25 minutes per pound, until the internal temperature reaches 165°, basting with the pan juices mixed with the sherry in which the prunes soaked. Add the potatoes and onions to the pan during the last hour of cooking time.

When the roast is cooked, remove it to a hot platter and let stand 15 minutes before carving. Remove the string. Surround with the roast potatoes and onions. Skim the fat from the pan juices and thicken them with the flour. Add the cream and cook over low heat until thickened. Season to taste with salt and pepper and serve with the pork. Serves 6.

When you carve the roast, you will get slices beautifully marbled with the prunes. The flavor will be like nothing you have ever tasted before and we are sure it will put pork at the head of your list. The pork is also excellent served cold with a spicy mustard sauce and dilled potato salad made with plenty of chopped onion and parsley.

ORANGE-GLAZED LOIN OF PORK

A 5- to 6-pound pork loin
1 or 2 cloves garlic, cut in slivers
Rosemary, salt to taste
1 can frozen concentrated orange juice, undiluted
Bitter orange marmalade
1 cup orange sections
½ cup fresh orange juice

Make incisions in the pork and insert the garlic slivers. Rub the roast lightly with rosemary and salt it well. Place on a rack in a shallow roasting pan and roast in a 325° oven, allowing about 25 minutes per pound. After the first 1½ hours, baste the roast with the undiluted orange juice. Roast for another 30 minutes, then spread the roast well with marmalade. Roast 30 minutes longer, then baste again with concentrated orange juice and add more marmalade, if necessary. The fat should be nicely glazed and there should be quite a lot of juice in the pan. When the meat has reached 165° (test by inserting a meat thermometer), remove it carefully to a serving platter or carving board and spread with another spoonful of marmalade. Skim the fat from the pan and combine the juices with the orange sections and fresh orange juice. Correct the seasoning. Serve the roast with the orange sauce and puréed yams. Serves 6.

Pork Shoulder

Pork shoulder makes a good roast, but tastes even better braised. For roasting, have the shoulder boned and tied to make carving simpler. If you can buy a shoulder with the skin on, do. Roast pork skin or crackling is too good to miss. If you are going to braise the meat, have the shoulder skinned, boned and tied. Try out the skin in a slow oven until crisp and crunchy; it makes a wonderful cocktail snack.

ROAST SHOULDER OF PORK WITH APPLES AND ONIONS

A 4- to 5-pound boned, tied shoulder of pork
Thyme, ground coriander
6 to 8 medium onions, peeled
8 cooking apples, cored
½ cup raisins
¼ cup chopped walnuts
8 tablespoons sugar
8 tablespoons butter
½ cup melted butter mixed with 3 tablespoons sugar
Salt, freshly ground pepper
1 cup heavy cream

Rub the shoulder well with a little thyme and ground coriander. Arrange on a rack in a roasting pan and roast in a 325° oven, allowing about 25 minutes per pound, until the internal temperature reaches 165°. After about 1¼ hours, add the onions to the pan. Baste with the pan juices and cook until tender but not mushy.

Meanwhile, remove a center band of skin from the cored apples. Stuff the cores with the mixed raisins, nuts, sugar and butter. Put them in a baking dish, add ½ cup water and bake in the oven with the pork until they are just tender, basting occasionally with the butter-sugar mixture.

Salt and pepper the pork well and remove it from the oven when it reaches 165°. Allow to rest on a hot platter for 10 minutes before carving. Drain the onions and arrange them around the meat. Serve the apples separately. Skim the excess fat from the juices in the roasting pan and combine the juices and cream. Bring to boiling point and cook down for several minutes. Season to taste and serve with the pork.

This coriander-flavored pork is wonderful cold. Serve with Vegetables Vinaigrette and French bread.

BRAISED PORK SHOULDER WITH CABBAGE

A 4- to 5-pound shoulder of pork, boned, rolled and tied
Pork fat or bacon fat
Salt, freshly ground black pepper
2 cups white wine
1 large head cabbage, shredded

Brown the pork quickly all over in pork or bacon fat in a deep kettle or Dutch oven. Season to taste with salt and pepper, add 1 cup wine, cover and simmer for 2 to 3 hours, or until the meat is tender.

Meanwhile, blanch the cabbage quickly in boiling salted water. Drain. Melt 6 tablespoons bacon fat in a large skillet, add the cabbage and braise over brisk heat until just colored. Add the remaining wine, 1 teaspoon salt and 1 teaspoon pepper. Cover the pan and simmer gently for 1 hour, stirring occasionally. Serve the pork with the cabbage, boiled potatoes and a selection of mustards.

In the following recipes cubed pork shoulder is combined with different ingredients to make an interesting ragout and goulash.

PORK RAGOUT

3 pounds pork shoulder, cut in 1½-inch cubes
Flour seasoned with salt
3 to 4 tablespoons fat trimmed from the meat
6 small onions, thinly sliced
3 cloves garlic, chopped
½ teaspoon thyme
½ teaspoon ground ginger
Dash of Tabasco
Broth or water
½ cup tomato purée
1 pound fresh snap beans

Dust the pork cubes with the seasoned flour. Try out the pork fat in a large kettle. When it is melted and crisp, add the onions and cook until delicately browned. Add the pork to the pan and brown all over. Add the garlic, thyme, ginger, Tabasco and just enough broth or water to cover. Bring to a boil, reduce the heat, cover and simmer gently or cook in a 325° oven for 2 to 2½ hours. Remove the lid and skim off the fat. Stir in the tomato purée and top with the snap beans. Cover and cook 30 minutes more. Taste for seasoning.

Serve the ragout with steamed potatoes. Serves 6.

PORK-AND-SAUERKRAUT GOULASH

3 pounds pork shoulder, cut into 1½-inch cubes
4 tablespoons pork fat or olive oil
3 large onions, chopped
2 sweet green peppers, seeded and cut in thin strips
1 tablespoon Hungarian paprika
½ bay leaf
½ cup water or stock
1 twenty-ounce can tomatoes or 5 fresh tomatoes, peeled, cored and chopped
1 twenty-seven-ounce can sauerkraut
Salt, freshly ground black pepper
1 cup sour cream

Sauté pork in a heavy skillet in the fat or oil until lightly browned. Add onions, green pepper and paprika. Sauté until vegetables are just limp. Add bay leaf, water or stock, tomatoes and sauerkraut. Cover and simmer very slowly for 1 hour, or until the meat is tender. Season with salt and pepper to taste. Serve very hot with sour cream spooned over goulash. Serves 6.

Fresh Ham

This is the uncured pork leg and a most versatile cut. It varies in size from 5 or 6 pounds up to 25 pounds and may be roasted with the bone in, boned and stuffed, or after marinating in wine, which gives it a really different and delightful flavor. Estimate about 1 pound per serving.

DRUNKEN PORK

A 6- to 8-pound fresh ham, boned and tied
2 to 3 cloves garlic, crushed
1 onion, thinly sliced
1 bay leaf
½ teaspoon ground cloves
¼ teaspoon ground ginger
¼ teaspoon ground or grated nutmeg
1 tablespoon salt
1 teaspoon crushed rosemary
Red wine
Beurre Manié
½ cup sultana raisins
½ cup pine nuts
Tabasco

Place the ham in a large, deep nonmetallic container with the garlic, onion, seasonings and enough red wine to cover. Turn it once and let it stand, covered, for 3 to 4 days in the refrigerator, turning every day.

When you are ready to roast it, remove from the refrigerator and let stand at room temperature for several hours, turning 2 or 3 times. Place on a rack in a shallow roasting pan and roast in a 325° oven, allowing 25 minutes per pound.

Baste frequently with the strained and heated marinade. When the internal temperature reaches 165°, remove the roast and keep hot. Skim fat from the pan juices, and if sauce has cooked down too much add a little more red wine. Bring to a boil. Thicken, if you wish, with Beurre Manié. Correct the seasoning, add the raisins, pine nuts and a good dash of Tabasco. Serve with the roast.

Pork Chops

The best chops are those cut from the loin or the rib section. Shoulder chops are not as thrifty a buy as they may seem, because of the amount of bone and fat. Have chops cut on the thick side (about an inch thick) if you are going to sauté them. Allow one good-sized chop per serving. This is a classic French way of cooking pork chops.

PORK CHOPS
CHARCUTIERE

4 pork loin chops, cut 1 inch thick
Pork fat or butter
2 large onions, finely chopped
Salt, freshly ground black pepper
1½ cups stock
½ cup tomato purée
1 teaspoon dry mustard
Beurre Manié
2 tablespoons finely chopped sour
  gherkins
Chopped parsley

Sauté the pork chops in pork fat or butter until nicely browned on both sides. Add the onions, cover the pan and let them cook down with the meat. Season with salt and pepper to taste. When the chops are cooked through, transfer them to a hot platter. Add the stock to the pan and bring to a boil. Mix in the tomato purée, mustard and ½ teaspoon pepper. Thicken the sauce with Beurre Manié and stir in the gherkins and parsley just before serving. Serve the chops with creamy mashed potatoes and serve the sauce separately. Serves 4.

Note: For heartier appetites, provide 2 chops per person. The same amount of sauce will be sufficient.

ROAST SPARERIBS

Many ways to prepare spareribs have been popularized these last few years, but we happen to feel that they are at their succulent best when merely roasted in the oven until crisp. Figure on at least 1 pound spareribs per person and try to get good country-style spareribs which have more meat on them.

Salt and pepper the spareribs to taste and arrange on a rack in a roasting pan. Roast in a 325° oven for 1 hour, turning twice during the cooking. They should be well browned and crisp. If you like, you can omit the salt and brush the spareribs with soy sauce before and during the roasting period.

Other Parts
of the Animal (Pork)

Pigs' ears, tails, feet and hocks are tasty bits of the pig that are often overlooked, yet they make wonderful eating if properly prepared, and they certainly qualify as economical food. If you like the rather resistant, gelatinous texture of the feet, you will also like the ears.

PIGS' EARS

Scrub the ears well and simmer them until tender in salted water with an onion stuck with 2 cloves, 1 carrot, a bouquet garni and some peppercorns. Drain. Serve them hot with a Vinaigrette Sauce or lemon butter; or let them cool, cut them in half, dip in beaten egg and dry bread crumbs and fry in deep fat at 360° for 3 or 4 minutes, or until browned. You can also cut them in strips and cook them slowly in butter with onions that have been sautéed until lightly browned.

PIGS' TAILS

Pigs' tails may be boiled like the ears for 2 hours with flavorings, then cooled, rolled in dry toasted crumbs and broiled slowly about 4 inches from the heat until they are heated through and nicely browned on all sides. Turn them often and watch carefully to see that they do not burn. Serve with English mustard or the sauce given below for Pigs' Feet St.-Menehould.

PIGS' FEET ST.-MENEHOULD

This is a famous way of preparing this part of the animal. Try to get feet that are cut long so you will have more meat. Scrub the feet well and wrap them carefully in pieces of cheesecloth. Wrap them very tightly (this prevents the skin from breaking during the long cooking process). Tie them securely and place them in a kettle with a bay leaf, an onion stuck with cloves, a carrot, 1 tablespoon of salt, a few peppercorns and a little thyme. Cover with water and bring to a boil. Simmer for about 4 hours or longer. Let the feet cool in the broth. When they are cool enough to handle, unroll the feet from the cloth, place them on a deep plate or platter, and pour a little of the broth over them. Chill.

When you are ready to serve them, remove the feet and roll them in dry toasted crumbs until they are well covered. Broil slowly until they are heated through and nicely browned on all sides. Watch them carefully so that they do not burn—keep them about 4 inches from the flame and let them cook slowly, turning often. Or they may be placed on a rack and baked in a 475° oven until brown.

Serve with . . .

PUNGENT SAUCE

6 shallots, finely chopped
3 tablespoons butter
1 tablespoon wine vinegar
1 tablespoon Worcestershire sauce
1 teaspoon dry mustard
3 tablespoons bottled Sauce Diable

Sauté the shallots in the butter, then mix in the vinegar, Worcestershire, mustard and Sauce Diable. Bring to the boiling point and serve.

PICKLED PIGS' FEET

Boil the pigs' feet as for Pigs' Feet St.-Menehould, then cool and unwrap them and place in a jar of spiced vinegar (2 cups white wine or cider vinegar combined with 1 bay leaf and 6 to 8 peppercorns). Leave in the pickle for a week before using. Serve cold. Good with beer and a salad.

JELLIED PIGS' FEET

Wash 6 or 8 pigs' feet well and put them in a kettle with 2 bay leaves, 1 teaspoon salt, 6 peppercorns, 2 cloves garlic, 2 onions stuck with 2 cloves each, 1 teaspoon tarragon, 2 cups white wine plus enough water to cover. Bring to a boil, skim off the scum, reduce the heat, cover and simmer gently for about 5 hours or until the meat is almost falling off the bones. Remove the feet from the broth and cool. Strain the broth, clarify it with a beaten egg white and an eggshell and strain through a cloth napkin.

Remove the meat from the bones and arrange in a mold. Top with a few sliced sour pickles, a few pistachio nuts and some diced cooked tongue. Cover with the broth and then with a layer of foil. Put a plate on top and weight it down. Chill until set, then turn out of the mold, slice and serve as an hors d'oeuvre or luncheon dish.

PIGS' HOCKS

Hocks may be boiled for 2 to 3 hours in the same manner as pigs' feet and served hot with horseradish or mustard sauce. Or, after boiling, cut the meat from the bones in large pieces, dip them in beaten egg, roll in dry crumbs and sauté in butter or pork fat until nicely browned. Serve with cooked white pea beans flavored with garlic, butter and parsley. This is good bourgeois cooking backed by long tradition.

Ham

Most of the hams sold in the markets have been "tenderized" and do not need long soaking or boiling. All you have to do is bake them. However, the aged and country-cured hams that can be bought in special food shops or ordered by mail have a much better flavor and texture. These need to be soaked, sometimes scrubbed, boiled, and skinned before they can be baked. Directions are usually included with the hams. Leftover ham is never any problem; there are always many ways to serve it, and the ham bone with any meat left on it can be used to make a good old-fashioned Split Pea Soup or Lentil Soup or for the wonderful Garbure Basquaise.

JAMBON EN CROUTE

Whole country ham, about 10 pounds
1 cup dry bread crumbs soaked in sherry or red wine

1 teaspoon thyme
1 teaspoon dry mustard
Ground cloves
½ teaspoon nutmeg
Pie pastry (double the amount
needed for a 2-crust pie)
Beaten egg yolk

Prepare the ham for baking. Soak, boil (allowing about 20 minutes per pound) and skin it, trimming off excess fat.

Combine the bread crumbs, thyme, mustard, a dash of cloves and the nutmeg. Rub the mixture well into the fat and surface of the ham.

Roll out the pastry dough until it is large enough to cover the top and sides of the ham, reserving scraps for decoration. Roll out the scraps and cut them into leaves, flowers or whatever shapes appeal to you. Cover top and sides of ham completely with the dough, molding it to the contours of the ham with your hands. Do not cover the bottom. Cut a hole in the center top of the dough and decorate the surface with the decorations, securing them to the crust with cold water. Brush the entire surface with beaten egg, and bake the ham in a 300° oven for 1¼ to 1½ hours. If necessary, raise the temperature a little toward the end of the cooking time to brown the crust. To serve, surround with glazed sweet potatoes and sautéed mushroom caps. Mustard sauce also goes well with the ham.

Note: If you prefer to use a tenderized, ready-to-eat ham, it will need some preliminary baking. Remove the skin and excess fat and place fat side down in a roasting pan. Add a pint of sherry or red wine to the pan, cover with foil and bake in a 350° oven for 1½ hours. Remove and cool. Spread breadcrumb mixture on ham, cover with pastry dough and bake as directed.

Here are some good ways to use up cold baked ham.

JAMBON PERSILLE

4 to 5 pounds cooked ham, cut into
  1-inch to 1½-inch cubes
2 envelopes gelatin
¾ cup water
3 cups consommé
½ cup white wine
¼ cup tarragon vinegar
1 teaspoon dried tarragon
⅓ cup chopped parsley

Arrange the ham cubes in a large glass or porcelain bowl. Soak the gelatin in ½ cup cold water. Heat the consommé, wine, vinegar and remaining ¼ cup water and add to the gelatin, stirring until dissolved. Cool the liquid slightly and add the tarragon and parsley. Pour the mixture over the ham, which should be covered by the liquid. Place a plate on top and weight it down. Chill until completely set and firm. To serve, unmold the ham and slice it, or cut it into thin slices in the bowl. Serves 8 to 10.

MOUSSE DE JAMBON FROID

4 tablespoons butter
4 tablespoons flour

1 cup milk
Salt, nutmeg, cayenne pepper
¼ cup brandy
½ cup heavy cream mixed with
   2 egg yolks
2 envelopes gelatin
½ cup cold water
½ cup hot stock
2 cups cold ham, ground very fine

Melt the butter in a saucepan and mix in the flour. Gradually stir in the milk and cook over low heat, stirring, until thickened. Season to taste with salt, ½ teaspoon nutmeg and a few grains of cayenne. Stir in the brandy. Mix a little of the hot sauce into the cream–egg-yolk mixture, then add it to the balance of the sauce, stirring until blended and thickened. Do not allow to boil. Soak the gelatin in the cold water, then dissolve it in the hot stock and blend it into the sauce. Mix in the ground ham and pour into a mold. Chill until firm and set. When ready to serve, unmold and decorate with thinly sliced cucumbers that have been marinated in 3 tablespoons wine vinegar with 2 tablespoons sugar, 3 tablespoons chopped parsley and a little chopped fresh dill. Serves 6 to 8.

This is a good dish for a summer luncheon party. Even though it is not expensive or hard to prepare, it looks and tastes special.

DEVILED HAM

2 cups freshly ground cold ham
   (trimmings from the bone are
   excellent)

4 tablespoons finely chopped sweet
   or sour pickles
Ginger, cloves, nutmeg
Homemade Mayonnaise

Blend the ham with the pickle (sweet or sour according to taste), a mere pinch of ginger, cloves and nutmeg and enough mayonnaise to make a spreadable paste. Pile into jars or crocks. This will keep for a week or so in the refrigerator. Excellent for sandwiches and snacks and for stuffings and seasonings.

Pork Sausage

In cities and towns where there are good French, German, Polish, Italian or Swiss butchers or pork stores you can usually find a delicious variety of excellent sausages. The French sausages are usually mild in flavor, except for the pungent garlic sausages. In Italian markets you will find sweet sausage with delicate seasoning and those that are stinging hot with pepper and basil and often anise. Polish markets have a variety of fresh sausages, most of which are highly spiced. American varieties of link sausage vary from heavily saged to delicately perfumed small links. Some are smoked.

To cook these sausages, poach them in water or in white wine for about 15 minutes, then pour off the water, add a little butter or oil to the pan and sauté the sausages until they are nicely browned and thoroughly cooked, turning once or twice. Drain on absorbent paper.

In German pork stores you will find bratwurst. Poach it for about 10 minutes in salted water, remove, dry and sauté very slowly in butter with finely chopped onions. With mashed potatoes and sauerkraut, this makes a wonderful dish.

ITALIAN SAUSAGES WITH PEPPERS

4 to 5 red or green bell peppers
12 to 18 Italian sausages, according to size
Olive oil
2 cloves garlic, finely chopped
Salt to taste
1 tablespoon red wine vinegar
2 tablespoons chopped Italian parsley

Although it is not essential, this dish is far better if you take the trouble to skin the peppers. Stick them on a fork and hold them over a gas flame, or place under the broiler, until the skin blackens and bursts. Scrape off the charred skin, seed the peppers and cut them in strips.

Blanch the sausages in boiling water for 6 or 7 minutes. Drain and brown them in 2 to 3 tablespoons olive oil, cooking slowly until done. Pour enough olive oil in a heavy skillet to cover the bottom of the pan. Heat oil, add the garlic and pepper strips and sauté gently until the peppers are just tender (skinned peppers take less time than the raw, unskinned). Cover the pan for part of the cooking time to tenderize the peppers, if you like. Season with salt and just before the peppers are done add the wine vinegar. Combine the peppers, sausages and parsley and serve with Polenta or rice. Serves 6.

CHOUCROUTE GARNIE

2 pounds salt pork, in one piece
3 tablespoons butter or goose fat
3 cans (27-ounce size) sauerkraut, well washed
8 to 10 juniper berries
2 cups white wine
1 cup stock or broth
1 potato, grated
8 knackwurst
2 Polish sausages (kielbasy)
8 bratwurst
8 slices ham
Boiled or steamed potatoes

Cut 12 slices from the salt pork chunk—it should be well streaked with lean. Parboil in water to cover for about 10 minutes. Melt butter or goose fat in the bottom of a deep kettle. Line the bottom of the kettle with the blanched pork slices. Add the sauerkraut, sprinkle with the juniper berries and pour the white wine over them. Push the remaining salt pork chunk into the center of the sauerkraut. Cover and simmer for 30 minutes, then add the stock or broth and the grated potato. Cook another 30 minutes. Just before serving, cook the sausages separately and heat the ham for a few minutes in a little white wine. Remove the salt-pork chunk and cut in slices. Arrange the sauerkraut in the center of a hot platter and surround with slices of salt pork, the knackwurst, kielbasy and bratwurst, and the ham slices, rolled, interspersing the meats and sausages with boiled or steamed potatoes. Serve with Dijon mustard and horseradish. Serves 8.

Choucroute Garnie is a favorite Sunday dish in France, and the leftover sauerkraut is used up the following day.

MONDAY KRAUT

Take a casserole large enough to accommodate the leftover sauerkraut and grease it. Put in a layer of about one third of the sauerkraut, then a generous layer of Gruyère cheese, another layer of kraut, a layer of cheese, and the remaining kraut. Top with a generous layer of buttered crumbs, at least ¼ inch thick. Bake in a 350° oven until the mixture is bubbly and the crumbs are lightly browned.

GARBURE BASQUAISE

This hearty and delicious soup-stew, a mixture of dried legumes, vegetables and sausages, is just the thing for a winter Sunday-night supper. It's also a good way to use up the end of the ham.

1 pound white pea beans
½ pound dried peas
1 ham knuckle, with meat
3 bay leaves
1 onion, stuck with 2 cloves
3 quarts water
6 potatoes, cut into small pieces
4 to 5 carrots, sliced
4 turnips, cut into small pieces
4 to 5 leeks, cut up
6 cloves garlic, chopped
1 teaspoon thyme
1 small head of cabbage, shredded
12 to 16 sausages

Soak the beans and peas overnight, unless they are of the quick-cooking type. Next day put them in a deep pan with the ham knuckle, 2 bay leaves, onion and water. After 1 hour, taste water for salt and add salt if necessary. (If the ham is salty, it may not need salting.) Cook until the beans are just tender but not mushy. Drain beans, reserving liquid; keep beans and ham bone warm while cooking vegetables. Cook the potatoes, carrots, turnips, leeks, garlic, thyme and remaining bay leaf in the bean liquid until tender. Add the shredded cabbage, the beans, the meat from the ham bone, and the sausages. Cook until the cabbage is just done. The soup should be thick enough almost to hold a spoon upright. At this point, you may, if you like, dish it into ovenproof bowls, top it with toast and grated Swiss cheese and put it under the broiler for a minute to glaze the cheese. Or simply sprinkle it with cheese and eat with plenty of French bread.

To make the garbure even more flavorful, you can add leftover cooked fowl—chicken, duck or goose. The sausages may be grilled and served separately or the garbure made with pigs' knuckles rather than the ham bone. The variations are endless, and they provide a good base for the imaginative use of leftovers. Serves 6 to 8.

GROUND MEAT

There must be ten thousand ways in which you can use ground meat, but you need a repertoire of only six or seven good and unusual recipes to maintain a reputation as an imaginative cook. You can vary these basic recipes with different combinations of seasonings and ingredients and create your own specialties.

To start with, here are three ways to make hamburgers, and a word of advice on buying it. It is no economy to buy the ready-ground beef sold for hamburger in supermarkets—this is pretty well fatted, and by the time it is cooked you won't have much meat left. The best hamburger is about 80 percent lean to 20 percent fat. Ask your butcher to grind top or bottom round and to add a small amount of beef suet to it as he grinds. A pound of hamburger will serve 4 if it is on a bun, but allow 8 ounces a serving if it is to be eaten on its own.

CHEESED HAMBURGERS

2 pounds chopped beef
2 tablespoons finely chopped onion
1 clove garlic, finely chopped
½ teaspoon salt
1 teaspoon freshly ground black pepper
⅔ cup grated sharp cheese
1 teaspoon Worcestershire sauce
Dash of Tabasco

Combine all the ingredients, blending well, and form into patties about 1 inch thick. Broil, or pan-broil with a little fat, until crusty brown on the outside and as done as you like them inside. The cheese melts through the meat and gives a pleasant texture that the usual cheeseburger lacks.

GRECIAN HAMBURGERS

2 pounds ground beef
1 medium onion, finely chopped
Salt, freshly ground pepper
2 tablespoons chili sauce

12 medium-thick slices eggplant
Flour
Bacon fat or butter
Tomato sauce

Mix the beef with the onion, 1 teaspoon salt, ½ teaspoon pepper and chili sauce. Form into 6 flat cakes. Flour the eggplant slices and brown them lightly in bacon fat or butter. Season with salt and pepper to taste and keep warm while you broil or pan-broil the hamburgers quickly. Place a patty between two slices of eggplant and serve with tomato sauce to which you have added a pinch of basil and 2 cloves finely chopped garlic sautéed for 1 minute in fat. Serves 6.

MUSHROOMBURGERS

1 pound mushrooms, finely chopped
1 medium onion, finely chopped
1 clove garlic, finely chopped
1 pound ground beef

1 teaspoon salt
1 teaspoon freshly ground black
pepper
4 tablespoons sour cream
Butter
3 tablespoons Worcestershire sauce

Combine the mushrooms, onion and garlic with the ground beef, salt, pepper and sour cream and blend well with your hands. Form into 4 patties. Sauté in butter until nicely browned on both sides and done to your taste. Just before removing patties from the pan, add the Worcestershire sauce and let it swirl around them. Serve with baked potatoes or German fried potatoes and a good sharp salad. With this and other ground-meat dishes, take a hint from the Scandinavians and serve a salad made with thinly sliced cucumbers, onion, chopped parsley, chopped fresh dill (if available) that have been marinated a little in a sauce of vinegar, salt, sugar and water. This sweet-sour combination should be served icy cold.

The following hamburger dish is called Lightning Stew. It bears no real resemblance to a stew, but it is easy, different and certainly quick.

LIGHTNING STEW

2 pounds ground beef
2 medium onions, finely chopped
1½ teaspoons salt
1 teaspoon freshly ground black
pepper
1 tablespoon dry mustard
½ teaspoon thyme

¾ to 1 cup red wine
Flour
Beef fat or bacon fat
1 can small carrots, drained,
or 1 package frozen carrots,
thawed
1 or 2 cans sliced mushrooms

Mix the ground beef with the onions, salt, pepper, mustard, thyme and about 4 tablespoons red wine. Mix thoroughly and roll into small balls about 1 inch in diameter. Dust them lightly with flour and brown in hot beef or bacon fat. Add the canned or frozen carrots, the mushrooms and their liquid and ½ cup or more red wine. Simmer until the vegetables are heated through. Serve with plain boiled potatoes sprinkled with chopped parsley.

Note: You can add to this quick stew any vegetables you like— canned, frozen or leftover. They will blend well with the other flavors. You may also use more wine if you like.

The true shish kebab made with lamb is an expensive dish, but if you like meat broiled on a skewer try this inexpensive version done with hamburger:

HAMBURGER KEBABS

1 pound hamburger
½ cup chopped nuts (any kind
except peanuts)
1 medium onion, finely chopped
½ cup chopped parsley
1 egg
1 teaspoon each salt, pepper,
oregano
French dressing

Mix the hamburger, nuts, onion, parsley, egg and seasonings well with your hands and mold onto 4 or 6 skewers in cakes about 6 or 7 inches long and 1½ inches in diameter. Soak in a good homemade French dressing for 1 hour before cooking (you can use it later for a green salad). Broil the kebabs quickly, turning often so that they brown nicely on all sides. They are delicious served with steamed rice or Rice Pilaf and onions French-fried until they are very crisp and chewy. Serves 4 to 6.

Note: The kebabs may also be made with ground lamb or mutton. If you make them with lamb, be sure to use pine nuts, they are traditional.

Meat Loaves

Meat loaf is most delicious when it is made with a combination of ground beef, veal and pork. Here is another dish that can be varied by using different seasonings.

BASIC MEAT LOAF

1 pound each ground beef, pork, veal
½ cup chopped green onions
½ cup chopped parsley
1 teaspoon salt
1½ teaspoons freshly ground pepper
½ cup fresh bread crumbs soaked in bouillon
½ teaspoon rosemary
Pinch of nutmeg
2 eggs, beaten
Bacon or salt-pork strips

Combine in a bowl the ground meats, green onions, parsley, salt, pepper, bread crumbs, rosemary, nutmeg and eggs. Mix thoroughly with the hands. Shape into a loaf. Arrange a layer of bacon or salt-pork strips in an earthenware baking dish or casserole and put the meat loaf on top. Top with a few strips of bacon or salt pork and bake uncovered in a 325° oven for 1½ to 2 hours. This is delicious hot, but even better if weighted down and served cold. Serves 6 to 8.

VARIATIONS

Bouquetière: Prepare as directed. Place in baking dish or casserole, top with strips of carrot and surround with whole baby carrots and small white onions. Bake at 325° for 45 minutes, then add small whole potatoes and turnips that have been parboiled for 10 minutes. Baste with pan juices and continue baking for 45 minutes more, or until thoroughly done.

Italian: Instead of the rosemary seasoning, add 3 finely chopped garlic cloves, 1 cup whole pitted ripe olives, ½ cup tomato purée and 1 teaspoon chopped fresh basil (or ½ teaspoon dried basil) to the meat mixture. Cover the loaf with a thin layer of tomato purée and top with bacon or salt pork strips. Bake as directed.

French: For the meat mixture, combine 1 pound pork, 1 pound veal and 1 pound chopped beef or pork liver with the seasonings given in the basic recipe. Add 1 cup red wine to the pan and baste frequently with the mixed wine and pan juices.

Mexican: Add to the basic mixture 1 tablespoon chili powder, 1 pinch cumin powder, ½ cup pine nuts and 3 finely chopped small green peppers. Baste with a combination of ½ cup tomato purée, ½ cup tomato juice, 3 finely chopped garlic cloves and 1 tablespoon chili powder.

Good accompaniments for these loaves when served hot are rice or mashed potatoes, and broiled or baked tomatoes. Accompany cold meat loaf with a rice or potato salad and perhaps hot asparagus with Hollandaise Sauce.

OLD-FASHIONED BEACH MEAT LOAF

2 pounds chopped beef, ground twice
1 pound chopped pork, ground twice
1 pound chopped veal, ground twice
1 large onion, chopped or grated
1 carrot, grated
1½ teaspoons salt
1 teaspoon dry mustard
1 teaspoon freshly ground black pepper
1 teaspoon rosemary leaves, crushed
½ bay leaf, crushed
⅔ cup fresh bread crumbs
2 eggs
3 tablespoons chopped parsley
Bacon or salt pork strips

Mix all ingredients but bacon or salt pork together and knead thoroughly. Press down. Form into a tight loaf and place on strips of bacon or salt pork in a shallow baking pan. Cover with more strips of bacon and bake in 350° oven, basting frequently, for 1½ to 2 hours, according to the size of the loaf. This is delicious hot, but even better cold, when it resembles a good pâté de campagne of the French provinces. It must not be baked in a loaf pan and it must be well pressed together with the hands before baking.

5
POULTRY

Topping the list of money-saving foods are chicken and turkey. Poultry is cheaper than most meats and, as a rule, it can be made to go farther. Furthermore, it is so versatile, with an affinity for all kinds of flavors and styles of preparation, that there is almost no limit to the number of interesting ways in which you can prepare it. As a leftover, it can become a different dish entirely.

Duck, we feel, has little part in eating better for less money. While the price is low, duck does not give the meat per pound that either chicken or turkey offers, and the number of ways to prepare it are limited by the nature of the meat and the high proportion of fat and bone. Goose has much the same drawbacks. It is more expensive and harder to get than turkey and, because of its rich covering of fat, will not give anywhere near the meat that a turkey of the same size yields. Accordingly, it seems wiser to eliminate these two birds from this book.

Flavor plays a big part in eating well, and fresh-killed chicken or turkey are infinitely superior to the frozen variety. If you live in the country, there should be no problem about getting fresh-killed birds, but if you live in the city it is advisable to find a butcher shop or market that has daily deliveries from a poultry farm. If you buy frozen poultry, cook it as soon as possible after thawing and never refreeze it once it has thawed.

CHICKEN

Leaving aside the tiny broiler and lordly, costly capon, both too expensive to be considered here, the chicken sizes that you will use most often are the broiler-fryer and the roaster for quick cooking, and the stewing fowl or hen for longer cooking, such as poaching and fricasseeing. Broiler-fryers are inexpensive, but stewing fowls are cheapest of all and have other advantages. There is the fat, for one thing. If you get a really fat bird, you will have a nice haul to render into shortening for baking and sautéing, and, after poaching, you'll have a goodly supply of broth that can be used for soups, sauces and stews.

When you buy a broiler-fryer, look for a bird with a firm, compact body and a soft-pointed breastbone, weighing between 2 and 3½ pounds, with a little fat on it.

A roasting chicken should weigh from 3 to 5 pounds, ready-to-cook weight, and have a compact body, broad through the breast, soft skin with enough fat underneath to keep it juicy and tender, and a pliable breastbone. When buying a stewing fowl, which will range in weight from 3 to 8 pounds, look for one that has a rigid breastbone and a fair amount of fat.

When buying chicken, estimate ½ to 1 pound per serving or, for 2-pound broilers, a quarter to a half chicken for each person.

BROILED CHICKEN

Have the broilers split and the backbones and necks removed. Before broiling, flatten the chicken by breaking the joints and removing the point of the breastbone. Wipe with a damp cloth and then rub well with butter or oil. Place skin side down on the greased rack of the broiling pan. Preheat the broiler. Broil about 3 inches from the heat for 15 minutes on the bone side, then season with salt and pepper, turn, brush with butter or oil, and broil a further 10 to 15 minutes on the skin side. Test by piercing the thigh joint with a fork or the sharp point of a small knife. If the juice runs clear, the chicken is cooked. Do not overcook. Season the skin side with salt and pepper and serve. If you like, you may rub the chickens with tarragon butter (see page 159) and baste with more tarragon butter during the cooking.

To *charcoal-broil*, brush with butter or oil and season with salt, pepper and paprika. Broil on a rack about 3 to 4 inches above the bed of coals, turning and basting often. Start broiling on the bone side and finish on the skin side. Test for doneness by inserting a fork into the thigh joint, as for oven broiling.

ROAST CHICKEN

Wash the bird and rub the cavity with a cut lemon. Sprinkle the cavity with salt and pepper and put in 2 tablespoons butter and any desired flavorings—peeled garlic cloves, sprigs of fresh tarragon or a handful of dried tarragon, dried rosemary, a couple of small peeled onions, a few sprigs of parsley. Truss and tie the chicken.

There is a good deal of talk about slow roasting and low temperatures in cooking poultry. I feel that you lose a good deal of flavor by roasting at a low temperature. Chicken is best roasted throughout at a high temperature; shrinkage is hardly enough to make any difference, and the meat remains juicier than when it is cooked at a low heat.

Rub the chicken well with butter (or arrange bacon strips over it) and arrange on its side on a rack in a roasting pan. Roast in a 375° oven for 20 minutes, then turn onto the other side and again rub with butter or cover with bacon. Roast another 20 minutes, then turn the chicken breast up and roast for a final 20 minutes, basting well with butter or a mixture of butter and white wine. Salt and pepper to taste and check for doneness by wiggling a leg—it should move easily. Cook a little longer if necessary, but do not overcook.

A good way to make a roast chicken go farther is to bone and stuff it. This, with salad and dessert, makes a superb meal. It pays to learn how to bone a chicken yourself. Boning needs a steady hand, infinite patience and a good sharp boning knife with a pointed tip. Once you have mastered the technique, you will soon be able to do it in minutes.

BONED STUFFED CHICKEN

5-pound roasting chicken
2 small onions, chopped
6 tablespoons butter
1 pound finely ground lean pork
½ pound ground pork liver
½ cup bread crumbs
1 teaspoon thyme
⅓ cup chopped parsley
1½ teaspoons salt
1 teaspoon freshly ground black pepper
3 ounces whiskey or brandy

Begin at the vent of the bird and gently and carefully cut the flesh away from the bones. Work along the backbone, removing small bits of bone and folding the flesh back as you proceed. Work on up to the leg joints, then slowly slip the flesh of the legs and thighs down, pushing it off the bones. Toward the very end of the drumsticks, cut through the bone with poultry shears, leaving the tip end of the leg bone to help hold the shape of the bird.

Then work on up the carcass, pushing the breast meat away from the bone. Treat the wings in the same way as the legs, slipping the flesh away toward the end but clipping through the bone near the wing tip so that you leave a small piece attached. Be very careful that you do not pierce the skin of the boned chicken and make holes in it. Finish working the flesh away from the upper backbones, and the job is done. The bird is now ready to be stuffed.

Sauté the onion in the butter, add the ground pork and cook for 5 minutes. Add the pork liver, crumbs, thyme, parsley, salt, pepper and brandy. Mix well. Spread the boned chicken out flat, stuff with the mixture, laying it in the center and pulling the skin around it to reshape into the chicken form, and sew it up. Butter the skin well and roast on a rack in a 350° oven, basting frequently with butter and the pan juices. It should take about 1½ hours to cook. Serve hot or cold, slicing right through the whole bird, stuffing and all. Serves 6.

Sauteed Chicken

This is one of the simplest, quickest and most delicious ways to prepare a broiler-fryer. The basic sauté can be varied by adding different flavorings and ingredients.

BASIC CHICKEN SAUTE

2 two-pound broiler-fryers, quartered
6 tablespoons butter
Salt, freshly ground black pepper

½ cup dry white wine
3 to 4 tablespoons chopped parsley

The chicken should be cut into four pieces—two halves of breast with the wings attached, and the two legs and thighs with part of the backbone. Wash the chicken in lukewarm water and dry thoroughly on paper towels. Melt the butter in a heavy 11- or 12-inch skillet with a tight-fitting lid. Add the chicken pieces and brown them on all sides. Season to taste with salt and pepper, reduce the heat, cover and cook very gently for about 5 to 8 minutes. Remove cover and rearrange the pieces so that they will cook evenly. Add ¼ cup wine, replace cover and cook 10 minutes more. Uncover and move the pieces of white meat to the top, leaving the dark meat, which takes longer to cook, on the bottom. Cover and cook until the chicken is just tender and done, but still juicy; this will take about 5 or 10 minutes more.

Remove chicken pieces to a hot platter. Add the remaining wine and the parsley to the pan, turn up the heat and boil, scraping up the brown glaze from the bottom of the pan with a wooden spoon. When the juices have reduced a little, pour over the chicken. Serves 4.

VARIATIONS

Red Sauté: Brown the chickens as directed and season with salt and pepper. Reduce the heat and add 3 tablespoons finely chopped onion and 1 small clove garlic, finely chopped. Cover and cook for 5 minutes. Remove cover, rearrange the chicken pieces, add the wine, cover and cook for 10 minutes. Move white meat to the top, add to the pan 3 medium-size tomatoes, peeled, seeded and chopped, cover and cook 10 minutes more. Correct the seasoning, remove the chicken, add 1 tablespoon chopped parsley and let the sauce cook down for 1 minute before pouring it over the chicken.

Sauté with White Wine and Herbs: Brown the chicken as directed. Add 1 medium onion, finely chopped, and 1 clove garlic, finely chopped, reduce the heat, cover and cook until almost done, rearranging the pieces as directed. When almost cooked, season to taste with salt and pepper and add 1 tablespoon each of chopped parsley, chives, chervil and tarragon (use fresh herbs where possible). Pour ½ cup dry white wine over the chicken, cover and let it cook down with the herbs, onion and chicken juices. Just before serving, add a few drops of freshly squeezed lemon juice. This is delicious with crusty fried potatoes and puréed spinach.

Lemon Sauté: Cook the chicken as directed for Basic Chicken Sauté, omitting the wine. Melt 3 tablespoons butter in a separate pan and let it brown slightly. Just before removing the cooked chicken, pour over it the juice of 2 lemons and the finely grated rind of 1 lemon. Cook for a minute, sprinkle with chopped parsley and remove to a platter. Pour over it the pan juices and the browned butter. In asparagus season, serve this dish with cooked asparagus lightly dusted with Parmesan cheese, arranging it around the chicken on the platter. With tiny new potatoes with chopped chives, crusty French bread and a bottle of chilled white wine, this makes a delicious spring luncheon.

Sauté with peppers: Brown the chicken as directed. Add 1 green pepper, finely chopped, 2 tablespoons chopped onion, 1 clove garlic, finely chopped, 4 diced pimientos and the liquid from the can. Reduce heat, cover and cook for 10 minutes. Add 2 large tomatoes, peeled, seeded and chopped very fine. Rearrange chicken pieces and let the mixture cook down. Turn the chicken in the sauce several times, then correct the seasoning and just before serving add 1 tablespoon chopped parsley and a few drops lemon juice.

SOUTHWESTERN SAUTE

This is a purely American version of the classic sauté.

2 two-pound broiler-fryers,
    quartered
6 to 8 slices bacon
Flour
Salt, pepper, cayenne pepper
2 teaspoons paprika
2 cloves garlic, finely chopped
1 small white onion, chopped
1 cup tomato purée
2 teaspoons chili powder
Pinch of basil
⅓ cup red wine
1 tablespoon chopped parsley

Prepare the chickens as for Basic Chicken Sauté. Fry the bacon in a skillet until crisp. Remove bacon. Dredge chicken pieces with flour and brown quickly on all sides in the hot bacon fat. Season with salt, pepper and cayenne to taste, and the paprika. Add the garlic and onion, reduce the heat, cover and cook for 10 minutes. Add tomato purée, chili powder and basil. Cover and simmer until chicken is done. Remove chicken, add wine to the pan and allow it to cook down for a minute. Pour the sauce over the chicken and sprinkle with the parsley.

Here are two other delicious ways to prepare a quartered chicken. One comes from the area of Normandy where apples and their by-products, cider and Calvados (we have substituted applejack), are widely used in cooking, the other is Hungarian in origin. Both turn a simple chicken into epicurean fare.

CHICKEN VALLEE D'AUGE

11 tablespoons butter
1 3½-pound frying chicken,
    quartered
Salt, freshly ground black pepper
½ cup cider (preferably dry)
5 to 6 good-sized cooking apples
¼ cup applejack or whiskey
3 tablespoons flour
1½ cups light cream
8 slices crisp toast

Melt 4 tablespoons butter in a skillet and brown the chicken pieces well. Sprinkle with salt and pepper to taste. Add the cider, cover the pan and simmer for 20 minutes, or until the chicken is tender. Meanwhile peel, core and thinly slice the apples into rings. Sauté them over low heat in 4 tablespoons butter. Keep warm while finishing the chicken.

When chicken is cooked, pour the applejack or whiskey into the pan, let it heat long enough for the fumes to ignite, then flame. When flames die down, remove chicken to a hot platter and keep warm while making the sauce.

Knead the flour with 3 tablespoons butter and add to the pan juices. Stir until smooth and thickened, then add the light cream and continue stirring until well blended and smooth.

Arrange the chicken on the toast, pour the sauce over it and serve with the sautéed apple rings. Serves 4.

PAPRIKA CHICKEN

3 tablespoons butter
3 tablespoons oil
2 tablespoons Hungarian
  sweet paprika
2 broiler-fryers, about 2½ pounds
  each, quartered
2 large onions, finely chopped
½ cup tomato juice or
  3 tablespoon tomato paste
  mixed with ¼ cup water
Salt to taste
¾ to 1 cup commercial sour cream
  mixed with 3 tablespoons flour

Melt the butter with the oil in a large skillet over medium heat. Add the paprika and cook a little, stirring well (this mellows the flavor and takes away the rawness of the spice). Put in the chicken pieces and brown very lightly all over. Push chicken pieces to one side of the pan, add the onion and stir until limp. Add the tomato juice or tomato paste and water. Season with salt. Turn heat very low and cook until chicken is just tender. Remove chicken to a hot serving platter or pile it on a mound of hot rice. Stir the sour cream-flour mixture into the pan juices and heat and stir just until the sauce simmers, about one to two minutes. Serve over the chicken or separately. Serves 4 to 6.

Poached Chicken

You can use either a roaster or a stewing fowl or hen for poaching. The hen is a better buy, as it runs larger and costs less per pound. The long, slow simmering needed to tenderize it also brings out the full flavor. It is getting harder to find hens in the markets, but they are definitely worth buying for the classic poached chicken dishes, or for casseroles and pies. When poaching, allow ½ to 1 cup water per pound of chicken. Add flavorings and bring the water to a boil. Skim off the scum, reduce the heat until the liquid is barely stirring, cover and cook until tender. A roasting chicken will take only 45 minutes to poach, a stewing fowl up to 3 hours.

One of the great French country dishes is Poule au Pot, or chicken in the pot, a popular Sunday dinner that provides plenty of leftovers for the next day. It is a very economical dish because it is made with a stuffed stewing fowl and, with the addition of meat, supplies the basis for a variety of meals.

POULE AU POT

A 6- to 7-pound stewing fowl
8 large onions
1 cup leftover cooked ham or pork
   or ½ pound pork butt
3 or 4 parsley sprigs
4 tablespoons butter
3 cups dry bread crumbs
1 teaspoon thyme
2 eggs, well beaten
1 ham butt or 3 to 4 pounds beef
   (short ribs, rump or brisket)
1 onion stuck with 2 cloves
8 carrots
1½ tablespoons salt
6 turnips, peeled

Clean the fowl of all inside fat and remove the neck, leaving the surrounding skin. Grind 2 of the onions with the leftover ham or pork, or the pork butt, and the parsley. Sauté the mixture in the butter and combine with the bread crumbs, thyme and eggs, mixing well. Stuff the fowl loosely with this mixture and sew it up tightly. (Put a piece of foil in the vent before sewing to make it watertight.)

Place the fowl in a pot with the ham butt or beef, onion stuck with cloves, 2 of the carrots, the salt and just enough water to cover. Bring to a boil. Skim off the scum, reduce the heat and simmer covered for 3½ hours or until the meat and chicken are tender. If the meat takes longer to cook, remove the chicken and keep it warm. Add the remaining onions and carrots and the turnips 1 hour before dinner.

For the first meal, serve the broth followed by a slice of chicken and stuffing with the vegetables; you may add a slice of the meat too if you wish. Serves 6.

Here are two ways to serve the chicken on the second day. The stuffing is delicious and usually firm enough to slice perfectly.

CURRIED CHICKEN AND STUFFING

Dip slices of leftover chicken breast and slices of stuffing in egg and crumbs and sauté them in butter or chicken fat.

After removing chicken and stuffing from the pan, add 1 cup milk, scraping up all the bits of stuffing and crumbs from the pan and blending them with the milk. Add 1 tablespoon curry powder and ¼ cup dry bread crumbs and stir over low heat until all the crumbs are absorbed by the milk; you may need to add more milk to get a smooth sauce. Taste for seasoning and serve poured over the chicken. Spinach *en branche*—plain spinach —is excellent with this, or a substantial green salad. Sharp cheese and crisp rolls or bread will be all you need to round out this hearty meal.

CHICKEN-AND-STUFFING HASH

1 large onion, finely chopped
4 tablespoons butter or chicken fat
1 cup chicken stuffing
1½ cups chopped leftover chicken
¼ cup chopped green pepper
½ cup chicken broth
½ cup heavy cream or evaporated milk
Salt, freshly ground black pepper, paprika

Sauté the onion in the fat until soft. Add the stuffing, chicken, green pepper and chicken broth. Blend well with the onion and cook, turning frequently, until the hash has a slight crust distributed through it. When the hash is thoroughly heated, add the cream or evaporated milk and let it cook down. Season to taste with salt, pepper and a good sprinkling of paprika. Serves 4.

Serve with plain boiled potatoes sprinkled heavily with finely chopped green onions and parsley, and sautéed pineapple slices. Chocolate roll or pudding makes a good dessert.

If you cooked beef with the Poule au Pot, you can have a really excellent and economical salad on the third day, ample for a main course and a beautiful sight if you have guests.

SUPER SALAD

Arrange Boston lettuce leaves on a large platter. Cut the beef in very thin slices and arrange down the center of the platter. Quarter 4 hard-cooked eggs and put these on either side of the beef. Add any bits of sliced chicken you may have left and garnish with sliced ripe tomatoes. Pour over all a good French dressing combined with chopped raw onion and chopped parsley. Top the beef with thin rings of raw red onion.

With the salad serve tiny new potatoes in their jackets, tossed with melted butter and caraway seeds. For dessert, have fresh fruit sprinkled with sugar and orange juice.

If, on the other hand, you cooked ham with your poule, here's the perfect way to finish it up:

WEDNESDAY'S LENTIL CASSEROLE

2 cups lentils
1 onion, stuck with 2 cloves
1 bay leaf
6 slices ham
Chicken and stuffing
Chicken broth
Buttered crumbs
Grated Parmesan cheese

Soak the lentils overnight in water to cover, unless they are of the quick-cooking variety that needs no soaking. To cook, add the onion and bay leaf and simmer gently until tender. Set aside until 1 hour before dinner. In a casserole, arrange a layer of lentils. Top with the ham, then make another layer of lentils, then add any chicken and stuffing that may be left, and finish with a layer of lentils. Pour over this any chicken broth that is left and the liquid from the cooked lentils. Bake in a 350° oven, covered, for 30 minutes. Reduce the heat to 300°, remove the cover and sprinkle the top with crumbs and cheese. Cook until the topping is crisp.

With a hearty salad of green beans, lettuce and onions and some crisp hot bread, this thrifty dish will serve 4 with good appetites or 6 who are not so ravenous. A glass of robust red wine goes well with this. You can use any combination of meat you wish.

Another magnificent and versatile dish that can be made with the economical hen is an old-fashioned chicken casserole. This will serve 6 or 8 diners exceedingly well for a fairly small outlay.

COUNTRY STYLE CHICKEN CASSEROLE

A 6- to 7-pound hen
Flour
Salt, freshly ground black pepper, paprika
6 tablespoons bacon fat or butter
6 young carrots, cut in strips
18 small white onions
1 turnip, cubed
1 teaspoon thyme
1 or 2 sprigs parsley
A few celery leaves
1 cup cream or evaporated milk
Beurre Manié (optional)

Cut the hen into serving pieces. Separate the legs from the thighs and the wings from the body and cut the breast into 3 pieces. Cut the back and the ribs into 2 pieces. Make broth with the giblets, using 3 cups water, and reserve. (Use the giblets for sandwiches.)

Roll the chicken pieces in flour seasoned with salt, pepper and paprika and brown quickly in the hot bacon fat or butter. Place the browned pieces in a casserole and add the carrots, onions, turnip, thyme, parsley and celery leaves. Add the reserved giblet broth, cover and cook in a 350° oven for 1½ hours, or until the hen is tender. Add the cream or evaporated milk and, if you want a thickened sauce, the Beurre Manié (small balls of butter and flour). Return to the oven for 15 minutes. Correct the seasoning. Serves 6.

Serve this flavorful dish with buttered noodles and a green salad. A Fruit Tart goes well as dessert.

VARIATIONS

Paprika Chicken Casserole: Omit the carrots and turnip and increase the onions to 24. Add 2 tablespoons paprika with the other seasonings and just before serving carefully mix in 1½ cups sour cream in place of the 1 cup cream. Do not thicken. Serve with noodles.

Chicken Casserole with White Wine: Instead of broth, use 2 cups white wine. Do not add cream. Thicken with Beurre Manié.

Chicken Casserole with Red Wine: When browning the chicken, also brown 3 slices salt pork, diced. Substitute 2 cups red wine for the broth and thicken with Beurre Manié.

Chicken Casserole with Tomatoes: For the basic vegetable mixture substitute 3 cloves garlic, chopped, 3 large onions, sliced, 2 green peppers, chopped, and 2 cups canned or stewed tomatoes with a pinch each of basil and thyme. Serve with seashell macaroni tossed with melted butter and grated Parmesan cheese.

If you are planning to serve a large number of people—say about 10 or 12—and want something substantial and good but easy on your pocketbook, buy a 5-pound fowl and make a delicious Tuscan Chicken Casserole. The recipe is rather involved, but it is the combination of various mixtures, cooked separately, that gives it a unique quality.

TUSCAN CHICKEN CASSEROLE

5-pound fowl
3 ribs celery
3 carrots
3 sprigs parsley
Salt, freshly ground black pepper
½ pound bacon, cut in slivers
2 medium onions, finely chopped
3 cloves garlic, finely chopped
1 green pepper, cut in fine julienne
1 cup soft black olives, pitted
¼ cup olive oil
6 large ripe tomatoes, peeled, seeded and quartered or 2 cups canned Italian plum tomatoes
3 tablespoons butter
1 teaspoon basil
3 tablespoons chopped Italian parsley
1½ pounds spaghettini
4 eggs
¾ cup grated Parmesan cheese

Truss the fowl and place it in a deep kettle with the celery, carrots, parsley sprigs, 1 tablespoon salt and water to cover. Bring to a boil. Boil 5 minutes, removing any scum that rises to the surface. Reduce the heat, cover, and simmer until the chicken is just tender. Remove it from the broth and when cool enough to handle remove meat from the bones and put into a 6- to 8-quart casserole. Strain the broth, skimming off the fat, and reserve.

While the chicken is cooling, fry the bacon in a skillet until crisp. Remove to absorbent paper and cook the onion and garlic in the bacon fat until soft. Put the bacon and onion-garlic mixture into the casserole with the chicken. Sauté the green pepper and olives lightly in the oil and add them to the mixture in the casserole. Simmer the tomatoes in the butter with the basil, breaking them up with a wooden spoon, until they are slightly cooked down. Mix in the parsley, salt to taste and plenty of freshly ground pepper, and add to the mixture in the casserole.

Cook the spaghettini in the chicken broth, adding water if necessary, until it is almost at the al dente stage. Drain and add to the casserole. Toss all the ingredients together and bake in a 375° oven for 15 minutes to blend the flavors. Lightly beat the eggs and mix in the cheese. Remove the casserole from the oven and pour the egg mixture over the top. Increase the heat to 450° and put the casserole back into the oven until lightly browned on top. This is not as time-consuming as it sounds if you cook two or three of the mixtures at the same time and then combine them. Serve this with a big salad of greens, hot French or Italian bread and a simple fruit or ice-cream dessert and you have a wonderful meal for a crowd.

Here is another good stretchable casserole that combines chicken with pasta.

VERNA ROSS'S CHICKEN CASSEROLE

6- pound fowl
1 onion stuck with 2 cloves
2 carrots
Salt, freshly ground black pepper
1 large onion, finely chopped
1 pound mushrooms, sliced
4 tablespoons oil or butter
2 twelve-ounce cans whole-kernel corn
2 packages frozen peas, preferably the tiny ones, thawed
A 29-ounce can Italian plum tomatoes
1 teaspoon basil
1 teaspoon oregano
1½ pounds seashell macaroni
1 cup bread crumbs
½ pound sharp cheddar cheese, diced

Cook the fowl with the onion, carrots, and 1 tablespoon salt in water to cover. When tender, remove and cool chicken and cut the meat into serving-size cubes. Strain the broth, skim off the fat and reserve to cook the macaroni.

Meanwhile sauté the chopped onion and mushrooms in the oil or butter until just limp. Season with salt and pepper to taste. Mix in the corn, peas, tomatoes, basil and oregano, and cook together for 5 minutes, breaking up the tomatoes with a wooden spoon.

While vegetables are cooking, cook the macaroni in the reserved broth with additional water, if necessary, until just al dente. Drain. Combine with the chicken and the vegetables, mixing well. Place in a 6-quart casserole or baking dish and correct the seasoning. Sprinkle top with the bread crumbs and dot with the diced cheese. Bake in a 375° oven for 20 to 25 minutes, or until nicely browned on top. Serve with a good tossed salad, crusty rolls and a light California red wine. This is also a nice dish for outdoor dining in summer. Serves 10 to 12.

Recently, while experimenting with the method of cooking a beef roast in foil in a low oven (see page 69), I decided to try the same method with a hen. It worked perfectly, and furthermore it required absolutely no attention.

FOILED FOWL

Take a sheet of heavy-duty aluminum foil large enough to completely cover the hen. Rub the hen with oil and sprinkle with salt and pepper. Place, breast up, in the center of the sheet of foil, add 4 or 5 peeled whole garlic cloves and bring the foil up over the breast of the bird, allowing an overlap of 3 inches. Close foil by folding together the top of the 3-inch overlap, and turn up the foil at either end of the bird to hold in the juices. Cook in a 250° oven for 4 to 5 hours. You can let it stay in the turned-off oven until ready to serve and it will remain moist and succulent.

Chicken in Parts

Every supermarket now carries a wide range of chicken already cut up and sold in parts—breasts, legs and thighs, wings, giblets and hearts. These are often a good buy, especially the less expensive parts such as wings, and can be turned into delicious dishes. For instance, as a less expensive variation on the Spanish paella, try making it with wings rather than the cut-up whole chicken.

PAELLA

Flour
12 chicken wings
Peanut oil
Salt, freshly ground black pepper
1 onion, finely chopped
2 cloves garlic, chopped
1½ cups rice
Chicken broth or water, heated to
  boiling
Pinch of saffron
1 or 2 Italian or Spanish sausages,
  sliced
½ cup chopped or canned
  tomatoes
24 clams and 12 shrimp, in their
  shells
3 pimientos, cut in thin strips
½ package green peas, cooked

Flour the chicken wings and brown them in oil in a skillet. When nicely browned, season with salt and pepper, remove and keep warm. Sauté the onion and garlic in the oil until soft. Add the rice and stir until well coated with oil and translucent. Pour over it enough boiling chicken broth or water to cover, season with salt, pepper and saffron, and let it cook down. Add the chicken wings, the sliced sausages, tomatoes and additional liquid, if necessary. When the rice is just beginning to get tender, add the clams and shrimp. Cook until the shrimp are pink and cooked through and the clam shells open. Nearly all the liquid should have cooked away at this point; if it has not, raise the heat until it evaporates, leaving the rice firm and the grains separate. Garnish with the pimiento strips and cooked peas. Serves 6.

FRICASSEE OF WINGS*

[This freezes well.]

12 to 14 chicken wings
1 onion, stuck with 2 cloves
1 bay leaf
1 teaspoon salt
A few celery leaves
1 or 2 parsley sprigs
3 tablespoons butter
4 tablespoons flour
½ cup heavy cream or evaporated
  milk

Salt, pepper, nutmeg
Lemon juice
Chopped parsley

Put the wings, onion, bay leaf, salt, celery leaves and parsley in a pan with water barely to cover. Bring to a boil, skim off scum, then reduce the heat and simmer until just tender, about 1 hour. Remove the wings and keep warm. Strain and measure the broth. Melt the butter in a saucepan and blend in the flour. Gradually stir in 1½ cups of the strained broth and cook, stirring, until thickened. Mix in the cream or evaporated milk and season to taste with salt, pepper and nutmeg. Add a good squeeze of lemon juice and a little chopped parsley. Put the chicken wings into the sauce and reheat slightly. Serve over rice. Green peas go well with this dish. Serves 6.

Don't be afraid to eat the wings with your fingers—that is the only way you can get all the goodness out of them. Finish off the meal with a Ginger Soufflé.

Chicken legs and thighs make a delicious pie.

FRENCH CHICKEN PIE*

[This freezes well.]

6 to 8 chicken legs and thighs, according to size
Flour
6 tablespoons butter
3 to 4 slices bacon, cut in pieces
2 onions, finely chopped
1 clove garlic, crushed
1 bay leaf

1 teaspoon thyme
½ pound mushrooms, sliced
¼ cup white wine
Salt, freshly ground pepper to taste
4 hard-cooked eggs, shelled and halved
Rich Savory Pastry (see below)
1 egg beaten with 1 tablespoon cream

Dust the chicken pieces lightly with flour and brown them on all sides in the butter. Add the bacon, onion, garlic and herbs. Cook until onion is just soft, then add the mushrooms and wine. Season with salt and pepper to taste, cover and simmer 45 minutes. Cool. Arrange the chicken pieces in a pie dish with the eggs and pour the mixture in the pan over them. Roll out the pastry to fit the top of the dish. (Reserve any excess pastry for another use, such as making a flan shell.) Top pie with the crust, cut a vent in the middle and place a small waxed-paper cornucopia in it to let the steam escape. Brush pastry with the egg-cream mixture and bake in a 375° oven for 25 to 30 minutes, or until the crust is thoroughly cooked and the chicken mixture heated through. Serves 6.

RICH SAVORY PASTRY

2 cups unsifted flour
¾ cup butter
3 hard-cooked egg yolks, mashed
2 raw egg yolks
½ teaspoon salt

Put the flour on a table or in a bowl and make a well in the center. Put the butter (this should not be ice cold, but not so soft as to be oily), the cooked and raw egg yolks and salt in the well. Mix the center ingredients to a paste with your fingertips, gradually incorporating the flour, until you have a firm, smooth ball of pastry dough. Work as quickly as possible to prevent the butter from becoming greasy. When the dough leaves the table-top or the sides of the bowl clean, wrap it in waxed paper or aluminum foil, and chill until firm enough to roll between sheets of waxed paper.

There is no part of the chicken that can't be used to advantage— one reason why it is a good idea to buy a whole bird and cut it up yourself. Backs and necks can be added to broth to increase its strength and flavor. They give very little meat, although you can manage to scrape off enough to make a small amount of chopped chicken for sandwiches. Giblets, on the other hand, can be turned into interesting and flavorful dishes and are usually very reasonably priced.

GIBLET SAUTE

1½ pounds gizzards and hearts
Flour
4 tablespoons butter
1 teaspoon salt
½ teaspoon freshly ground black pepper
¼ teaspoon thyme
4 tablespoons dry sherry or white wine
1 clove garlic, finely chopped
4 tablespoons chopped parsley

Clean and trim the gizzards and hearts and flour them well. Melt the butter in a skillet and sauté the giblets briskly until they are well browned. Season with the salt, pepper and thyme and add the wine. Cover and simmer for 1 hour. Add the garlic and let it cook until soft, then add the parsley. Serve on steamed rice. Serves 4.

VARIATION

Hungarian Giblets: Cook the giblets as directed, then add ½ pound sliced mushrooms with the garlic and a little more butter. Sauté until just cooked through, then stir in 1 cup sour cream. Serve on buttered noodles.

TURKEY

Turkeys today are a vast improvement over those of twenty years ago. They are plumper, more compact and yield as much as 50 percent more meat than formerly. They are also much more tender, which shortens the cooking time and prevents the meat from drying out.

You can now buy turkeys weighing from as little as 4 pounds to as much as 30 or 38 pounds. Smaller birds, weighing from 4 to 9 pounds, can be roasted or cut up and broiled, sautéed, braised or barbecued. (If you don't feel like buying a whole turkey, you can also get it cut into parts like chicken.)

If you compare the price per pound of turkey with that of a roasting chicken, you will find it is often a more economical buy. Large birds of 20 pounds and over are the best for roasting from the point of view of flavor and price, as they have a higher proportion of meat to bone weight. If you know a few ways to use up cold turkey, larger turkeys are definitely a better buy.

In this chapter you will see how you can take advantage of the saving represented by buying a 16- or 20-pound turkey and planning a series of meals around it.

Freshly killed turkeys are the most desirable, but these are pretty hard to find. To get a turkey that has been freshly killed and hand-plucked, you need a special poultry dealer. The turkeys sold in markets come packaged frozen and "ready-to-cook," which means that the bird has been fully eviscerated and processed; "pan-ready," "table-dressed," "oven-ready" and "eviscerated" are other packaging terms that mean the same thing.

When you buy a turkey for roasting, estimate about 1 pound per person ready-to-cook weight. This will allow for plenty of second helpings and leftovers.

Frozen whole turkeys should be thawed before cooking, preferably slowly. After thawing, rinse the bird with cool water, drain, and pat dry. It can then be stuffed and roasted or prepared otherwise as desired.

After stuffing a turkey, truss it by tying the legs together with string and then tying the string around the tail. Turn the wing tips under the wings on either side of the bird. Rub well with olive oil and arrange on one side on a rack in a roasting pan. It is almost impossible to give hard and fast rules about the length of time a turkey should roast. Broadly speaking, a 16-pound turkey roasted in a 325° oven will take 3¾ to 4 hours, but this timing is approximately. A more accurate way is to take the internal temperature with a meat thermometer inserted into the thickest part of the thigh. According to how well-cooked you like your turkey, it should register between 175° and 185°. If you take the turkey out of the oven when the thermometer registers 170° and let it stand for 20 to 25 minutes before carving, the internal temperature will rise to 180°. Another way to test for doneness is to puncture the skin at the thigh joint to see if the juices run clear.

With the open-roasting method, the turkey should be roasted on one side for a third of the total cooking time, then on the other for a third of the time, and lastly on its back for the remainder of the time, so that the breast browns. To keep the breast and legs moist you can cover the bird with well-oiled cheesecloth and baste it through the cheesecloth with oil and butter, or cover it with strips of salt pork or bacon and baste occasionally with the pan juices.

When the turkey is done, remove it from the oven and allow to stand for 20 to 25 minutes before carving. If you are serving 4 people, you will use only part of one side of the breast and the meat from one leg and thigh. Cut the remainder of the meat from the bones and store it separately. Save the wings and the bones for the curry, and wrap the carcass to be used for broth. It is just as easy to slice from a large piece of meat as it is from the bone. Wrap and store leftover stuffing separately, too.

Six Meals from a 16-Pound Turkey

If you buy a bird of this size for a small family, you really save money, and under proper refrigeration the leftover turkey will keep for at least 2 weeks; if you have a freezer you can keep parts of it much longer.

FIRST DINNER

*(Recipes marked * either follow or appear elsewhere in this book)*

Cream of tomato soup with
croutons
Roast Turkey with Bread and
Sausage Stuffings*
Mashed yellow turnips
Pan-browned potatoes
Turkey Gravy*
Strawberry Sorbet*

ROAST TURKEY

16-pound turkey
1 lemon
Bread stuffing
Sausage stuffing
Olive oil
Bacon slices

Rinse and dry the turkey and rub the inside with a cut lemon. Stuff the body cavity with bread stuffing and the neck cavity with sausage stuffing. Stuff lightly, as the stuffing will expand during cooking and if the neck cavity is stuffed too tightly it may burst. (Any leftover stuffing may be cooked in a covered casserole and basted with the pan juices for the last half hour of roasting time.) Fasten the neck skin to the back of the turkey with a skewer, and sew up the tail opening or close it with a piece of crumpled aluminum foil.

BASIC BREAD STUFFING

½ pound (or more) butter
1 cup finely chopped shallots,
onions, or spring onions
8 cups (approximately) fresh bread
crumbs, crusts and all
1 tablespoon fresh tarragon (or
more to taste) or 2 teaspoons
dried tarragon, moistened in a
little white wine for 1 hour
1 cup finely chopped parsley
1 tablespoon salt, or to taste
1½ teaspoons freshly ground black
pepper

A basic bread stuffing is exceedingly accommodating because it lends itself to all kinds of additions and flavorings. Fresh bread crumbs, made in the blender or on a rather coarse grater, are preferable to commercial packaged crumbs.

The rule for figuring out the proper amount of stuffing is easy to remember: Approximately 1 cup per pound of bird. This works very well unless you want stuffing for only one meal, in which case this quantity is excessive. So, starting from the maximum, reduce the amount of stuffing to suit your needs.

Place the butter and the shallots or onions in a sauce pan and allow the butter to melt over low heat. Do not sauté the shallots. Combine with the crumbs and other ingredients and toss lightly. Add more melted butter if needed, and taste for seasoning. This amount makes about 10 cups stuffing.

SAUSAGE STUFFING

2 pounds rather fat shoulder or loin of pork (about 60 percent lean and 40 percent fat), ground coarsely
1½ teaspoons salt
1 teaspoon freshly ground black pepper
½ teaspoon ginger
1 teaspoon or more of the same herb used in the Bread Stuffing
Large dash Tabasco
½ teaspoon crushed anise seeds

Blend all ingredients lightly but well. Makes 3 cups stuffing.

SECOND DINNER
(*Recipes marked * either follow or appear elsewhere in this book*)

Celery, radishes, green onions
with Dunking Sauce
(*see suggestions on pages 44–46*)
Scalloped Turkey*
Green salad
Apple Charlotte*

SCALLOPED TURKEY

12 ounces noodles, cooked until tender and drained
1 cup cold turkey stuffing
2 cups diced cold turkey
1 pound mushrooms, sliced
½ cup finely chopped onion
Butter
¼ cup chopped parsley
8 hard-cooked eggs, sliced
2 cups turkey gravy or Béchamel Sauce
Buttered crumbs

Make a layer of half the cooked noodles in the bottom of a deep 2½-quart baking dish. Add the stuffing and turkey. Sauté the mushrooms and onion in butter and add to the dish with the parsley and sliced hard-cooked eggs. Add turkey gravy or Béchamel Sauce and top with the remaining noodles. Dot with butter and sprinkle with buttered crumbs. Cover and bake in a 350° oven for 25 to 30 minutes. Remove cover for last 10 minutes of cooking time. Serve with a crisp salad and drink a chilled rosé wine. Serves 6 to 8.

THIRD DINNER

(Recipes marked * either follow or appear elsewhere in this book)

Curried Turkey Wings and Bones*
with rice and curry
accompaniments
Fresh fruit

CURRIED TURKEY WINGS AND BONES

2 large onions, chopped
2 tablespoons butter
1 apple, cored but not peeled, finely chopped
1 green pepper, seeded and finely chopped
2 tablespoons curry powder
2 cups turkey broth or chicken broth
Turkey wings, disjointed
Turkey leg and thigh bones (with some meat left on them)
Leftover turkey gravy or 1 can cream of mushroom soup diluted with evaporated milk
½ cup seedless white grapes

Sauté the onion in the butter until soft. Add the apple and green pepper and cook until tender. Mix in the curry powder and cook for a few minutes to remove the raw taste. Mix in the broth and simmer for 30 minutes, then add the turkey wings and bones and cook until they are heated through. Mix in any leftover turkey gravy, or mushroom soup mixed with evaporated milk. Season to taste and mix in grapes. Serve with Steamed Rice, chutney, chopped salted peanuts, thinly sliced cucumbers dressed with oil and vinegar, and baked bananas. Beer is good with this.

FOURTH DINNER

(Recipes marked * either follow or appear elsewhere in this book)

Clam–Tomato Broth*
Turkey Divan*
Noodles with buttered garlic croutons
Green salad with raw mushrooms
Chocolate Roll*

CLAM–TOMATO BROTH

Heat equal quantities of clam broth and tomato juice with a little cooked rice. Add a dash of sherry just before serving.

TURKEY DIVAN

Cover the bottom of a large flat casserole with cooked broccoli. Arrange slices of turkey on top and mask with Sauce Mornay (rich cheese sauce). Sprinkle with grated Parmesan cheese and put under the broiler for a few minutes to glaze.

FIFTH-DAY LUNCHEON

(Recipes marked * either follow or appear elsewhere in this book)

Turkey Tonnato*
Bean salad vinaigrette
Granita di Caffè*

TURKEY TONNATO

Make 2 cups Homemade Mayonnaise flavored with lemon juice and

1 tablespoon onion juice. Mix with a 7-ounce can white-meat tuna, flaked, and 2 finely chopped anchovies. Marinate for several hours in the refrigerator to mellow the flavors. Slice turkey thin and arrange on a serving platter, mask with the tuna sauce and garnish with cherry tomatoes and black olives.

SIXTH-DAY LUNCHEON

(Recipes marked * either follow or appear elsewhere in this book)

Turkey–Tomato Consommé*
Caesar Salad*

TURKEY–TOMATO CONSOMMÉ

Simmer all the bones and scraps with water and tomato juice, an onion stuck with 2 cloves and a good pinch of thyme. Cook until rich and flavorful. Strain and serve. You can add rice or noodles to the soup if you wish to make it heartier.

Six Meals from a 20-Pound Turkey

Another money-saving idea is to buy a large turkey and have it cut in halves or quarters. If you have a freezer, you can put parts of it away, cooked or raw, for weeks. Or you might roast part of it for one dinner and poach the rest.

FIRST DINNER

(Recipes marked * either follow or appear elsewhere in this book)

Thinly sliced tomatoes with basil and oil
Roast Turkey Hips*
Cranberry mold
Creamed Cabbage with Noodles*
Lemon Pudding* with Brandy Sauce*

ROAST TURKEY HIPS

Remove the legs and thighs from the turkey by cutting through the thigh joints and removing each leg and thigh in one piece. Rub well with butter or oil and a little dried thyme, salt and pepper. Roast in a 450° oven for 20 minutes, basting twice during that time with melted butter and white wine. Reduce the heat to 350°, cover with a piece of aluminum foil and continue roasting until tender, about 1 to 1½ hours, removing the foil for the last 20 minutes to crisp the skin.

SECOND DINNER

(Recipes marked * either follow or appear elsewhere in this book)

Turkey Mole*
Polenta*
Thin-sliced cucumbers and onions dressed with oil and vinegar
Cream cheese and guava paste with crackers

TURKEY MOLE

1 turkey breast and wing
1½ teaspoons salt

2 medium onions, chopped
Bacon fat or oil
2 cloves garlic
2 tablespoons chili powder
1 small dried hot red chili pepper
1 cup ground nuts (almonds, walnuts, peanuts or cashews)
2 ounces bitter chocolate
1 cup ripe olives (optional)

Cut the turkey wing into 2 pieces and the breast into 3 or 4 pieces. Place in a large kettle with enough water to cover, and bring to a boil. Add the salt, reduce heat and simmer for 30 minutes. Meanwhile brown the onion in the fat or oil. Add to the turkey with the garlic, chili powder, chili pepper, nuts and chocolate. Cover and simmer until turkey is tender and the sauce well blended and thickened by the nuts. Correct seasoning. If you wish to include olives, add them 10 minutes before serving. Serves 4. Serve with sliced Polenta, the cucumber-and-onion salad and beer.

THIRD DINNER

(Recipes marked * either follow or appear elsewhere in this book)

Turkey Pot Pie*
Buttered young turnips
Sliced oranges and grapefruit
sprinkled with rum or kirsch

If you have poached the rest of the turkey, you should have another breast and wing, the bones and scraps and a fair amount of turkey broth. Some of these odds and ends can be turned into a pot pie.

TURKEY POT PIE*

[This freezes well.]

4 tablespoons butter
5 tablespoons flour
1 cup turkey broth
½ cup white wine or dry vermouth
½ cup evaporated milk or light cream
Salt, pepper, nutmeg
2 cups poached turkey, cut into large dice
¼ pound mushrooms, quartered or 1 small can sliced mushrooms
1 can small white potatoes
A few strips of pimiento or green pepper
Pie crust

Melt the butter, blend in the flour and cook until lightly colored. Gradually stir in the broth, wine and milk or cream. Cook, stirring, until smooth and thickened. Season to taste with salt, pepper and nutmeg. Combine the sauce, turkey and vegetables and put into a baking dish or deep pie dish. Put an egg cup in the center to hold up the crust. Top with your favorite pie crust, rolled out rather thick. Slash 2 or 3 vents in the crust and brush it with milk or water. Bake in a 450° oven for 15 minutes, reduce the heat to 350° and continue baking for about 20 minutes. Serves 4.

FOURTH-DAY LUNCHEON

(Recipes marked * either follow or appear elsewhere in this book)

Reuben Sandwiches*
Cole Slaw*
Dill pickles

REUBEN SANDWICHES

For 4 persons, spread 4 large slices of rye or pumpernickel bread with Russian dressing. On each one put, in this order, a slice of cold turkey, a slice of ham, a slice of Swiss cheese, lettuce, more Russian dressing, and finally cole slaw. Top with another slice of bread. Serve with more cole slaw, dill pickles and beer.

FIFTH-DAY LUNCHEON

(*Recipes marked * either follow or appear elsewhere in this book*)

Artichokes Vinaigrette*
Turkey and Almond Crêpes*
Orange Sherbet*

TURKEY AND ALMOND CREPES

2½ cups diced poached turkey
2 cups turkey or chicken broth, heated
4 tablespoons butter
4 tablespoons flour
1 teaspoon tarragon
1 teaspoon salt
2 tablespoons bourbon
1 cup heavy cream
3 egg yolks
¾ cup toasted salted almonds
12 crêpes (see Basic Crêpe Mixture)
Grated Parmesan cheese

Cover turkey with ½ cup broth and keep warm. Melt the butter and blend in the flour. Cook 2 to 3 minutes, without browning, then stir in the remaining 1½ cups broth. Cook, stirring, until thick-

ened. Stir in the tarragon, salt and bourbon. Combine a little of the sauce with the cream which has been mixed with the egg yolks. Gradually stir into the hot sauce and stir over medium heat until thickened; do not allow to boil. Add about half the sauce to the turkey and broth, and stir in the toasted almonds. Spoon turkey mixture onto crêpes and roll up the crêpes. Arrange in a gratin dish. Combine the cheese with the remaining sauce, pour it over the crêpes and glaze in a 450° oven or under the broiler. Serves 4.

SIXTH-DAY LUNCHEON

(*Recipes marked * either follow or appear elsewhere in this book*)

Turkey Soufflé*
Risi e Bisi*
Baked Bananas flambéed with rum*

TURKEY SOUFFLE

4 tablespoons butter
3 tablespoons flour
1 cup turkey broth or milk
Salt, pepper, nutmeg
4 eggs, separated
1 cup ground turkey

Melt the butter in the top of a double boiler and blend in the flour. Stir in the broth or milk and cook over hot water, stirring, until thickened. Season to taste with salt, pepper and nutmeg. Allow to cool slightly, then mix in the egg yolks, well beaten, and the turkey. Mix well. Finally, stiffly beat the egg whites and fold them in. (For a puffier soufflé, add an extra egg white.) Pour into a buttered soufflé dish and bake in a 400° oven for 25 to 35 minutes. If you wish, serve the soufflé with a Béchamel Sauce made with turkey broth and milk or light cream. Serves 4.

BROILED TURKEY

Only very young, fresh-killed turkeys weighing from 3½ to 5 pounds broil successfully. Split the turkey and remove the breastbone and backbone. Rub well with oil, salt, pepper and paprika. A clove or two of garlic, finely chopped, may be rubbed into the skin and along the bone of the bird; this gives the turkey a delicious flavor.

Adjust the broiling pan about 4 to 5 inches from the heat and broil the turkey, bone side to the heat, for approximately 25 minutes, basting occasionally with a little melted butter. Turn at the end of 25 minutes, brush with butter or olive oil, and broil until nicely browned and cooked through, about 18 to 25 minutes more. Be careful not to overcook, or the white meat will be dry and uninteresting.

Serve the broiled turkey with matchstick potatoes and a good salad.

VARIATION

Marinate the turkey in 1 cup white wine, ½ cup Japanese soy sauce, 3 cloves garlic finely chopped, ¼ cup olive oil, and 1 tablespoon Tabasco. Turn the turkey several times during the marinating period. Broil as directed and baste with marinating liquid. Serve with fried rice and tiny cooked green beans with crisp, crumbled bacon and onion.

6

VEGETABLES

Fresh vegetables, more than any food in this country, tend to vary in flavor, quality and cost according to area, season and supply and demand. By shopping around and going a little out of your way you can usually find good buys in vegetables at any time of year. In ethnic sections of the larger cities the prices are generally lower and the selection wider than in the supermarkets. Offbeat vegetables like Swiss chard, fava beans, fennel, salsify, kohlrabi and parsley root turn up here. Chinese markets, of course, carry vegetables called for in Oriental cooking such as bok choy and snow peas, and Italian markets usually offer unusual salad greens and herbs like arugala, dandelion greens and basil, while Spanish-American markets flaunt a fascinating crop of exotic Caribbean root vegetables and fiery chili peppers.

Seasonal Buys

Summer is the time to seek out roadside stands selling fresh farm produce—lettuce and tomatoes, cucumbers and corn, beans and peas, peppers and squash, onions and scallions, carrots, beets, potatoes, spinach, eggplant and, later in the year, pumpkins. Vegetables are always cheaper in season, when the farmers are anxious to dispose of their rapidly maturing crops. Very few of us have the storage space required for canning or freezing our own vegetables, but you can always buy a bushel basket of ripe red tomatoes and turn them into a glorious soup, sauce or purée. A word of caution about summertime vegetable-buying in the country. Of late, a rash of so-called "farmers' markets" has sprung up in the popular vacation areas. Many of them have nothing to do with local farms but are actually little more than outlets for leftover produce that hasn't sold in the cities. It is trucked back, weary and wilted, to be displayed, ostensibly, as the fresh local product. A keen eye will soon learn to tell this bogus merchandise from the authentic article. Local vegetables are usually small, firm and dewy fresh, sometimes with the dirt still clinging to their roots; lettuces, in particular, often have the roots left on. The cucumbers are unwaxed, the tomatoes have the healthy blush and green-streaked top that show they have been picked when sun-ripened. They look, in short, like what they are —vegetables straight from the garden, at their peak of flavor and freshness.

Fresh vs. Frozen

Many people, accustomed to shopping in supermarkets, look on frozen vegetables as a way of life. They are unwilling to take the brief time and trouble to prepare their own fresh beans, spinach, peas and broccoli (or even to peel and cook their own potatoes). However, the price-conscious should reflect on this fact: flavor apart, frozen vegetables seldom can compare in price, pound for pound, with fresh. You have only to look at the price of a package of frozen asparagus to realize that fresh asparagus, although one of the more expensive vegetables, is definitely the better buy. However, there are times when the fresh product is expensive, in short supply or not as good as it might be, and then certain frozen and canned vegetables come into their own. The tiny frozen peas are excellent, so is the corn, and when mushrooms are expensive or hard to find, the heat-in-the-bag mushrooms do very well as a substitute. Canned vegetables, which have greatly improved of late, are good buys in terms of value for the dollar. Among the better canned vegetables are the corn, tiny peas and baby beets. Canned tomatoes are excellent, cheaper and infinitely better than the tasteless, pallid wintertime selection in supermarkets. Canned asparagus and canned celery hearts, while expensive, are among the better canned vegetables, and canned green beans, if marinated, are good in salads or as part of an hors-d'oeuvre platter.

A final word on the subject of vegetables. Properly cooked, fresh vegetables can elevate an otherwise routine meal to the class of fine eating. The most important thing to remember is that, generally speaking, no vegetable can be drowned in water and overcooked without losing all its flavor, texture and character. Treat the humble, inexpensive vegetable gently; it can give you superb food at little cost.

Artichokes

Artichokes, most often served hot with melted butter or Hollandaise Sauce, or cold with Vinaigrette, are actually more versatile than they are allowed to be. Like other vegetables, they can be converted to a satisfying main course by being stuffed—either in the center or between the leaves. When you buy artichokes, look for those that are uniformly green, without brownish streaks or spots, and have tight leaves. For each person, choose a fine large artichoke. Trim the top off or leave it intact, as you prefer, and cut the stem end flush with the artichoke bottom so that it will stand upright. Remove some of the outer leaves. You can trim the point from the remaining leaves with scissors if you wish. Cook the artichokes in boiling salted, acidulated water until they are just tender (test to see if a leaf pulls out easily), about 40 minutes. Drain well, upside down, and when it is cool enough to handle, remove the choke and the center leaves. If they are to be served hot, return to the pan to reheat in a steamer over hot water. If they are to be served cold, cool and then chill in the refrigerator.

Hot artichokes may be stuffed with creamed oysters, creamed oysters and turkey, or creamed seafood mixtures.

Stuff cold artichokes with chicken salad, lobster salad, Codfish Salad, mixed-seafood salad, Mussel Salad, or a modified Salade Niçoise, without the lettuce.

HERBED STUFFED ARTICHOKES

Wash the artichokes and cut off about ½ inch from the leaf tips. Trim the stem end level so that it will stand upright. Make a stuffing by combining ½ cup dry bread crumbs, ¼ cup grated Parmesan cheese, ½ cup chopped parsley, ¼ cup chopped chives, 1 tablespoon grated onion, ½ clove garlic, grated, and 4 tablespoons softened butter. Press the stuffing down well within the side leaves and into and across the top. Tie a string around the artichokes to keep the stuffing in place. Arrange stuffed artichokes in an earthenware casserole with about 1 inch water in the bottom. Dribble olive oil over the artichokes, cover and bake in a 350° oven for 1½ hours, or until they are thoroughly tender and the leaves pull out easily. Serves 4. Serve as a first course or as a luncheon entrée with a salad of greens and a ripe-olive dressing.

Asparagus

There is no reason to deny yourself the pleasure of eating asparagus because of the cost. Just wait until it is in season and plentiful and the price drops accordingly. To enjoy asparagus at its best, choose tender young shoots and do not overcook them; they should be still crisp and just bitey. And if you have never eaten asparagus raw, try it. You are in for a rare treat, it is so elegantly brittle and flavorful this way. Serve it with a Green Goddess Salad Dressing, Mustard Mayonnaise or a Vinaigrette Sauce flavored with finely chopped anchovy fillets. The Chinese have a way with asparagus that also retains its tender freshness.

CHINESE ASPARAGUS

Clean and trim 2 pounds asparagus, preferably the thinnest stalks, and with a sharp knife cut them in long, thin diagonal slices. Put them into a colander or large sieve and wash well. Bring to a boil a large pot of salted water. When water is boiling rapidly, plunge the colander of asparagus in and keep it there for 2 minutes. Remove and drain well.

Melt 6 tablespoons butter in a large skillet, add the asparagus and stir over low heat, tossing lightly as for a salad, for several minutes, until the asparagus is well coated with butter—don't skimp on the butter. Serve at once. Asparagus cooked this way is perfect with fish or with broiled or roasted meats. Serves 4.

DUTCH ASPARAGUS

Clean 2 pounds medium-size asparagus and boil in salted water. (My favorite method is to lay the stalks flat in a shallow skillet with just enough boiling salted water to cover them and cook them, uncovered, just until the tips are tender; the stalks will still be bitey.)

While the asparagus is cooking, hard-cook 6 eggs. Drain the asparagus well and place on a napkin in a serving dish. Surround with the hot halved hard-boiled eggs. Cream 1 stick (¼ pound) sweet butter, adding lukewarm water drop by drop as you cream, until it has the consistency of Hollandaise. Serve each person asparagus, an egg and some of the butter sauce. The egg is crushed with a fork and blended with the creamy butter and a tiny dusting of nutmeg to make a paste. Dip the asparagus in the sauce mixture and eat. Dutch etiquette requires the use of a fork and spoon —the fork for eating the asparagus, the spoon for the saucing—but I find it easier to eat the asparagus with my fingers. This will serve 4 to 6, depending upon appetites.

Green Beans

One pound of green beans will serve 4 people. Select young beans —the larger, knobby ones are older and will be tough—and be sure they are fresh. A good way to test them is to break one in half. It should snap easily with a crisp feel.

If the beans are very tiny, leave them whole. Otherwise, you can cut them into 1-inch lengths or into long strips, French style. Cook them uncovered in a very small amount of boiling salted water (just enough to cover) until they are barely done. They should have some bite left. Dress them with butter and freshly ground black pepper if you like.

If you want to "fancy" beans up a bit, try some of these suggestions:

1. Sliver some blanched almonds —¼ to ½ cup—and brown them in butter. Add cooked green beans to the pan and toss them around lightly.

2. Melt butter in a skillet, add cooked green beans, stir them about a bit, and sprinkle with ¼ cup of grated Parmesan cheese. Mix well.

3. Chop 3 or 4 strips of bacon and fry until crisp. Remove the bacon bits, pour off part of the fat and add 1 medium onion, finely chopped. Brown the onion, return the bacon bits to the pan and add cooked green beans. Toss all together.

Beets

Two pounds of fresh beets will serve 4 to 6 people. As with green beans, be sure to buy only young beets if you want to have a tender, tasty vegetable. If the young beets are out of season and only the older, larger ones are available, you would be wiser to buy tiny ones canned whole.

Do not peel beets. Cut the tops off, leaving about 2 inches of stem attached. Put into just enough boiling salted water to cover, cover the pan and cook until tender, about 20 to 30 minutes. When they are tender, rinse in cold water and slip off the skins. If they are very tiny, serve them whole, dressed with butter. Larger beets should be sliced.

Here are some ways to dress up this colorful vegetable:

1. Melt 3 tablespoons butter in a skillet, add 1 medium onion, finely chopped, and cook slowly until just transparent. Add tiny whole beets or sliced beets and toss them about.

2. Melt butter in a skillet, add chopped onion and cook. Add beets and 1 to 2 tablespoons chopped parsley. (Or you can omit the onion and add half parsley and half chives.) Toss these about and spoon sour cream—about 4 to 6 tablespoons—over all. Let the cream heat through, but do not let it boil. Sprinkle liberally with freshly ground black pepper.

Broccoli

One pound of broccoli will serve 2 people. In young, tender broccoli, the budlike heads are tiny and tightly packed. If the buds are a paler green and have begun to open, the vegetable is old and will be tough. Before cooking broccoli, always soak in cold water with a teaspoon of salt for 15 to 20 minutes to bring out any tiny insects that may be lurking inside.

Cut off the toughest part of the stalks, and peel the lower sections of the stalks if the skin is tough. Split the larger bunches so that all stalks will be the same size. Cook uncovered in a very small amount of boiling salted water until just tender, about 10 to 15 minutes. As with green beans, broccoli should still be bitey when done. It is wise

to prop the heads up out of the water, or tie the broccoli in a bunch and stand it up in the pan; otherwise the heads may become mushy before the stalks are done. Serve dressed with melted butter flavored, if you wish, with lemon juice.

Broccoli is a vegetable that is especially suited to dressing up. Here are some suggestions:

1. Melt butter in a skillet and add fine toasted crumbs. Pour the buttered crumbs over cooked broccoli.

2. Top cooked broccoli with grated Parmesan cheese and run it under the broiler to brown.

3. Dice 2 or 3 strips bacon and fry until crisp. Remove the bacon bits, drain off some of the fat and add 1 medium onion, chopped. When the onion is cooked, return the bacon to the pan to reheat, and pour this combination over the cooked broccoli.

4. Heat 4 tablespoons olive oil or peanut oil in a skillet. Add a crushed clove of garlic, and sauté until colored slightly. Add cooked broccoli, and sauté until just heated through. Sprinkle the top with grated Parmesan cheese and some freshly ground black pepper. (Leftover broccoli can be treated this way and served on top of cooked spaghetti for an excellent main dish. Pass extra cheese and perhaps some crisp bacon bits.)

Brussels Sprouts

Brussels sprouts are usually sold in pint or quart baskets. One quart will serve 6 people.

Trim off the stem and the discolored leaves and soak in salted water for 15 minutes. Cook uncovered in boiling salted water to cover until just tender, not mushy —about 15 minutes. (Brussels sprouts are particularly unattractive when overcooked; they fall apart and turn a grayish color.) Drain well. Serve with butter. You might pass some vinegar or lemon juice, as some people like a dash of tartness with this vegetable.

Here are some special methods of preparing sprouts:

1. Cut 4 to 6 strips of bacon into small pieces and fry until crisp. Remove the bacon bits and pour off some of the fat. Sauté 1 finely chopped medium onion and when it is cooked add the bacon bits and one quart cooked sprouts. Heat through and serve.

2. Melt 4 to 6 tablespoons butter in a large skillet and add 1 quart Brussels sprouts. Toss them in the hot fat until they are well seared and wilted on the outside. Turn the heat down, sprinkle with salt and pepper to taste, cover and simmer until the sprouts are just tender, about 10 to 15 minutes. Add a dash of lemon juice, 1 tablespoon grated onion and a touch of basil before serving.

Cabbage

A 2-pound head of cabbage will serve 4 people. Besides the well-known common cabbage, there are two varieties available in many areas—the savoy cabbage, which has a curly leaf, and the red cabbage. The savoy cooks the fastest of the three kinds and is very tender. Red cabbage takes the longest, but is very colorful and attractive. Add a few drops of vinegar to the water when you cook red cabbage, so that it will keep its color.

Shredded cabbage cooks quickly. Only a few minutes in a small amount of boiling salted water will make it tender. Do not overcook cabbage or you will have a tasteless mess on your hands and a strong smell all through the house. Quartered heads of cabbage take about twice as long to cook. Serve cabbage with butter or margarine.

Here are some ways to use cabbage in tasty and hearty dishes:

1. Shred cabbage and cook covered in a small amount of boiling salted water for 5 minutes. Drain it and use half to line a large casserole. Add ½ cup of rich cream sauce or Béchamel Sauce, and sprinkle with freshly grated black pepper and a little grated Parmesan cheese or sharp cheddar. Add the rest of the cabbage and pour another ½ cup of sauce over the top. Add more pepper and more cheese, and top with buttered crumbs. Bake in a 375° oven for 10 to 15 minutes, or until the sauce bubbles and the top is browned.

2. Shred a head of red cabbage. Heat 3 or 4 tablespoons of fat— pork, bacon or ham—in a large skillet. Add the cabbage and 1 medium onion, chopped. Cover and simmer for several minutes, turning the cabbage now and then. Season with salt and pepper and add 1 cup red wine. Simmer for 10 minutes or so and add 2 tart apples, diced, sprinkle with brown sugar and pour about 1 tablespoon of

vinegar over all. Cover again and simmer until the apples and cabbage are tender. This hearty dish goes well with any kind of pork.

3. Grease a large casserole with bacon or ham fat. Add a quartered head of cabbage. Sprinkle the cabbage with salt, pepper and 1 medium onion, chopped. Pour ¾ cup of bouillon (this can be made with a bouillon cube) into the dish and top with pork sausages. Cover and bake in a 350° oven for about 1 hour.

Carrots

Two pounds of carrots will serve 6 people. The larger, older carrots are fine in stews and for flavoring in soups or broths, but if you are planning to serve carrots as a separate vegetable, try to get the young ones, the tinier the better. If they are very tiny they need not be peeled; otherwise just a bit of scraping will do.

Very young carrots may be cooked whole; slightly larger ones may be cut in rounds or cut lengthwise. Cook in a very small amount of boiling salted water until just tender. Serve with butter.

The carrot is a much mistreated vegetable. In many homes the only time you see it outside of a stew or soup is in a heavy cream sauce or combined with some other vegetable. Actually, tender young carrots are quite able to stand on their own, and there are several ways to treat them so that they become a truly elegant dish.

1. If you have tiny carrots, try steaming them whole in butter.

Melt 4 tablespoons butter in a large skillet and lay the carrots in rows in the butter. Turn the heat down, cover and steam gently just until tender. Season and serve with the pan juices poured over them.

2. Dress cooked carrots with butter, chopped chives and parsley, and a bit of oregano.

3. Melt 2 tablespoons butter in a skillet, add an equal amount of honey and toss cooked carrots in this mixture until they are glazed. Season and add a dash of lemon juice.

4. Steam tiny green onions in a skillet with butter until just tender, add cooked carrots and toss together.

Cauliflower

A 2- to 3-pound head of cauliflower will serve 4 people. As with broccoli, be careful when selecting the cauliflower to pick a head that is tightly packed. It should be snowy white; a yellowish tinge means the vegetable is old.

Clean the cauliflower before cooking. Cut off the stem end, remove the green leaves and soak the head in 2 quarts cold water with 1 teaspoon salt for 30 minutes to bring out any insects.

You may cook the head whole or cut it into flowerets. Of course, a whole head makes a more attractive way of serving. Cook the head, stem end down, in boiling salted water to cover, in a covered pan, until just tender, about 20 to 25 minutes. Do not overcook, or it will turn dark and mushy and begin to break apart. Serve dressed with butter.

There are several ways to dress up boiled cauliflower:

1. Brown slivered blanched almonds in butter and pour over the cooked cauliflower.

2. Brown fine toasted bread crumbs in melted butter and pour over the cooked cauliflower.

3. Place cooked cauliflower head in a baking dish, season with pepper, dot with butter and sprinkle with grated cheese (Parmesan, cheddar or Switzerland Swiss). Heat in a 450° oven until the cheese melts.

4. Place cooked cauliflower in a buttered baking dish and cover with 1 cup Béchamel Sauce or rich cream sauce. Sprinkle with ½ cup grated Parmesan cheese and ⅓ cup browned buttered bread crumbs. Cook in a 450° oven until the cheese is melted and the top is browned and bubbling.

5. Place cooked cauliflower in a baking dish, sprinkle with buttered crumbs and crumbled crisp bacon. Dot with butter and put in a 450° oven for a few minutes.

Celery

One large head of celery will serve 4 people. Buy the green, or pascal, celery; you get more for your money and it is tastier and crisper. Always wash celery thoroughly, as there is often a great deal of grit around the base of the stalks. Trim, but do not discard the leafy tops; they are excellent for flavoring soups and stews and, if tender, can be added to green salads. Remove any very tough strings, cut the celery into bite-size pieces and cook in enough boiling salted water to cover, in an uncovered pan, until just tender. Serve dressed with butter.

Celery is so delicious that it seems unnecessary to do anything special to it, yet there are at least two ways to treat it that are superb:

1. Brown slivered blanched almonds in butter and pour over cooked celery.

2. Slice whole celery stalks lengthwise, heart and all. Melt 4 tablespoons butter in a large skillet, add the celery and brown lightly over fairly high heat, turning once. Add ½ to 1 cup beef or chicken broth (or dissolve a bouillon cube in hot water), lower the heat, cover and simmer until the celery is barely tender. Season to taste. Serve with the pan juices. This braised celery is equally delicious hot or cold.

Note: For a hurry-up version of braised celery, simply heat canned celery hearts in chicken broth.

Corn

Corn is certainly one of our most important vegetables—and one of the most typically American. Yet in spite of its great popularity, many people still insist on spoiling it by overcooking. Buy only young, fresh ears—as fresh as possible—in their husks. Keep the corn cool and damp in the refrigerator (or, preferably, buy just before cooking) and don't peel off the husks and the silk until just before cooking. Cook very briefly—3 to 5 minutes is ample—in boiling water to cover. Do not add salt; it toughens the kernels. Drain and serve immediately with plenty of butter and salt and pepper. Feast on corn when it is in season. Provide at least 2 ears per serving. Fresh corn is so good "as is" that it seems heresy to do anything other than cook it simply. But if you want to serve it some other way than on the cob, try the following recipe.

SAUTEED CORN

To serve 4, slice the kernels from 8 ears of corn. Melt 3 or 4 tablespoons butter in a skillet, add the corn and sauté gently about 5 minutes, stirring and tossing with a fork. Season with salt and freshly ground pepper. You may vary this recipe by adding cream (about ½ cup) to the sautéed corn, or by cooking a green pepper, seeded and cut into strips, or 4 chopped green onions in the butter before you sauté the corn.

Eggplant

Eggplant is an extremely versatile vegetable, but for some reason it is often neglected by American cooks. It is hearty food, and when dressed up with bacon or cheese or some sauce it makes an excellent main dish for a luncheon.

Eggplants come in various sizes, from very small on up to huge ones weighing 2 or more pounds. One weighing about 1½ pounds will serve 4 people. Choose eggplants that are firm and free from bruises.

SAUTEED EGGPLANT

The simplest way of preparing this vegetable is to sauté it. Peel the eggplant and cut it into ½-inch-thick slices. Dip the slices into flour, season with salt and pepper, and sauté in hot olive oil and butter until brown on both sides and tender.

Here are several ways to vary sautéed eggplant:

1. Serve with a tomato sauce.
2. Top with grated Parmesan cheese and put under the broiler for a few minutes.
3. Serve topped with grilled tomato slices and sautéed onion rings.
4. Sprinkle with bits of crisp fried bacon and grated cheese.

In combination with other foods in a casserole, eggplant can be the main dish in a meal:

BAKED EGGPLANT

Peel and pare an eggplant and cut into ½-inch slices. Dip in seasoned flour and brown lightly in oil and butter. Arrange the slices in a greased casserole in layers with thin onion rings, green pepper rings and tomato slices. Dot each layer generously with butter, or sprinkle with oil and season with salt and pepper. Top the whole with buttered crumbs and grated Parmesan cheese, mixed. Bake in a 350° oven for ½ hour, or until the vegetables are tender. Serves 4.

STUFFED EGGPLANT

Halve 2 small eggplants lengthwise and scoop out the flesh. Chop it rather coarsely and sauté in ⅓ cup olive oil with 2 cloves garlic, finely chopped. In a separate skillet, sauté 2 cups bread croutons in olive oil flavored with a clove of garlic. Combine the eggplant pulp, croutons and 16 to 20 finely chopped anchovy fillets and toss well. Season to taste with salt and pepper and add the grated rind of 1 lemon and 2 tablespoons lemon juice. Stuff the eggplant shells with this mixture and drizzle olive oil lightly over the top. Place in a baking dish, surround with a little warm water and bake in a 375° oven for 35 minutes. Serves 4.

Fennel

Fennel, or finocchio, as it is called by the Italians, has feathery tops that look rather like dill. The bulb, with its strong anise, or licorice, flavor, is delicious sliced and eaten raw, like celery, or braised.

BRAISED FENNEL

Trim the tops from 2 or 3 heads of fennel and cut them in quarters. Melt 5 to 6 tablespoons butter in a skillet and brown the fennel pieces slightly. Add 1 cup broth, cover the skillet and let the fennel poach— not boil—until just tender. Season to taste and serve with butter and chopped chives.

Leeks

Leeks are hard to find in markets in some areas, but if you can buy them they are well worth using as a vegetable for their tasty, delicate flavor. The French, who call them poor man's asparagus, serve them cold in a Sauce à la Grecque as an appetizer or salad (see Vegetables à la Grecque). They are equally delicious braised. Allow 2 to 3 leeks per serving, depending on size.

BRAISED LEEKS IN BRANDY

Trim 12 leeks, cutting off the root end and all but 1 inch of the green tops and wash thoroughly under cold running water, pulling the layers apart to wash out the sand and grit that settles between them. Brown them in 3 tablespoons olive oil in a skillet, season with 1 teaspoon salt and ¼ teaspoon thyme, and add ⅓ cup consommé and ¼ cup brandy. Reduce heat and simmer until just tender enough to be pierceable. Add the juice of ½ lemon and taste for seasoning. Sprinkle with chopped parsley and serve hot as a vegetable; or chill, dress with a little more oil and lemon juice and serve as a first course.

Mushrooms

Mushrooms have so many uses in the kitchen that it would be difficult to think of cooking without them; they lend their delicate unique flavor to everything from subtly sauced dishes to soups and stews, and as a garnish they are supreme. Like asparagus, they are equally delicious raw—sliced thin and tossed in a salad. Mushrooms should not be peeled (unless they are old, with a wrinkled, tough skin), soaked in water or washed, but should merely be wiped off with a damp cloth or dampened paper towels. One of the most interesting ways to use mushrooms is to make Duxelles, a concentrated mushroom paste for which the mushrooms are chopped fine and cooked very slowly in butter until they lose all their liquid and turn black. This may seem like an extravagance, but actually it isn't. Just a spoonful or two of Duxelles in a stuffing, sauce or filling will permeate the whole with a wonderful essence-of-mushroom flavor. Buy mushrooms when they are cheap and make up the Duxelles. It will keep for weeks in a screw-topped jar in the refrigerator, for months in the freezer.

DUXELLES

Wipe 3 pounds of mushrooms and chop as finely as possible, stems and all. Melt ½ pound butter in a large skillet, add the mushrooms and cook over very low heat, stirring occasionally, until all the moisture has evaporated and the mushrooms have reduced to a dark, thick mass; this may take up to 2 hours. Season with salt and refrigerate or freeze until needed. When ready to use, you may add sautéed shallots or chopped parsley to the Duxelles when you reheat it. This is delicious in omelets, in stuffed tomatoes—anywhere you want a strong mushroom taste.

Onions

To most people, an onion is an onion. Actually, there are many vegetables belonging to the onion family, including chives, leeks, shallots and garlic, to mention just four. The onions most generally found in our markets are the medium-sized cooking onion with the yellow-brown, papery skin; the larger round yellow-skinned globe or Spanish onion, which has a rather sweeter flavor; the sweet red-skinned Italian onion; the small white onion; and the young green onion, or scallion.

Almost every American cook is familiar with the boiled onion with cream sauce or butter, the fried or sautéed onion and the grilled onion slice usually served with steak or hamburger. Here are some ways the onion family can give you more eating pleasure at very little cost:

1. Select small, fresh green onions, clean them and place them flat in a skillet. Add several tablespoons of butter, cover tightly and steam until tender. Season to taste with salt and freshly ground black pepper.

2. Select medium-sized yellow globe onions, allowing 1 onion per serving. Peel, place in a baking dish and add enough beef bouillon (or hot water in which you have dissolved a bouillon cube) to cover the bottom to a depth of 1 inch. Dot with butter, season with salt

and pepper and bake, covered, in a 350° oven for about 1 hour, or until the onions are just tender. Remove the cover, sprinkle with your favorite grated cheese, and return to the oven until the cheese melts.

3. Select 1 medium-sized yellow globe onion per person. Peel and parboil in salted boiling water for about 20 minutes. Remove the center portion of each onion, chop very fine and mix with pork sausage or any other seasoned ground meat. Stuff the onions with the mixture, arrange in a buttered casserole and bake in a 350° oven until the meat is done. This, of course, is to be served as a main dish.

Parsnips

Mostly you see parsnips, those tapering yellowish root vegetables, in the bundles of soup vegetables sold in supermarkets. Few people think of serving them as a vegetable, though their sweet flavor can be an absolutely delicious complement to roast meat—especially lamb.

PARSNIP PUREE

Peel parsnips and boil in salted water until soft. Purée by putting through a food mill and then beat in a liberal amount of butter, nutmeg to taste and a little Madeira wine. Pile into a baking dish, sprinkle dry bread crumbs on top, dot with butter and heat in a 350° oven until the crumbs are lightly browned.

Peas

Fresh peas are good only when they are truly fresh and young. If they are out of season, it is better to rely on frozen peas. Two pounds of unshelled fresh peas will serve 4 people. Do not shell the peas until you are just ready to cook them. They lose their sweet garden flavor if they stand around.

As with other green vegetables, peas are too often overcooked in too much water. Just a small amount of boiling salted water will do. Cover and cook them just until they are tender. Serve with plenty of butter.

For variations, try the following suggestions:

1. Cook peas with tiny new green onions.

2. Sprinkle peas with bits of crisp bacon.

3. (This French method of cooking green peas retains all their flavor.) Melt several tablespoons of butter in a skillet, add the peas and cover them with several fresh lettuce leaves that have been rinsed in water. Steam the peas very slowly under the lettuce until they are just tender. Season to taste. You will be surprised at the unusually good flavor they have.

Peppers

Peppers are another vegetable that Americans seem to treat in only one manner. Generally they are served stuffed and are viewed as a ready answer to the leftover problem. They deserve to be appreciated for themselves alone; a good serving of sautéed green-pepper strips is a delicious addition to almost any dinner plate.

Select firm, fresh peppers, and allow at least one of a good size for each serving. To prepare them, wash, seed and cut them in ½-inch strips. Sauté gently in hot oil or butter until just tender. Season to taste. Here are some variations:

1. Sauté with tiny new green onions until just tender.

2. Sprinkle with grated Parmesan cheese just before removing from the skillet.

3. Sauté in oil—not butter—and add a dash of wine vinegar or lemon juice just before removing from the fire. Prepared in this way, the peppers may be served either hot or cold, as a relish.

Potatoes

The ever-present potato is too often taken for granted. In many American homes potatoes are cooked almost every day, and I'm afraid little thought goes into the process; they are usually served up indifferently boiled or mashed. Properly fixed, however, potatoes can be a most delicious vegetable.

Select 1 large or 2 small potatoes for each serving. If you are buying the tiny new potatoes, you will want 4 to 6, or even more, per person. If you plan to boil, mash or scallop the potatoes or to roast them with meat, the regular variety will do. If you are planning to bake them, the larger Idaho potatoes are superb. They do have an excellent texture. However, they are more expensive.

The major mistake made in cooking potatoes is, as usual, overcooking. When you boil potatoes, test them with a sharp fork. They are done when you can pierce them easily. Do not let them get mushy and watery. Serve them with plenty of salt, freshly ground black pepper and butter.

BAKED POTATOES

Many people like to eat the skin of baked potatoes, so rub each one with fat (butter, oil, bacon fat and beef fat are excellent) before you put them into the oven; this keeps the skin smooth and soft. Make a small slit in the top skin—just enough to let the steam escape during cooking. Bake in a 375° oven for 30 minutes to 1 hour, according to the size of the potatoes, or until the inside tests soft when pierced with a fork. Split open the tops of the baked potatoes and add a good-sized lump of butter to each one. Season with salt and freshly ground pepper and pass more butter, salt and pepper.

VARIATIONS

1. When potatoes are done, slit open and scoop out the insides. Mash or rice the pulp and add 1 tablespoon butter, salt and pepper to taste, and 1 tablespoon chopped parsley or 1 tablespoon each chopped parsley and chives. Mix well, put back into the shells, dot

with additional butter and return to the oven to heat through.

2. Instead of the herbs, add 1 tablespoon sharp grated cheese to the mashed-potato mixture. Return to shells and sprinkle with paprika.

3. Serve plain baked potatoes with sour cream, chopped chives, salt and pepper; or scoop out the insides and combine them with these ingredients, return to shells and reheat. You may substitute crumbled bacon for the chopped chives.

4. Follow directions for Variation 1, using either chopped parsley or chopped chives. Sprinkle the filled potatoes with grated Parmesan cheese and buttered crumbs and reheat.

STUFFED POTATOES

Bake 3 large potatoes in a 350° oven for 1 hour. Remove them and slice each one horizontally. Remove pulp from insides without breaking the skins, leaving a thin layer of pulp around the inside of the skin. Press the potato through a sieve or food mill and mix in 1 ounce butter, 2 tablespoons grated Parmesan cheese, and salt and a little nutmeg to taste. Beat well with a wooden spoon. Put into a pastry bag with a large round tube and pipe into the potatoes, around the sides of the skin, leaving a hollow in the center. Put a few dots of butter into the bottom of each hollow, then break an egg into the center of each halved potato. Sprinkle with salt and pepper and replace in the oven just until the whites are set; the egg

yolks should still be liquid. Serve immediately.

POTATOES ANNA

Butter well a large shallow baking dish or pie pan (Teflon-coated pans are excellent for this) or a heavy iron skillet and arrange on the bottom an overlapping layer of potatoes that have been peeled and cut into very thin slices. If the dish is round, arrange the slices in a spiral. If it is square or oblong, arrange them in rows. Season to taste with salt and freshly ground pepper and spread or dot liberally with butter. Repeat the layers until the dish is full and all the potato slices (you will need 1 sliced potato per person) used. Spread butter lavishly over the last layer and bake in a 400° oven for 30 to 40 minutes, or until the potatoes test tender with a toothpick or a fork. Turn the baking dish upside down on a large platter or plate so that the potatoes come out in a solid mass, crusty side up.

SCALLOPED POTATOES

Peel the potatoes and slice them rather thin. Grease a large baking dish with butter or margarine and place a layer of potato slices on the bottom. Season with salt and pepper and dot with more butter. Add another layer of potato slices and season again. Proceed until all the potatoes are used up. Pour milk into the dish until it almost covers the potato slices, cover the dish and bake in a 375° oven for 30 minutes. Remove the cover and continue baking until the potatoes are done and the top is browned.

Add slices of onion to the layers. Or add grated cheese to each layer of potatoes. Or sprinkle each layer with chopped parsley.

Spinach

Two pounds of leaf spinach will serve 4 people. If you buy spinach that comes with the stem and the root, it will probably be very sandy. It must be washed thoroughly under running water to loosen all the grit. (If you buy the already cleaned spinach sold in packages, you need only rinse it lightly.) Cut off the root and the larger stems. For cooking, spinach needs no water other than what clings to the leaves after washing; its own natural juices furnish all the additional moisture needed. Put the washed spinach into a pan, sprinkle lightly with salt and cook over low heat, covered, until the leaves are thoroughly wilted and tender—this should only take a few minutes. Drain well, season to taste and serve with plenty of butter. For those who like a tart flavor to their spinach, serve with lemon wedges or a good wine vinegar.

VARIATIONS

1. Heat olive oil in a skillet and add a chopped garlic clove. Toss the spinach in the garlicky oil. Season with salt and pepper.

2. Add grated onion or finely chopped green onions to the butter before you put it on the spinach. Garnish with sliced hard-cooked egg.

3. Chop the spinach coarsely and mix with ½ pound sliced, sautéed mushrooms. Season to taste.

4. Add 2 tablespoons chopped chives and 1 teaspoon dried tarragon (or 1 tablespoon chopped fresh tarragon) to the butter before putting it on the spinach. Season with salt and pepper and serve with lemon wedges.

5. Chop the spinach coarsely after cooking. Melt 2 tablespoons butter in a skillet and add 4 tablespoons heavy cream. Blend the chopped spinach into the mixture, season to taste and serve.

Note: Other leafy greens such as Swiss chard, beet or turnip tops, collards, dandelion greens, mustard greens, chicory or kale may be cooked according to the directions given for spinach.

Tomatoes

Tomatoes are used extensively in salads, soups and various sauces, but many cooks forget how good they can be as a hot vegetable. Baked, fried, stewed, broiled—any way you fix them, they have a refreshing quality as well as a colorful appearance. Buy 1 large or 2 small tomatoes for each serving.

Recipes often call for tomatoes to be peeled before cooking. To do this, plunge tomatoes into boiling water for 1 minute, drain and plunge at once into cold water. The skins will then slip off easily.

STEWED TOMATOES

Peel and core the tomatoes and cut them into quarters. Place them in a pan, season to taste with salt and freshly ground pepper, and simmer very gently until just done. Taste for tartness and if it seems necessary add a little sugar. Add butter and serve.

VARIATIONS

Sauté sliced onion rings in butter or oil and add them to the tomatoes. If you like the flavor of basil, add a little of the herb to the tomatoes as they cook.

Some people like their stewed tomatoes thickened a bit. To do this, add cubes of bread that have been fried until very crisp in butter, margarine or olive oil.

PENNSYLVANIA-DUTCH TOMATOES

This is a famous version of the fried tomato—one that has been served for generations in the eastern part of Pennsylvania. The unusual combination of flavors is a treat. Use either ripe or green tomatoes for this dish. Slice, dredge with flour and season with salt and pepper. Cook very slowly in butter. Just before turning the slices, sprinkle each one with brown sugar. Sprinkle the tops with brown sugar after turning. Watch to see that the sugar and butter do not burn.

When the tomato slices are nearly done and lightly browned, add a goodly amount of cream or evaporated milk to the skillet—enough to cover the bottom up to ½ inch or more. Continue cooking until the cream is hot and thoroughly blended with the butter and sugar. Serve the tomatoes with the creamy sauce poured over them.

BAKED TOMATOES

Hollow out each tomato, removing the seeds and center pulp. Combine the pulp with any of these mixtures to use as a stuffing for the tomatoes: chopped mushrooms, grated garlic, chopped parsley, salt, pepper and dry bread crumbs; any leftover meat ground up, chopped onions, chopped parsley, bread crumbs, salt, pepper and a little dry mustard; sautéed chopped green pepper and green onion, corn, salt and pepper. Add a little butter to the stuffing, fill the tomatoes, dot with more butter, sprinkle with grated cheese and place in a greased baking dish. Add a little water to the dish to prevent the tomatoes from sticking. Bake in a 375° oven about 20 to 30 minutes, or until the tomatoes are done.

GREEK STUFFED TOMATOES

Cook 1 cup long-grain rice in 2 cups salted water until just tender. Drain. Sauté 2 finely chopped garlic cloves and ½ cup pine nuts in ⅓ cup olive oil. Combine with cooked rice and season with 1 teaspoon salt, ½ teaspoon pepper and ½ teaspoon rosemary. Cut the tops from 6 large ripe tomatoes and scoop out the seeds and pulp. Stuff with the rice mixture and arrange in a baking dish. Combine ½ cup oil, ¼ cup tomato purée and 1 tablespoon lemon juice and pour over the tomatoes. Bake in a 350° oven for 30 minutes, basting from time to time with the pan juices. The tomatoes should still be firm and the rice and flavorings blended. Serves 6.

Note: The stuffed tomatoes may be served cold, as a first course, with the addition of a little white-wine vinegar.

Turnips

Turnips, like parsnips, are often overlooked as a vegetable, yet their flavor and texture can make a pleasant change from the usual run of accompaniments to meat and poultry.

RUTABAGA PUREE

For 4 servings, peel and dice 2 large rutabagas, or yellow turnips, and cook in boiling salted water until just tender. Mash well with a potato masher or put through a ricer or food mill. Season to taste, add plenty of butter (at least 6 tablespoons) to the purée and whip thoroughly. Heap into a serving dish and sprinkle with paprika. You may also blend in sour cream or heavy cream if you like. Serve with roast pork, turkey or game.

WHITE TURNIPS WITH MUSHROOMS

Peel and slice small white turnips and steam in butter, covered, until tender. Combine with sliced, sautéed mushrooms and toss.

Zucchini

The small Italian summer squash known as zucchini is a tender morsel that can be fixed in a variety of ways. Buy 1 pound to serve 4 people. Leave the zucchini un-peeled and cut it in medium-thin slices. Cook very gently in a covered pan in a small amount of boiling salted water until just barely tender. Zucchini is much better when still a little firm rather than mushy. Drain and dress with butter, salt and freshly ground black pepper.

Zucchini combines excellently with a variety of seasonings and other vegetables. Try some of these combinations:

1. Sauté sliced zucchini in 2 or 3 tablespoons olive oil seasoned with a chopped garlic clove. Season to taste with salt and freshly ground black pepper.

2. Add 2 tomatoes, peeled, seeded and diced, to the pan when the zucchini are about half sautéed. Just before the mixture is done, sprinkle the top with grated Parmesan cheese, cover the skillet and let the cheese melt.

3. Add a little chopped fresh basil or dried basil to the zucchini-and-tomato mixture.

4. Sauté green-pepper strips and red Italian onions rings in olive oil

or butter. When they are slightly colored, add sliced zucchini and sauté a few more minutes. Add tomato wedges and finish cooking. Season to taste with salt and freshly ground black pepper.

5. Sauté little green onions in butter with zucchini slices. Season to taste.

6. Fry 3 or 4 strips of bacon until crisp. Remove from the skillet. Cook zucchini slices in the hot bacon fat and serve garnished with the bacon, crumbled.

Zucchini, eggplant, onions, tomatoes and peppers all combine in the marvelous Provençal dish of stewed vegetables called Ratatouille, which may be served either hot or cold. Hot, it is delicious with lamb or cold roast meat or as an omelet filling. If you are serving it cold as a salad, let it cook down slightly more and add a touch more oil and a little lemon juice or wine vinegar. Freshly chopped parsley sprinkled on top makes a colorful and pleasing garnish. Or serve Ratatouille cold as a first course, topped with anchovy fillets and capers.

RATATOUILLE

1 large or 2 medium eggplants, unpeeled and thinly sliced
½ cup olive oil
2 medium onions, thinly sliced
2 cloves garlic, thinly sliced
4 or 5 small or 2 large zucchini, thinly sliced
1 red or green pepper, thinly sliced
4 to 5 tomatoes, peeled, seeded and chopped or 29-ounce can Italian plum tomatoes, drained
2 teaspoons salt
1 teaspoon freshly ground black pepper
1 teaspoon or more basil
½ teaspoon ground coriander

Salt the eggplant and leave for 1 hour. Rinse and press. Heat the oil in a large shallow pan which has a cover, add the onion and sauté until just soft and wilted. Add the garlic, the drained and pressed eggplant (if large, cut into smaller pieces), and the zucchini. Mix well together and cook over medium heat for 5 minutes. Add the red or green pepper and mix with the cooked vegetables. Cover and cook for 15 minutes, removing the cover once or twice to stir the mixture. Add the tomatoes and mix in. Simmer uncovered for 45 minutes to 1 hour, or until the vegetables are well blended and cooked down slightly. Add the salt, pepper, basil and coriander and cook a few minutes longer. Taste for seasoning. If the Ratatouille is to be served cold, cool and chill, and garnish with chopped parsley.

VARIATIONS

1. Add sliced mushrooms during the last 10 minutes of cooking.

2. For a cold Ratatouille, add thinly sliced fennel with the red or green pepper.

7

SALADS
and
HERBS

You can always count on salads and herbs to make a simple meal more interesting to the eye and pleasing to the palate. Although the tossed green salad has practically become an American cliché, when it is properly prepared, varied and seasoned there is really nothing better. Add to it pieces of leftover meat and poultry and some cheese or eggs, and you have a Chef's Salad substantial enough for luncheon. Summer and winter, salads never lose their appeal, because they can be varied to suit the season. Nothing tastes better on an early-spring day than a Salade Niçoise, while a rich Turkey Salad can lift the spirits in those gastronomically letdown days after Christmas. Beans, rice, eggs, sausage, cheese, fish and shellfish, bacon, all manner of fresh and canned vegetables—there is almost nothing that can't be put together to make a good salad. With a repertoire of salads at your fingertips, you will never be at a loss for a good meal.

Herbs, natural partners to salad, are also a prime cooking ingredient in their own right. Without them there would be no luscious Sauce Béarnaise, no Pesto for pasta, no *omelette fines herbes*. It is well worthwhile to cultivate not only herbs, but also a knowledge of their many, essential functions in cooking.

TOSSED GREEN SALAD

A good tossed salad adds zest to any meal and can be varied and added to at will. One of the major faults in preparing salad is unimaginativeness. Many people use nothing but iceberg lettuce—over and over and over again—although this is just one of the many greens now available in American markets. Look for romaine, escarole, endive, chicory, watercress, tiny new spinach, leaf lettuce, Boston lettuce, bibb lettuce, field salad and tender celery tops. Any of these, alone or in combinations, will make a delightful crisp salad.

Wash the greens thoroughly and freshen them in icy water. Drain well. Roll them in a towel or paper towels and put them into the refrigerator to crisp.

Be sure the greens are dry when you use them. Nothing is worse than a soggy, wilted mass in the salad bowl. Try to prepare the salad at the very last minute and it will keep its freshness. Break or tear (do not cut) the greens into small pieces and arrange them in your bowl. Now dress them with a simple French dressing: use 3 to 4 parts olive oil to 1 part wine vinegar or lemon juice; salt and pepper to taste. Pour this over the salad greens and toss lightly. Be sure each leaf is bathed with the oil-and-vinegar mixture.

There are many ways to vary the basic Tossed Green Salad by adding bits of this and that. Here are some suggestions:

1. Add finely cut celery and thin green-pepper strips. Top with onion rings.

2. Add tomato wedges, sliced radishes, sliced cucumbers and chopped little green onions.

3. Add tomato wedges, chopped chives and a little chopped fresh basil. Or add a pinch of dried basil to the dressing when you mix it.

4. For a hearty luncheon salad in the summer, add tomato wedges, onion rings, radishes and top with strips of cheese and cold meats.

5. Spice up the dressing with a little dry mustard, or a dash of Worcestershire sauce, or a little grated garlic.

6. Add any leftover cold vegetables such as green beans, carrots, peas, cauliflower, broccoli, and top with onion rings.

GARDEN SALAD PLATE

Almost any cold vegetable or combination of cold cooked vegetables can make a delicious salad. This version is as simple as anything could be.

Chill a large plate or platter, line it with salad greens and arrange on it any selection of vegetables you choose, such as peeled thinly sliced tomatoes, cucumbers, shredded cabbage, green onions, radishes, carrots, cooked cauliflower, cooked broccoli, cooked green peas or string beans. Have a bowl of French dressing and one of mayonnaise and let each person make his own selection.

VARIATION

For a heartier salad, suitable for a summer-evening supper, slice leftover cold meat and fish and arrange on a platter. Surround with mounds of cold cooked vegetables on greens. Garnish with onion rings and mayonnaise.

WILTED SPINACH SALAD

4 tablespoons olive oil
1 large or 2 small cloves garlic, crushed and chopped
2 tablespoons soy sauce
½ cup thinly sliced water chestnuts
Freshly cracked pepper, salt to taste
2 tablespoons lemon juice
1 pound spinach, washed, dried and crisped
2 hard-cooked eggs, coarsely chopped

Cook olive oil and garlic over medium heat for 2 minutes. Add soy sauce, water chestnuts and pepper. Cook for 1 minute, tossing water chestnuts. Add lemon juice and blend. Then add spinach and toss as you would a salad until spinach is just wilted. Taste for salt and correct seasoning if necessary. Transfer to salad bowl and garnish with chopped egg. Serves 4.

CAESAR SALAD

This salad, when properly assembled, is one of the most delicious of all. It should be mixed at the last moment and never allowed to stand.

10 tablespoons olive oil
4 tablespoons butter
4 slices bread, crusts removed, cubed
3 cloves garlic, thinly sliced
1 whole clove garlic
2 heads romaine, washed, dried, and crisped
18 to 24 anchovy fillets, cut into pieces
Fresh lemon juice to taste
Freshly ground black pepper
Salt, if needed
1 egg, coddled for 1 minute
Freshly grated Parmesan cheese

Combine 2 tablespoons olive oil and the butter in a skillet over moderate heat. Add the bread cubes and sliced garlic, and toss until the croutons are brown and crisp. Drain on paper toweling.

When ready to serve, rub the interior of a salad bowl with the whole garlic clove. Add the romaine, broken into manageable pieces. Pour remaining oil over this, and toss well. Then add the croutons, the anchovies, lemon juice and freshly ground pepper to taste. Toss again lightly and then taste for salt. Finally, break the coddled egg into the bowl and add a good fistful of grated Parmesan. Toss the salad well and eat at once. Serves 4.

CELERY SALAD

1½ to 2 bunches pascal celery
8 or 9 tablespoons olive oil
3 tablespoons lemon juice
1 teaspoon dry mustard
1½ teaspoons salt

Wash the celery well, keeping the bunches intact. Cut through the bunches in fine slices, leaves and all. Place in a salad bowl and toss with a dressing made by combining the oil, lemon juice, mustard and salt. Mix well and let the salad stand for an hour or so before serving; the longer it stands and the more wilted it becomes, the better it tastes. Taste for seasoning before serving. Serves 6.

Note: You may use mayonnaise diluted with wine vinegar or lemon juice instead of the oil dressing. Season it highly with mustard.

CUCUMBERS WITH YOGHURT

5 slender cucumbers
1 teaspoon salt
1 cup yoghurt
1½ teaspoons vinegar flavored with 1 crushed clove of garlic (let garlic stand in vinegar 1 hour, then discard)

½ teaspoon dried dill weed or
1 tablespoon chopped fresh dill
1 tablespoon minced fresh mint
leaves

Peel cucumbers, quarter lengthwise
and remove seeds. Slice very thin,
put into a bowl and sprinkle with 1
teaspoon salt to draw out bitter
juices. Mix yoghurt, vinegar and
dill weed until smooth, and combine with drained cucumbers. Serve
chilled in a glass bowl, sprinkled
with the mint. Serves 6.

Cole Slaw is the quintessential
American vegetable salad, served in
every luncheonette. These two versions are råther out of the ordinary:

COLE SLAW

Cut a 2-pound cabbage into thin
shreds, sprinkle lavishly with salt
and allow to stand, covered, in the
refrigerator for several hours. Wash
and drain.
Make a spicy dressing with 4
parts olive oil to 1 part wine vinegar, 1 teaspoon celery seed, 1 teaspoon mustard seed, a bay leaf,
freshly ground pepper to taste and
½ cup shredded onion. Bring this
to a boil, cool slightly, pour over
the cabbage and chill thoroughly.
When it is cold, correct the seasoning and chill again before serving. Serves 4 to 6.

QUICK COLE SLAW

2-pound cabbage, shredded
1 cup mayonnaise

½ cup sour cream
Juice of 1 lemon
1 tablespoon (or to taste) sugar
1 teaspoon dry mustard
Salt, freshly ground black pepper to
taste

Soak the cabbage for 1 hour in
salted water. Drain well. Combine
all the remaining ingredients thoroughly and pour over the cabbage.
To vary the flavor, add 1 tablespoon horseradish to the dressing.
Serves 4 to 6.

There are many versions of potato salad. This one is unusual and
delicious.

HOT POTATO SALAD

3 pounds small new potatoes,
   unpeeled
1 pound bacon
3 large onions, chopped very fine
½ cup vinegar
6 scallions, chopped very fine
Salt, pepper to taste
12 hard-cooked eggs

Cook the potatoes in boiling salted
water until just tender. Plunge into
cold water and peel at once. Cut
into quarters while still warm.
While the potatoes are cooking,
fry the bacon until crisp. Remove
the bacon and crumble it. Add the
chopped onions to the hot bacon
fat and cook until just faintly
colored. Add the vinegar, chopped
scallions, salt and pepper and blend.
Pour this sauce over the potatoes
and toss well. Garnish with crumbled bacon and quartered hard-
cooked eggs.

BEAN SALADS

Very few people ever think of making salads with cooked dried beans and chick-peas, yet they are not only good and interesting, but hearty enough to make a summertime luncheon. Bean salads go well with pork and sausage dishes.

RANCHO SALAD

1 twenty-ounce can kidney beans, drained
1 twenty-ounce can cannellini beans, drained
1 one-pound can chick-peas, drained and rinsed
1 large onion, coarsely chopped, or 12 green onions, coarsely chopped
3 pimientos, chopped
3 celery stalks, chopped
12 to 18 stuffed olives, sliced
2 green chili peppers, chopped
⅓ cup chopped parsley
½ cup olive oil
3 to 4 tablespoons wine vinegar
2 cloves garlic
1 teaspoon salt
1 teaspoon freshly ground black pepper

Mix the beans, chick-peas, onion, pimientos, celery, olives, chili peppers and parsley. Combine remaining ingredients to make a dressing and shake well in a screw-top jar. Pour dressing over salad and toss well. Leave for an hour or two in the refrigerator to marinate. Remove garlic. Serve on a bed of greens and garnish with sliced tomatoes. Serves 6 to 8.

BEANS PRIMAVERA

This unusual salad of beans and tuna may be made with the regular dried pea beans or with canned cannellini beans, which are available in some of the larger chain stores or in Italian groceries.

1 pound pea beans or 3 twenty-ounce cans cannellini beans
2 seven-ounce cans solid-meat tuna
3 cloves garlic, chopped
¼ cup chopped parsley
¼ cup finely chopped fresh basil
Olive oil
Wine vinegar
Salt, freshly ground black pepper

If you use the dried beans, soak them overnight in water to cover. Next morning, drain, add fresh water to cover, salt to taste, 1 bay leaf and an onion stuck with 2 cloves. Bring to a boil, reduce the heat and simmer until the beans are done but still firm, not mushy. Drain well. They should be mixed with other ingredients while still hot. If you use the canned beans, drain them, wash them in cold water and drain again.

Mix the beans with the tuna broken into pieces, garlic, parsley and basil. Add oil and vinegar, salt and pepper to taste. Chill for a few hours. Before serving, sprinkle with a little additional chopped parsley.

This cold bean salad can be served as fork food, in hollowed-out, well-drained tomato shells as a first course, or as a snack on pieces of toast or crisp crackers. Serves 8 to 10.

SEAFOOD SALADS

And now for some more salads made with seafood, especially that good old standby, tuna, one of the essential ingredients in the wonderful south of France specialty.

SALADE NIÇOISE

6 medium potatoes, boiled and sliced
½ cup finely chopped onion
1 tablespoon or more chopped basil
3 tablespoons chopped parsley
1 teaspoon salt
½ teaspoon freshly ground black pepper
¾ cup olive oil
¼ cup wine vinegar
3 ripe tomatoes, peeled and cut into sixths
Tuna in olive oil (amount to taste), broken into chunks
20 to 30 anchovy fillets
4 to 6 hard-cooked eggs, quartered
Green-pepper rings
Black olives
Romaine or Boston lettuce

Toss the potatoes and onion with the basil, parsley, salt, pepper, oil and vinegar. Garnish with the remaining ingredients. Serves 6 as a main course at luncheon.

Note: You can vary Salade Niçoise to taste by adding or changing ingredients—substituting red-onion rings for the chopped onion, adding artichoke hearts, pimiento strips or crisp fried croutons. However, a good Salade Niçoise should always contain tuna, anchovies, tomatoes, eggs and black olives for a nice contrast of flavors.

TUNA SALAD

For each serving:
1½ cups greens
1 cup imported oil-packed tuna, drained
1 sliced hard-cooked egg
2 tablespoons capers
¼ cup onion rings
¼ cup diced avocado
Vinaigrette Sauce

Arrange greens in a salad bowl. Add tuna, egg, capers, onion rings and avocado. Dress with a plain Vinaigrette Sauce.

VARIATIONS

To greens and tuna, add:
1. Thinly sliced fennel, chopped onion. Serve with a plain Vinaigrette.
2. Black olives, 2 or 3 chopped anchovies, onion rings, and cherry tomatoes. Serve with a Vinaigrette flavored with fresh dill.

SHRIMP SALAD

For each serving:
1½ cups greens
1 cup cooked shrimp
¼ cup onion rings
¼ cup orange sections
1 tablespoon capers
1 teaspoon chopped chives
Vinaigrette Sauce flavored with chopped chives

Arrange greens in a salad bowl. Add shrimp, onion rings, orange sections, capers and chives. Dress with the Vinaigrette Sauce.

VARIATIONS

To greens and shrimp add:
1. Fresh dill, capers and finely chopped chives. Serve with plain Vinaigrette.
2. Avocado slices and capers. Serve with a garlic-flavored Vinaigrette.
3. Peeled and cubed cucumber and chopped fresh tarragon. Serve with a tarragon-flavored Vinaigrette.
4. Hard-cooked-egg wedges, black olives. Serve with a plain Vinaigrette.

SCANDINAVIAN HERRING SALAD

1 twelve-ounce jar herring tidbits, cut julienne
1 cup diced ox tongue
1 cup diced cooked veal
1 crisp apple, unpeeled, diced
1 cup diced cooked potatoes
Mayonnaise
2 hard-cooked eggs, quartered
Chopped parsley and chopped green-onion tops
12 canned baby beets, drained

Combine herring, tongue, veal, apple and potatoes, and toss with mayonnaise. Garnish with eggs, chopped parsley and onion. Surround with a ring of baby beets. Serves 4.

CODFISH SALAD

1 pound filleted salt codfish
Olive oil
Wine vinegar
2 cloves garlic, finely chopped

1 large or 2 medium red Italian onions, thinly sliced
1½ pounds potatoes, unpeeled
Salt, freshly ground black pepper
¼ cup chopped Italian parsley
A handful of pine nuts

Soak the codfish overnight in cold water, changing the water once. Wash and place in a saucepan with water to cover. Bring to a boil, reduce the heat and cook until the fish flakes easily when tested with a fork. Do not overcook. Drain. When cool enough to handle, break into large flakes. Add 2 to 3 tablespoons oil and 1 tablespoon vinegar, the garlic and onion.

Boil the potatoes in salted water until just tender. Drain and plunge into cold water. When cool enough to handle, peel and slice and combine with the cod. Add a few more tablespoons oil and vinegar to taste and a few grinds of pepper. Chill for several hours before serving. Just before serving, toss gently and taste for seasoning; you may need additional oil and vinegar. Garnish with parsley and pine nuts. Serves 4 to 6 as a first course or part of an hors-d'oeuvre table. It may also be served as a main dish at a summer luncheon.

MUSSEL SALAD

Cook the mussels as for Moules Marinière (see Chapter 3), but do not pour the broth over them. Instead, cool the mussels and remove them from the shells, picking off the black edges. Marinate for 2 hours in a good Vinaigrette Sauce made of 3 parts oil to 1 part wine vinegar with salt and pepper to taste and a touch of mustard.

When mussels are well marinated, add ½ cup finely chopped green onion and toss well with mayonnaise. Arrange on greens. Serves 2.

SARDINE-AND-EGG SALAD

For each person, arrange on a bed of shredded greens 1 to 1½ sliced hard-cooked eggs, about 10 to 12 sardines and a few slices of cucumber. Sprinkle with lemon juice and serve with a good mayonnaise.

HEARTY SALADS

Almost anything goes into a salad— leftover meats, seafood, eggs, sausages, cheese, rice, whatever happens to be on hand. And the more you add, the more of a meal the salad becomes. First, a good way to use up the holiday bird:

TURKEY SALAD

3 cups white turkey meat
½ cup walnuts
Salad greens
1 cup sour cream
1 cup mayonnaise
1 teaspoon tarragon
2 tablespoons chopped parsley
Capers, sliced hard-cooked eggs, black olives

Toss turkey with walnuts and arrange on a bed of greens. Blend together the sour cream, mayonnaise, tarragon and parsley. Spoon lavishly over the turkey and garnish with capers, eggs and olives. Serves 6.

Or last night's poached chicken:

MACADAMIA-CHICKEN SALAD

2 cups cold white chicken meat
1 tablespoon fresh finely chopped tarragon or 1 teaspoon dried tarragon soaked in 2 tablespoons white wine
1 cup mayonnaise
1 cup sour cream
Salt, pepper to taste
⅔ cup macadamia nuts
Salad greens
4 hard-cooked eggs, quartered
¼ cup capers

Combine the chicken and tarragon. (If using dried tarragon, soak it for 45 minutes in the white wine.) Add mayonnaise to sour cream and beat well. Taste for seasoning. Reserve some of the mayonnaise mixture for garnish and toss the chicken and nuts with the remainder. Arrange salad on a bed of greens and garnish with the reserved mayonnaise mixture, the eggs and capers. Serves 4 to 6.

For more substantial fare, add potatoes or cold cooked rice, as in the three recipes following:

CHICKEN, POTATO AND BEAN SALAD

1½ cups diced cooked potatoes
1½ cups diced cooked chicken
1½ cups finely cut cooked string beans

12 anchovy fillets
3 tablespoons capers
2 tablespoons chopped basil
Vinaigrette Sauce
Lettuce leaves
4 tomatoes, quartered

Combine potatoes, chicken, string beans, anchovy fillets and capers. Sprinkle with basil. Dress with Vinaigrette Sauce. Arrange on lettuce leaves in a bowl and garnish with tomato quarters. Serves 4.

RICE SALAD ITALIENNE

3 cups cooked rice
3 pimientos, cut in strips
1 green pepper, cut in strips
12 green onions, finely chopped, or ⅔ cup chopped red Italian onions
1½ cups chicken or turkey breast, cut into julienne strips
18 large stuffed olives, sliced
18 large black olives, sliced
18 anchovy fillets, coarsely cut
1 teaspoon dried or 2 tablespoons chopped fresh basil
Garlic-flavored French dressing
Tomato wedges, quartered hardcooked eggs, capers

Combine first 9 ingredients and toss with the French dressing. Garnish with the tomato wedges and quartered hard-cooked eggs. Sprinkle with capers. Serves 6.

CHICKEN-AND-ARTICHOKE SALAD

1½ cups cold cooked rice
½ cup diced cooked chicken
½ cup diced ox tongue
½ cup chopped green onion
¼ cup chopped parsley
Vinaigrette Sauce
1 package frozen artichoke hearts, cooked and chilled
2 tablespoons chopped tarragon

Toss rice, chicken, tongue, onion, and parsley with Vinaigrette Sauce. Garnish with artichoke hearts and sprinkle with tarragon. Serves 4.

Did you think there was only one way to make a Chef's Salad? Here are seven:

CHEF'S SALAD

This dieter's favorite has no standard recipe and is likely to be an impromptu production. In restaurants, it is usually composed of a large quantity of torn or shredded greens, topped with strips of ham, chicken, turkey and cheese and served with a Vinaigrette Sauce, a blue-cheese dressing or Thousand Island dressing. Below are suggested combinations of ingredients to add to the greens for the Chef's Salad of your choice. You can invent your own combinations ad infinitum.

1. Julienne of ham, turkey, Emmenthaler cheese.
2. Julienne of ham and tongue, Bel Paese cheese.
3. Julienne of tongue and chicken, Emmenthaler or Gruyère cheese.
4. Julienne of corned beef and tongue, Muenster cheese.
5. Shrimp, lobster chunks.
6. Crabmeat cubes, lobster chunks.

7. Julienne of cold roast beef and turkey, cheddar cheese.

The next four salads are good for buffets or outdoor eating.

SPECIAL BEEF SALAD

4 cups cold boiled beef or half boiled and half corned beef, cut into ¾-inch to 1-inch dice
2 cups thinly sliced green onions
2 cups thinly sliced celery
1 cup shredded green pepper
2 cups thinly sliced cold boiled potatoes
2 cups tomatoes, peeled and cut into wedges, or 2 cups cherry tomatoes
¼ cup chopped parsley
¼ cup capers
1 cup thinly sliced raw mushrooms
1 cup or more mustard-flavored Vinaigrette Sauce
Romaine or chicory leaves
6 hard-cooked eggs, halved
Parsley sprigs
Olives

In a mixing bowl combine the first nine ingredients and toss lightly with the Vinaigrette Sauce. Arrange romaine or chicory leaves around a serving ravier or a bowl, and heap the tossed mixture into the center. Top with the hard-cooked eggs, a few parsley sprigs, and olives. Serves 4 to 6.

KNACKWURST SALAD

6 knackwurst
1 medium onion, finely minced
6 sour pickles or sweet gherkins, thinly sliced
1½ tablespoons Dijon mustard
1 cup mayonnaise
3 tablespoons sour cream
Romaine
Chopped parsley, chopped gherkins
Hard-cooked eggs, halved

Cook the knackwurst, cool and skin them. Slice rather thin and combine with the onion, sliced pickles, mustard and mayonnaise. Toss well. Add the sour cream and toss again. Arrange on a bed of romaine and garnish with chopped parsley and chopped gherkins. Surround with halved hard-cooked eggs. Serve with thin buttered pumpernickel. Serves 6.

GERMAN SALAD

4 large knackwurst
1 cup julienne of Gruyère or Emmenthaler cheese
½ cup diced celery
1½ cups cooked sliced potato
6 green onions, chopped
Mustard Mayonnaise

Simmer knackwurst in hot water for 15 minutes. Drain, cook, peel and slice. Combine with cheese, celery, potato and onions, and dress with Mustard Mayonnaise. Serves 4.

TONGUE AND SPINACH SALAD

1½ cups julienne of tongue
2½ cups spinach leaves
½ cup crisp bacon bits

⅓ cup shredded fresh horseradish or 2 tablespoons prepared horseradish
Vinaigrette Sauce

Toss tongue, spinach, bacon, and fresh horseradish with Vinaigrette Sauce. (If prepared horseradish is used, mix it into the sauce.) Serves 4.

And when you are stuck for a quick, good luncheon dish, you'll usually find cheese, eggs, bacon and salad greens in the refrigerator— and there are the makings of your salad.

BACON AND EGG SALAD

8 slices (½ pound) bacon
2 large heads romaine or 1 large head leaf lettuce and 1 bunch watercress
6 hard-cooked eggs
4 chopped green onions
1 teaspoon salt (approximately)
Freshly ground black pepper to taste
3 tablespoons wine vinegar

Cook the bacon until crisp. Drain and crumble, reserving about ½ cup of the bacon fat. Wash the romaine or the leaf lettuce and watercress well. Dry thoroughly and put into a large bowl, tearing the leaves with your fingers. Shell and chop the eggs and scatter them, with the crumbled bacon, on top of the lettuce. Add the chopped green onions. Sprinkle the salad with salt and pepper and pour over it the vinegar and reserved bacon fat. Mix gently but thoroughly. Serves 4.

SALADE DE FROMAGE DE ZOLLIKOFFEN
(Swiss Cheese Salad)

⅓ pound Swiss cheese, cut into 1-inch cubes
4 hard-cooked eggs, chopped
1 teaspoon dry mustard
1 teaspoon grated horseradish
½ teaspoon salt
½ teaspoon freshly ground black pepper
Pinch of cumin seed
⅓ cup sour cream
Salad greens

Mix the cheese and eggs and season with the mustard, horseradish, salt, pepper and cumin. Add the sour cream and toss lightly. Serve on a bed of greens. Serves 4.

HERBS

During medieval times and in the age of the Renaissance, knowledge of herbs was part of one's educational and social background. Herbs were used in a multitude of ways in the medicines sold by apothecaries, in household remedies, in love potions, in cosmetics and, of course, in cooking. The proper home had its own herb garden, the produce of which was as much a part of family life as salt. In America, the chemists and the drugstores have taken over the job of supplying us with medicines, perfumes and creams, with the result that Grandmother's pennyroyal tea for what ails you, love powders, and the sprigs of lavender and homemade pomander balls for the linen closet have all disappeared. So, for the most part, have the herb garden and, unfortunately, herbs in the cooking pot.

Lately there has been a revival in America of interest in herbs—a revival that all of us who enjoy good living and fine food welcome heartily, provided one goes about cultivating a real understanding of the culinary uses of these fascinating plants.

As with most growing things, the fresh herb out of the garden has the best flavor. If you grow your own (and even a city dweller can make good use of a window box or a few pots on the windowsill or the terrace), remember to dry or freeze some for out-of-season use. You can also, in the growing season, make up batches of herb-flavored butters and sauces and store them in the freezer.

It really is not at all difficult to grow herbs. You can buy seeds at every dime store these days, or get the young, sprouting plants from nurseries.

Make the Most of Herbs

If you live in a city, you will find the best selection of fresh herbs in the markets in the foreign sections of the town, although certain things like dill and tarragon are now becoming so popular that the better supermarkets and vegetable markets have taken to stocking them.

Although it is obviously cheaper to grow and dry your own herbs, there will always be times when you have to depend on the dried commercial variety. It pays to be cautious when buying herbs in jars or tins. The quality and strength vary remarkably. You can usually depend on the better-known brand names; Spice Islands is one of the very best. There is a tendency among most packers to powder herbs too much—to such an extent, I feel, that they lose their potency. When you find dried or dehydrated herbs that are large-leaved and filled with a fine perfume, they should prove excellent. Certain specialty cooking stores are now carrying the dried herbs from Provence. By all means buy these if you see them. A tip I recently learned that brings out more flavor in dried herbs is to warm them slightly in a low oven before using them. This I have found to work amazingly well.

Buy dried herbs only when you need them and in small quantities. They soon lose their power on the kitchen shelf, and every time the jar is opened some of the freshness is dissipated.

Don't feel that you must have every herb listed here or in the cookbooks. You can get along just buying a few good ones that you are apt to use most frequently. Poor-quality herbs are worse than none at all. Always use the nose test on herbs. Some will have the smell of old grass, others will tingle the nose with a wonderful bouquet.

Don't overwork herbs. There is no reason why every dish must be dosed with herbs, either fresh or dried. And don't mix herbs together indiscriminately. Certain ones complement each other; your nose should tell you whether or not the perfumes of the herbs blend well. It is never wise to overseason, and to "overherb" is folly. To use herbs successfully, one must become herb-conscious, which means "to study the individual aroma of the herbs, to learn to distinguish them, to love them and to use them," as Leonie de Sounin so charmingly put it in her book *Magic in Herbs*.

In this chapter we discuss the most common and essential cooking herbs and for each one give a recipe that shows it to best advantage. The more familiar you become with herbs, the more ways you will find of using them to give your food added flavor at very little cost.

Sweet Basil

Sweet basil is the only member of the large family of basils used for cooking. It is a hardy annual with a pungent, delightful odor. If you live in one of our larger cities, walk through the Italian section and you will see huge pots of this bright-green herb on the windowsills.

The flavor of basil is especially good with tomatoes, and any dish using them is enhanced by its addition. It is also good with other vegetables. One of the most superb of the Italian sauces for pasta is Pesto, made with basil.

PESTO

2 cups fresh basil leaves
3 cloves garlic
½ cup pine nuts
1 cup parsley sprigs
½ cup grated Romano cheese
½ to 1 cup olive oil

You can make Pesto by whirling all the ingredients in a blender or by pounding them in a mortar until they form a soft paste. The amount of oil used depends on the method. If you are using the blender, it is best to make the Pesto in two batches, using enough oil each time to cover the blades of the blender—about ½ cup.

If you use a mortar and pestle, add the oil, a little at a time, until the paste has reached the proper consistency. It should not be too runny. Taste the Pesto and add a little salt, if necessary. Makes about 2 cups.

To store unused portion of Pesto, place in a screw-top jar and cover with a film of olive oil. Refrigerate or freeze.

Chervil

This delicate feathery herb is a member of the parsley family, and its dainty greenness is a beautiful addition to any garden plot. It has such a subtle flavor that it seems to need the companionship of a more robust herb to bring out its charm. Either chive or parsley will do, but we think the chive does the better job. Chervil is used by the French as one of the *fines herbes* added to such things as omelets and Vinaigrette Sauce, but its exquisite flavor is best appreciated in a simple salad.

CHERVIL IN SALAD

Combine a few leaves of chervil with some chives and add to romaine. Make a simple dressing of olive oil, salt, pepper (freshly ground) and a little touch of lemon juice or wine vinegar. Toss all together.

A little chervil is also excellent with a Hollandaise Sauce for fish, and it blends beautifully with tarragon in a Sauce Béarnaise for steak or roast beef.

Chive

Common in many American gardens, its delicate tubes topped with purple blossoms, chive is the most refined member of the onion family. It is probably the most widely used food accent, and rightly so, for no one really interested in good food could possibly do without it. Chive has a lovely flavor by itself and also blends nicely with other herbs.

Chives are happy additions to salads; they give many vegetable dishes a distinct lift. Chopped and blended into meat sauces or sprinkled on the top of soups, they turn an everyday meal into something festive. Here is a recipe making a special thing of the chive—a dish, in fact, that is built on its entrancing flavor.

VEAL WITH CHIVES

2 thick veal chops
Flour
4 tablespoons butter
Salt, freshly ground black pepper
½ cup white wine or beef stock
½ cup finely cut chives
2 tablespoons chopped parsley

Dredge the chops lightly in flour and brown them quickly on both sides in the butter. Season to taste with salt and pepper. Reduce the heat, add ¼ cup wine or stock, cover and simmer for 20 minutes, or until tender. Add the chives and parsley and the remaining wine or stock. Turn the chops several times so that they become nicely coated with the herbs. Serve them with the pan juices poured over them. Tiny new potatoes and tiny green peas go well with this wonderful spring dish. And if you really want to be festive, drink a bottle of well-chilled white wine. Serves 2.

Dill

This lacy, delicately flavored herb is used in many dishes. Americans have never found as many uses for dill as have Swedes, Germans and Russians. The fresh sprigs of this herb mix well with many vegetables and with salads and fish. Cucumbers with sour cream and fresh dill are remarkably good. New potatoes with butter and finely chopped fresh dill are delicious. If you are serving cold poached fish with mayonnaise, fresh dill will make it taste ambrosial. For hot fish, try Dill Butter.

DILL-MUSTARD MAYONNAISE

1 cup Homemade Mayonnaise
2 tablespoons fresh dill
1 tablespoon Dijon mustard
Sugar to taste

Combine all ingredients. This makes a rather sweet-sour mixture, and a teaspoon or so of lemon juice can also be added to sharpen the flavor.

DILL BUTTER

Cream ½ pound soft sweet butter with 1 tablespoon minced fresh dill, 1 teaspoon lemon juice and a dash of Tabasco sauce. Serve at room temperature.

Marjoram

Sweet marjoram, or pot marjoram, is one of the most popular of herbs, although it has less character than many of the others and seems to us to be less useful in great cookery.

Try it in salads; with certain meats, such as beef; with boiled chicken; and with vegetables such as carrots, spinach and turnips.

CARROTS WITH MARJORAM

9 tablespoons butter
12 whole small young carrots
½ teaspoon salt
Marjoram
2 tablespoons honey

Melt the butter in a saucepan and add the carrots, salt and a good pinch of marjoram. Cover and cook very gently over low heat until the carrots are just tender. Add the remaining butter and the honey and let the mixture boil up for 3 minutes, shaking the pan so that the carrots are covered and glazed with the sauce. Serves 4.

Mint

There are a great many varieties of mint here and there in this country. Acres of it grow in Indiana, Michigan and the Pacific Northwest. It is the easiest of herbs to grow; in fact, once you start it you have a hard time getting rid of it.

The mint in julep, in mint sauce and in summer decoration for food is usually the spearmint, although what is called cat mint, white mint or sometimes pennyroyal is also used.

Mint should never be cooked with food. It is an herb to add when things are ready to serve. Use it with young new potatoes, with peas, with sautéed greens.

SAUTEED DANDELION GREENS

This is a spring dish, distinguished in flavor and simple to prepare. It is popular in the north of Italy, where people cultivate the dandelion. If you have the patience to go out into your garden in the early spring and dig up the tender leaves of the weed you will curse later on in the year, you can easily prepare Sautéed Dandelion Greens. Italian markets sell them, too, a slightly less arduous way of procuring your greens.

½ pound fat smoked bacon, cubed
2 cloves garlic

Dandelion greens
1 tablespoon finely chopped fresh
   mint
1 tablespoon lemon juice
Salt, freshly ground pepper

Cook the bacon with the garlic until it is cooked through but not hard and crisp. Add a good-sized bowl of dandelion greens and let them cook down very quickly in the bacon fat. When they have wilted down, add the mint and lemon juice. Season to taste with salt and pepper. This is really fine eating.

Oregano

Here is an herb that is a favorite throughout the Orient, in all Latin countries and in Spanish America. It gives that secret charm to such things as shish kebab, to the famous dishes of Mexico, to the marinades and basting sauces of the Caribbean cooks. The zest of this wild marjoram far exceeds that of the cultivated member of the family.

Try oregano in your stuffings for meat and fowl. Try it if you marinate anything. Once you get used to its rather different flavor, you will want to use it freely.

BASTING SAUCE FOR
BARBECUED MEATS

This is a sauce very popular in the Caribbean for basting pig and fowl roasted outdoors. It is simple and pungent and can be used in your back-yard barbecue with great success. The Caribbean version is made with sour orange juice. We seldom find the sour orange here, so we substitute the mixture of juices below.

Blend together 1 cup olive oil, ½ cup orange juice mixed with a little lemon or lime juice, 3 cloves garlic, crushed or pounded, 1 tablespoon salt, 1 teaspoon freshly ground pepper, and chopped fresh or dried oregano to taste—about 1½ tablespoons fresh or 1½ teaspoons dried.

Use this Basting Sauce for pork, poultry or beef.

Parsley

There are a great many people who go through life believing that parsley is just something to decorate a plate. They have never cultivated the joy of tasting its somewhat acrid tang. Parsley can be introduced into practically any dish with good results, and without it many dishes seem flat and uninteresting. Its robustness makes it a great pusher for other, more delicate flavors, but its own flavor will never overwhelm anything else.

We are accustomed to the curly parsley, but there is also the plain-leaved or flat parsley, which has a somewhat different flavor and is used to a great extent by the Italians. Originally an Egyptian plant, this plain-leaved variety must have caught the fancy of the ancient Roman gourmets, who no doubt brought it to Italy. It is often called Italian parsley here.

Use parsley in salads and for flavoring roasts, sauces, fish, soups, stews. Here are two special ways of serving it:

PARSLEY BUTTER

Cream 3 or 4 tablespoons chopped parsley with sweet butter and a little lemon juice. This is delicious on broiled steak or fish.

FRIED PARSLEY

Use only the curly variety for this. Drop parsley sprigs into deep hot fat and fry for 1 minute, or just until crisp. Drain and serve with fish or steak.

Rosemary

This herb figured in ancient legends and in the early books of the Bible. It has long stems with long needle-like leaves and a fragrance that is like an incense or a rare perfume. In fact, it was used for centuries in perfume making. It decked the church during celebrations and was used in ancient times in place of myrrh.

The culinary uses of rosemary were forgotten for a long time and are just now coming back into popularity. Again it is the Italians more than any other group who use it for flavoring. It is traditional with them that the paschal lamb be perfumed with rosemary when it is placed upon the table. In the south of France, where Niçoise cookery is a mixture of French and Italian, rosemary steals into many of the dishes and great bunches of the wild herb are thrown onto the coals when lamb is being roasted. Rosemary is simple to grow and can be found potted in most nurseries and seed shops and occasionally in the neighborhood vegetable store. In a garden, it is both decorative and pungent. Rosemary lends flavor and fragrance to an Orange-and-Onion Salad, a combination strong enough to take its authority.

ORANGE-AND-ONION SALAD

2 large oranges
2 large red Italian onions
Chicory
4 tablespoons olive oil
1 tablespoon lemon juice
Salt, freshly ground pepper
Fresh rosemary leaves

Peel and thinly slice the oranges and onions, removing all the bitter white pith from the oranges. Arrange on a bed of chicory. Combine the oil, the lemon juice, and salt, pepper and fresh rosemary leaves to taste, and pour over the salad. Serves 4.

Sage

Sage is a commonly used, often overused, herb. It grows wild in many parts of the world and is cultivated both here and abroad, the broad-leaved variety with the frosty-green sheen being most popular.

Because of its strong, heavy flavor it must be applied with great care. In fact, most American housewives lean on it too heavily in their poultry stuffing, and American farmers and meat packers tend to overdo sage in their sausages. Sage does, however, have an affinity for pork and can be used sparingly in certain dishes, such as this traditional English pie.

PORK-AND-APPLE PIE

4 pounds (about) lean pork, finely chopped
4 to 5 apples, peeled, cored and thinly sliced
2 medium onions, finely chopped
1 teaspoon sage
Salt, pepper
Stock or bouillon
Mashed Potatoes
Melted butter

Arrange alternate layers of pork and apples in a deep baking dish. Sprinkle each layer with a little chopped onion, sage and salt and pepper to taste. Moisten with a little stock or bouillon. Cover with a thick mashed-potato crust and brush well with melted butter. Bake in a 325° oven for 1½ to 2 hours, or until the pork is thoroughly cooked. Serve with crisp bread, pickled walnuts and beer. Serves 6 to 8.

Sorrel

Many children know this tender green plant as "sour grass." It grows wild in some parts of the country, is easily cultivated almost anywhere, and can be bought in Italian and French markets in the larger towns. Its faintly tart flavor is wonderful in

stews. It can be eaten as a green vegetable combined with other vegetables; or used to make soup; or added to salads.

SORREL AND SPINACH

Wash 1 pound sorrel and remove the coarse stems. Cook 2 packages frozen spinach according to directions on the box. When the spinach defrosts and begins to cook, add the sorrel and cover tightly. The sorrel will be done when the spinach is cooked. Chop and dress with butter and a small grating of garlic.

Summer Savory

This is a little-known herb that is usually planted only by those who start an herb garden and, with great gusto, insist on including everything in the herb line. Its delicate flavor is very pleasant and makes a nice addition to many vegetable dishes—especially those in which cabbage and Brussels sprouts figure, as it seems to take the edge off their sometimes overly strong flavor. But it is as a flavoring for roast leg of lamb that it really attains its true glory.

ROAST LEG OF LAMB WITH SUMMER SAVORY

Make incisions in a leg of lamb and insert slivers of garlic and leaves of summer savory. Rub the leg well with garlic and summer savory and place on a rack in a roasting pan.

Roast at 325°, allowing 14 to 15 minutes per pound, until it reaches an internal temperature of 140°. A leg of 5 to 7 pounds will take between 1¼ and 1¾ hours. Baste from time to time with the pan juices and season with salt and pepper during the last 15 minutes of cooking. Remove from the oven and allow to stand 10 minutes before carving.

Tarragon

Tarragon is perhaps the most delightfully flavored of all herbs. It is difficult to grow unless you are an experienced gardener, but you can buy it fresh in most large cities. Also, the Spice Islands dehydrated tarragon is excellent.

This herb was once used for medicinal purposes in the belief that it was an antidote for the bite of a mad dog, but now it is appreciated for its delicate, pungent taste and its wonderful perfume. A bit of chopped fresh tarragon lifts any green salad into a special class. It is sheer delight in summer in aspics with chicken, eggs or fish. Tarragon used for flavoring a chicken sauté or a roasting chicken will add a zip to these inexpensive dishes and make them taste luxurious.

TARRAGON CHICKEN

Combine 4 tablespoons butter and 2 tablespoons chopped tarragon and rub on the outside and inside of a roasting chicken. Put the trussed chicken on a rack in a roast-ing pan and roast in a 350° oven for 18 to 20 minutes per pound, basting with a mixture of 4 tablespoons melted butter, ½ cup white wine and 1 tablespoon chopped tarragon. When the leg moves easily, the chicken is cooked. A 4-pound chicken should take about 1 hour and 15 minutes.

Thyme

Thyme is one of the oldest known culinary herbs. Its praises were sung by the ancient Greeks, who were fond of the honey from Mt. Hymettus, where the bees fed on the blossoms of wild thyme. And William Shakespeare must have delighted in it, for he gave it a place in one of his loveliest lines: "I know a bank whereon the wild thyme grows." Shakespeare was probably thinking as much of its wonderful perfume as of its taste, for to sit on a bank of thyme is to surround yourself with a lovely odor. A bunch of thyme will perfume an entire room.

Next to parsley and chive, thyme is probably the most companionable of herbs. It blends with practically anything. The French use it constantly mixed with other herbs, and it is probably one of the commonest flavors, although its taste is so subtle that often the average person doesn't even realize its presence.

Use thyme in poultry stuffing—as a change from sage—in stews and all other meat dishes, in soups, in marinades, in any dish of mixed flavors.

Here is a dish that is a delightful snack with cocktails or, to take the place of a rich dessert, after luncheon or dinner:

THYME CHEESE

Mix together 4 ounces cream cheese, 2 or 3 tablespoons heavy cream, ½ clove garlic, minced, and about 1 teaspoon fresh thyme leaves or about half that amount if dried. Add a few grains of salt and chill for an hour in the refrigerator.

OTHER SEASONINGS

There are a few other seasonings, apart from dried spices, that are just as important in cooking as herbs— in some cases, more so than herbs— and that perform the same kind of function. The first of these is something no good cook can be without.

Garlic

This member of the onion family is one of the oldest seasonings known, and its popularity never wanes. Originally it was used in China before the invention of the wheel. It has covered the globe, but it has somehow, in American minds, become associated with Latin cookery. Actually, it has a place in every cuisine.

The clusters of cloves grow together with an outer covering. When the bulbs are dried, you may separate the cloves or not, as you wish. Green garlic peeled and spread on bread and butter is a delectable dish.

When garlic is cooked for a long time, most of its powerful pungency evaporates and only the essence of the flavor remains. For this reason it is perfectly feasible to use in a dish what would seem to most people like an inordinate quantity of garlic.

CHICKEN WITH 40 CLOVES OF GARLIC

2 plump fryers, quartered, or
  8 chicken legs
4 ribs celery, thinly sliced
⅔ cup olive oil
6 sprigs parsley
1 teaspoon tarragon
2½ teaspoons salt
¼ teaspoon freshly ground pepper
A dash of nutmeg
40 whole cloves garlic, peeled
Flour and water

Rinse chicken in cold water and pat dry with paper towels. Put the oil into a heavy casserole with the celery, parsley and tarragon. Add the chicken pieces and sprinkle with 1 teaspoon salt, the pepper and the nutmeg. Turn chicken several times so that all surfaces are coated with oil. Toss in the 40 peeled garlic cloves, sprinkle with remaining salt and put lid on casserole.

Make a heavy, thick flour-and-water paste and, with your hands, press it all around the rim where the lid and the casserole meet, making an even, tight seal. Cover the lid and the circle of paste with a layer of foil. Bake in a preheated 375° oven for 1½ hours. Do not remove the lid or the foil during the baking period. At serving time, remove foil and flour seal. Serve the chicken with hot toast or thin slices of pumpernickel and spread the soft, buttery garlic cloves on top. Serves 6.

Ginger

This root or rhizome has many applications in the field of fine foods. The green ginger root is used in cookery by the Chinese, the Japanese and several other national groups. Ginger root is also sold candied, preserved and canned. Jamaica ginger is used for powdered ginger. It is becoming much easier to obtain the fresh ginger root these days. In any form of Oriental cooking, fresh ginger is almost obligatory, but in a pinch you can use the ground.

CHICKEN TERIYAKI

½ cup soy sauce
½ cup white wine, sherry or sake
1 to 2 tablespoons fresh ginger root, chopped, or 1 teaspoon ground ginger
1 or 2 cloves garlic, chopped
1 teaspoon grated orange rind
¼ cup peanut oil
2 frying chickens (about 3 pounds each), split for broiling

Mix the first 6 ingredients and pour the mixture over the chickens, ar-

ranged flat in a porcelain, glass or enameled-cast-iron pan. Refrigerate from 1 to 24 hours for the chicken to absorb the flavors of the marinade. When ready to broil, remove chicken from marinade and drain well. Place on a grill over charcoal or on the broiler rack, bone side up, and broil slowly for about 15 minutes. Turn and broil on flesh side for about 10 minutes. Test for doneness. If the chicken is broiled in the oven, it should be about 5 inches from the heat. If over charcoal, it should be 6 to 7 inches from a not-too-hot bed of coals. The chicken may be brushed with the marinade during broiling, if you wish. Serves 4.

Horseradish

Although it is the root of the horseradish that we use, this plant has beautiful foliage. In the past, when people had front and back gardens, the horseradish plant graced many a perennial border. It grew originally in the Orient but gradually spread to Europe as a wild plant and was later cultivated by Europeans for its pungent accent with meats.

If you take the trouble to grate the fresh root instead of buying it already mixed with vinegar—and, I'm afraid, a little turnip sometimes—you will have a wonderful fiery condiment with twice the power and pungency of the commercial product.

For sauces you may add some

vinegar or mix the horseradish with sour cream or whipped cream.

HORSERADISH APPLESAUCE

A mixture of horseradish and applesauce is excellent with pork dishes and pot roast. To each 1½ cups applesauce add about 2 tablespoons freshly grated horseradish, according to taste. Flavor with a little grated nutmeg and chill thoroughly.

Horseradish complements beef, pork, some fish (such as carp and bass), tongue, corned meats and pastrami. Some people like it mixed with French mustard on ham or corned beef. Chopped beets and horseradish are often mixed together, as the slight sweetness of the beets makes a pleasant contrast to the sharpness of the horseradish.

Here is a recipe for the very hardy person, and one that stimulates thirst—if that is your object:

OLD ENGLISH HORSERADISH CANAPES

Spread rounds of pumpernickel or rye bread with butter that has been mixed with dry mustard. Cover with freshly shaved horseradish and garnish the edges with finely chopped hard-cooked egg.

Shallots

This rather refined and delicate member of the onion family is much in demand among those who practice foreign cookery. It is more pungent than onion and more delicate in flavor than garlic—ideal for seasoning. In Europe shallots are as common as other varieties of onions, but for some unknown reason they are hard to come by in this country. If you look in foreign markets in most large cities you may find these russet-skinned bulbs, or try the fancy fruit and vegetable shops. They are so excellent as flavoring in many dishes that if it is difficult for you to get them you should plant some and dry your own. They are available at good seed houses and are not difficult to grow.

STEAK SAUCE

Chop enough shallots to make ½ cup. Sauté lightly in 4 tablespoons butter, just until soft; do not let them brown. Add ½ cup white wine and 1 tablespoon wine vinegar and let the mixture boil up. Add ½ teaspoon salt and finally melt ¼ pound butter with the other ingredients. Served with steak or hamburgers, this is sensational.

8

CHEESE
and
EGGS

It would be no exaggeration to say that cheese and eggs are the best friends a budget-minded cook can have. Both are high in protein, filling and nourishing and can be used in literally thousands of ways. You could have cheese and egg dishes every day of the year without even beginning to exhaust their possibilities. The French have perfected the most delicious variations on the egg in their soufflés, crêpes, omelets and quiches. Cheese has equal stature in the cooking habits of nations around the world. We have the Swiss to thank for that great party dish, Fondue; the English, for Welsh Rabbit. These versatile products of the hen and the cow have a natural affinity, and many of the greatest dishes arise from a combination of the two. With a hunk of cheese and a dozen eggs in the refrigerator, you need never be at a loss for the makings of a delicious meal.

CHEESES

It has taken a long time for true appreciation of good cheese to get started in America, but we now import cheese from nearly every European country, from Canada and from some of the South American countries, in addition to producing many excellent cheeses of our own. We have definitely become a cheese-eating nation and are growing more so every year, as a glance at the shelves of any good cheese store will prove.

Generally speaking, there are several distinct types of cheese. There is the natural cream cheese, which is not cooked and not fermented. Our Philadelphia cream cheese is a noble example.

Then there are the fermented, uncooked cheeses. Examples are the soft, creamy cheeses such as Brie, Camembert and Pont l'Évêque; and the harder ones, such as Roquefort and blue cheese.

Notable among the cooked cheeses are the Emmenthal and Gruyère of Switzerland, the Parmesan of Italy and the Port Salut of France, Canada and the United States.

Cheeses that taste better when ripe and creamy—such as Brie, Camembert, Liederkranz, Pont l'Évêque—should be left in a warm spot (this means room temperature) for several hours before serving. Chilled cheese has little aroma and its true flavor will not emerge. In fact, almost any cheese, except for the delicate cream and double-cream cheeses, is better off out of the refrigerator for quite some time before being eaten.

Perhaps you have always eaten cheese with crackers. If so, try it sometime with a fine crusty piece of French bread or a crisp hard roll or some fine rye bread or pumpernickel. I believe you will agree with most Europeans and all lovers of fine eating that the blending of bread and cheese is more delicious than the cheese-and-cracker combination. By all means, try butter with most cheeses. It seems to enhance their flavor.

Choices for a Cheese Tray

When you are serving a cheese tray, try to offer the greatest possible variety. Have one of the soft cheeses (a fine ripe Camembert, for instance), two of the dry cheeses (a fine Emmenthal from Switzerland and a really good aged cheddar from the United States or Canada) and possibly a fine cream cheese for those who don't like strong flavors. Add a good wedge of Roquefort or bleu and you will have a really fine selection. Have plenty of rolls or bread and butter and also some pears and apples, both of which go wonderfully with many cheeses, from cheddar to the Italian Taleggio and Bel Paese.

If you are having a midnight snack with beer, choose some of the "louder" cheeses—Limburger, Tilsit, Port Salut, beer cheese, a good Muenster and certainly a huge piece of imported Swiss. These will require thinly sliced rye and pumpernickel, some rolls and French bread, and crackers of the hardier sort. You might have a couple of pots of mustard around for this sort of gathering, for some people always appreciate it with cheese.

For a simple luncheon or supper, try a menu of a big tossed salad and a tray of different cheeses, such as a Gorgonzola, a dry Provolone, Gouda, Edam and a large wedge of good cheddar. And if you are rounding out a dinner party with cheese rather than dessert, a perfect ripe Brie or Camembert is almost obligatory.

Don't think that having a selection of cheeses out at one time is a waste or an extravagance. If you are careful about wrapping them in foil and plastic wrap and keeping them moist in the refrigerator, most cheeses will last for a long time. For this reason alone (apart from the fact that it also costs less than lots of little canapés and is nowhere near the trouble), cheese is economical party food.

Here are some of the best-known cheeses available in this country. Most of them can be purchased in the average community and all of them may be ordered from specialty food shops throughout the country.

Asiago: A skim-milk cheese similar to Parmesan, popular in the United States and Europe. Like Parmesan, good for grating.

Bel Paese: A soft but firm creamy cheese made in Italy and also in the United States. It is mild, delicately flavored and delicious with fruit or with rolls and butter. It should be kept at room temperature for several hours before serving. It keeps well, and if allowed to age it ripens into an excellently flavored sharp cheese.

Bleu or blue: There are many different varieties of this blue-veined cow's-milk cheese made in this country and in Denmark and France. Two of the finest from France, only recently available in this country, are Bleu de Bresse and Bleu d'Avergne. Maytag blue is a superb domestic version from Iowa, hailed by the gourmets but presently available only by mail order from the source. Aged until it develops a distinctive and distinguished flavor, bleu cheese becomes creamier as it ripens, but it is not classed as one of the soft cheeses.

Boursin and Boursault: Two very similar soft, creamy French cheeses that have caught hold amazingly in this country; it is now even possible to find them on the shelves of better supermarkets. They come plain or with seasonings, such as garlic and *fines herbes.* The seasoned types are good with cocktails, the plain with a green salad.

Brie: This delicious soft, creamy cheese made from whole milk must be thoroughly ripened to be at its best. It is thin and yellow-crusted (the crust is edible, of course), and the finest comes from the village of Meaux in the part of the French countryside known as Brie, not far from the Champagne area. Brie has a strong odor and its flavor is supremely good. Definitely one of the choicest cheeses.

Excellent versions of Brie are made in Illinois and California.

Camembert: Madame Harel, the French farmer who originated this cheese, has been immortalized with a statue in the tiny Norman town of Camembert. Camembert has much the same texture as Brie, but it is thicker, is smaller in diameter, and evidently is ripened by different organisms, as the flavor is entirely different. Camembert has been successfully copied in many parts of France and America, so there are many different varieties. It is at its creamiest and best when runny and soft—but not when there is an ammonia odor. Eat the crust as well as the cheese, merely scraping the powdery white mold off first. Always let Camembert stand at room temperature for several hours before eating.

Cantal: A French cheese, the closest thing to cheddar that France produces.

Cream: This is probably the most widely used cheese in the United States, not only as a dessert cheese but also for cooking. "Philadelphia cream," "regular cream" and various trade names all identify the same type of light, delicately flavored soft cheese. It is delicious mixed with a little sour cream and served plain or sprinkled with caraway seeds. It also combines beautifully with jams and jellies for dessert or breakfast and is exceedingly good with fresh fruit, especially pears.

Cream brick: This is an aged cheese similar to some of the European cheeses. Ripe-smelling and rather strong, it can be flavorful and creamy. It is not always available in the Eastern states, but is very common in parts of the West and Northwest.

Crema Dania: A smooth, soft, rich cheese from Denmark that usually comes two foil-wrapped pieces to a box. Like Boursin and Boursault, Crema Dania has become so popular that it is now a staple of the better supermarkets.

Cheddar: This is the most common of the cheeses in this country and Canada. Called "store cheese," "rat cheese," "American cheese" and about twenty other names, it is the old standard for eating and cooking. It varies in quality from the less than mediocre to top excellent. Some of the fine aged cheddars from the Northwest, the Northeast and Canada can take their places alongside the very great cheeses of any country. Some cheddar has been colored a deep orange, other varieties are almost cream color, and some are almost white. It has a creamy, almost rubbery consist-

ency when young. Later it matures into a flaky, firm texture, and when really aged and ripe it becomes somewhat crumbly. It comes in small and large wheels—all the way from 5 pounds to giants of 1,000 pounds. Cheddar not only is a good cheese for the cheese tray, but is indispensable in cooking.

Chèvre: A goat's-milk cheese, almost chalky in texture, with a rather heavy distinctive flavor. It comes in small and large cylindrical loaves and is at its best when there is green mold on the outside skin.

Edam: The famous round red cannonball cheese from Holland. It can be mild or a little sharp, depending upon its age. The proper way to use it is to make an incision at the top and cut out a small round from which the rest of the cheese may be reached and extracted. The small round acts as a lid and is replaced each time cheese is scooped out. Some fanciers like to treat the cheese to brandy or sherry when they open it, and let it mellow for a few days before they use it. Edams made in this country are similar in flavor and texture to the Dutch product.

Emmenthal: This is the cheese that is commonly called Swiss—the one with the big eyes. It has been imported from Switzerland for many years and has been made in this country just about as long. To my taste after years of cheese eating, neither the American nor the French Emmenthal has the flavor of the genuine Swiss product. Perhaps it is the pasturage, or perhaps it is the aging process, but there is a difference. Both the Swiss and the American products come in tremendous wheels which are made from a cooked paste and aged for varying lengths of time to achieve the almost waxy texture and the huge glistening eyes. This is a perfect cheese for the table, besides being one of the greatest cooking cheeses in the world. The drier it gets the more delicious it is, grated for cookery. Combined with grated Parmesan it makes a wonderful topping for many foods.

Gorgonzola: This is to Italy what Roquefort cheese is to France. The true Gorgonzola comes from a town of that name near Milan, but there are different varieties made elsewhere, and several excellent ones in the United States. It is a creamy, richly flavored cheese with blue veins that becomes softer and creamier than most other blue cheeses and has a tendency to develop a riper flavor. Remarkably good with fruit, or with French or Italian bread and butter and a good robust red wine.

Gouda: This is the junior version of Edam. It is often very young and on the rubbery side when found in the markets. Give it a little time to age and dry out. Gouda is a fairly good melting cheese for sandwiches and for toasting.

Gruyère: Another Swiss cheese, creamier, richer in flavor and smoother in texture than Emmenthal and without holes. Gruyère is in the class of the four or five really great cheeses of the world and is very popular in this country. Its melting quality is superb, and it is the only really suitable cheese for the classic Fondue.

Jack: A light creamy cheese with a delicate flavor, very popular in the West and the Southwest. Use it in cooking and as a regular eating cheese.

Liederkranz: An American cheese, belonging to the family of the soft crusted cheeses, that recently celebrated its one-hundredth anniversary. When properly aged, it has a flavor of great distinction and a soft, creamy texture. One of the most widely available cheeses.

Limburger: A creamy cheese that develops a tremendously strong odor and flavor. There have been many jokes about Limburger, but it is not as powerful as the jokes would have you believe. Even so, it overwhelms almost everything else. Not to be classed with the great cheeses.

Mozzarella: A soft Italian cream cheese with a somewhat vague flavor when eaten straight, but a most important ingredient in Italian cooking. It melts magnificently and adds greatly to such dishes as Lasagna and eggplant Parmigiana.

Muenster: A mild cheese rather like a young cheddar with a slightly acid flavor. An excellent lunch cheese and good in sandwiches, but a cheese you tire of with crackers or fruit. It grows a little dull.

Parmesan: This hard cheese of Italy—and made very well in the United States too—is one of the most valuable kitchen aids in the entire cheese family. It has a salty, pungent flavor and mixes well with highly seasoned foods. It is practically impossible to melt and is used finely grated. I suggest you buy a piece of Parmesan—which will keep indefinitely in your refrigerator—and grate it as you need it. The difference in flavor from the canned or bottled variety is pronounced, and there is much less waste, therefore less expense. When you grate Parmesan, use the finest grater.

Pont l'Évêque: At its best, this whole-milk cheese has a delicious creaminess and rich flavor. It is made in molds—usually square— and cured for about four months, during which it develops a heavy crust and the typical odor of ripe cheese. Keep at room temperature several hours before serving.

Port Salut: This creamy cheese is made in Denmark, the United States and France and is pretty generally available around the country. To achieve its best flavor it should not be kept cold.

Ricotta: An Italian skim-milk cheese, similar to a sieved cottage cheese, that is widely used in cooking. Now made in the United States and available in supermarkets.

Romano: Another of the hard cheeses for grating. It has a more decided, more acid flavor than the average Parmesan. A blend of the two is delicious. Or use them interchangeably.

Roquefort: Regarded by many people as the greatest of all cheeses. It is made only in Roquefort in the mountains of central France, from sheep's milk. Roquefort is aged in caves for many months, at very low temperature, before it is ripe enough to be shipped. The townspeople themselves prefer it when it has aged at least twice as long as the ones we receive in this country. The cheese is very white, with even blue veins all through it, and is always marked "Roquefort," a marking no other cheese may carry.

Sage cheese: A version of cheddar cheese, highly flavored with sage. You will either love it or detest it, depending on your taste for that herb.

Stilton: This is the British version of a blue cheese, rich in flavor, creamy in texture, and well veined.

Taleggio: A soft, creamy, very gracious cheese from Italy. Extraordinarily good with fruit and as a breakfast cheese.

Teleme: A soft, delicious creamy cheese made in California.

CHEESE DISHES

And now for some cheese recipes, beginning with the supreme versions of melted cheese.

WELSH RABBIT

The old standard Welsh Rabbit will always be popular with men. Although we hardly think of it as an evening snack, that, strangely enough, is when it is most often served. I happen to prefer it for Sunday brunch or supper.

1 tablespoon butter
1 pound American sharp cheese or cheddar
1 cup ale or beer
Salt, cayenne
1 teaspoon dry mustard
1 egg, beaten

Melt the butter in a chafing dish or the upper part of a double boiler and add the cheese and ale or beer. Stir over the hot water until the cheese is melted and creamy. Season with a little salt, a few grains of cayenne and the mustard. Just before serving, stir in the beaten egg. Serve at once, on buttered toast, before it gets stringy or leathery. Serves 4.

FONDUE

1 clove garlic
1½ pounds Gruyère or Emmenthal cheese, grated
1 cup dry white wine
4 teaspoons potato flour or cornstarch dissolved in 2 ounces kirsch
Cubed French bread for dipping

Rub an earthenware casserole with the garlic. Put the cheese and wine into the casserole, put an asbestos mat under it and cook the wine-and-cheese mixture over medium heat, stirring constantly, until the cheese is melted. Add the potato flour or cornstarch dissolved in the kirsch and stir well until the Fondue is creamy. Transfer the casserole to an electric or alcohol heating unit and provide cubes of French bread to be dipped into the Fondue. (See that each cube has some crust, so that it does not fall apart.) If the Fondue gets stringy, just stir in a little more kirsch.

CHILI CON QUESO

2 cloves garlic, finely chopped
1 twenty-eight-ounce can Italian plum tomatoes
Salt, freshly ground black pepper
2 cans peeled green chilies, seeded and finely chopped
1½ cups rich cream sauce
1 pound shredded jack or medium-sharp cheddar cheese

Combine the garlic, tomatoes and salt and pepper to taste. Cook down for 20 minutes over medium heat, stirring occasionally. Add the chopped chilies (be sure to remove the seeds before chopping) and cook, stirring, until the mixture is thick and pasty. Add cream sauce and cheese and place in a chafing dish or electric skillet set at low heat. Stir until the cheese is melted and the dip smooth. Do not let it boil or the cheese will become stringy. Serve warm with breadsticks, fritos, small pieces of crisp tortilla, celery or cucumber sticks for dipping.

In France, a popular first course in restaurants is a Croque Monsieur. It is really just another version of the Toasted Cheese Sandwich, but an interesting diversion.

CROQUE MONSIEUR

For each serving, butter 2 slices of white bread and remove the crusts. Have a good slice of Swiss Emmenthal cheese and cooked ham for each sandwich. Put the sandwich together and butter the outside. Sauté on both sides in a skillet until the sandwich is toasted and the cheese melted. Serve very hot.

TOASTED CHEESE SANDWICHES

½ pound sharp cheddar cheese, shredded
2 tablespoons chopped chives
½ teaspoon salt
1 teaspoon dry mustard
2 eggs, separated
8 slices bread
Butter

Mix together the cheese, chives, salt, mustard and egg yolks. Stiffly beat the egg whites and fold in. Spread the mixture on half the bread slices and top with the remainder. Butter the outsides of the sandwiches liberally and brown on both sides in a buttered skillet until the cheese is thoroughly melted.

FRENCH-TOASTED CHEESE SANDWICHES

Make a batter with 3 eggs and 1 cup milk, seasoned with salt and cayenne pepper to taste. Arrange a slice of cheese (Swiss, cheddar or any other) between two slices of buttered bread and press together firmly. Dip into the batter and brown on both sides in hot butter or margarine until the outside is slightly crispy and the cheese melted. This makes enough batter for 4 sandwiches.

Cheese spreads make good fare for cocktail time.

BLUE-CHEESE SPREAD

From Roquefort or blue cheese, you can make a basic spread that will keep for weeks in the refrigerator. It's good for canapés, for cheese rolls, for sandwiches and for snacks.

Mash 1 pound of Roquefort or blue cheese with ½ pound of butter and ½ pound of cream cheese. Whip them well together, flavor with a good shot of brandy or whiskey and beat again. Add a few grains of cayenne pepper and taste —you may decide you would like more liquor or more blue cheese. Store in small crocks and use as needed. The flavor can be varied by using sherry, Madeira or red. wine in place of the spirits.

TANGY BLUE CHEESE AND CHEDDAR SPREAD

¾ cup beer or ale
¾ pound aged cheddar cheese, coarsely grated
⅛ pound blue cheese, crumbled

½ teaspoon dry mustard
1 tablespoon soft butter
2 dashes Worcestershire sauce
1 dash Tabasco
1 teaspoon coarsely chopped chives
   or onions

Put the beer or ale and the cheddar cheese into a blender and blend for 20 seconds, or until smooth. (If you don't have a blender, beat together until smooth.) Add the remaining ingredients and blend or beat until smooth and well mixed. Spoon into a crock or serving dish and chill. Garnish with chopped chives before serving. Makes about 2½ cups.

CHEDDAR-CHILI SPREAD

½ pound sharp cheddar, grated
   (2 cups)
2 canned peeled green chilies,
   chopped
½ canned pimiento, chopped
1 small clove garlic, grated
Few drops Tabasco
½ cup softened butter
3 to 4 tablespoons cognac, sherry
   or bourbon
Salt to taste

Have all the ingredients at room temperature. Mix in the bowl of an electric mixer or mash with a fork by hand. If the mixture seems too stiff to spread, add cream or milk, a few teaspoons at a time, until it is of a good spreading consistency. Serve in a crock or, for a more unusual presentation, form the mixture into one large or two small balls or logs and roll them in chopped toasted nuts or chopped

parsley or chives. Serve on a cheese board or tray with a knife and surround with crackers, Melba toast, cocktail rye or slices of French bread.

You can also make the spread into a dip by adding more milk or cream until it has the right dunking consistency. This tastes especially good with raw vegetables such as celery, carrot sticks, cucumber sticks, radishes, endive, cherry tomatoes, snow peas.

To freeze the cheese balls or spread, wrap in polyethylene freezer bags and seal tightly. Thaw several hours before using. To freeze the dip, transfer to moisture- and vapor-proof freezer containers. The mixture will separate when thawed, but stirring will bring it back to the original consistency.

LIPTAUER

1 pound (2 8-ounce packages)
   cream cheese
2 ounces (½ stick) butter
2 tablespoons heavy cream
Chopped onion, chopped anchovy
   fillets, chopped chives, capers,
   radish roses

Mix the cream cheese, butter and cream until fluffy in the small bowl of an electric mixer, or beat by hand. Shape into a mound on a decorative platter and surround with the onion, anchovy, chives, capers and radish roses. Serve with small pieces of thinly sliced rye bread (not the sweet variety) and a knife to spread the cheese mixture and chosen seasonings on the bread.

FARMER'S CHEESE

Cream or cottage cheese mixed with coarsely chopped raw vegetables and served with sour cream is exceedingly pleasant for lunch in summer or after a curry dinner. You can buy this cheese already prepared in some areas, but if you make your own the vegetables will be crisper. Use radishes, onions, scallions, celery, parsley, green pepper, any herbs you like. In fact, let imagination be your guide.

Now for some delicious dishes that star those natural partners, cheese and eggs.

CHEESE PUDDING

3 eggs, beaten
1½ cups milk
1 teaspoon dry mustard
Salt, paprika
4 slices buttered bread, cut into
    1-inch cubes
⅔ pound sharp cheddar cheese, cut
    into 1-inch cubes

Combine the eggs and milk and season with the mustard, salt to taste and a dash of paprika. Mix in the cubed bread and cheese and pour into a buttered casserole. Bake in a 325° oven for about 45 minutes. Serve plain or topped with Tomato Sauce or mushroom sauce. Serves 4.

STEAK DE FROMAGE VAUDOIS

10 eggs
½ cup milk
2 tablespoons melted butter
2 tablespoons brandy
1 cup flour
1 teaspoon baking powder
1¼ to 1½ pounds imported
    Gruyère, Swiss, cheddar or
    Muenster cheese
Butter
Salt, freshly ground pepper

Beat 2 of the eggs slightly and mix in the milk, melted butter and brandy. Sift the flour with the baking powder, add to the liquid and blend thoroughly. The batter should be the consistency of heavy cream, so if it seems too runny add a little extra flour.

Cut the cheese about ½-inch thick and then into 3- by 6-inch strips. Dip each strip into the batter until well coated. Sauté in butter in a skillet, turning once. When the cheese strips are nicely browned on both sides, arrange them in a baking dish. Beat the remaining 8 eggs lightly and season to taste with salt and pepper. Pour the egg mixture over the cheese and bake in a 375° oven until the eggs are cooked and delicately browned and puffy on top. Serves 4.

EGGS SWITZERLAND

8 eggs
4 tablespoons cream
Salt, freshly ground black pepper
¼ pound Swiss or Gruyère cheese,
    grated

Butter 4 individual casseroles well. Break 2 eggs into each and add 2 tablespoons cream, being careful not to let the cream cover the egg yolks. Season to taste with salt and pepper and sprinkle with the grated cheese, again being careful not to get any on the yolks. Bake in a 350° oven until the whites are set and the yolks just glazed over. This will take about 10 minutes. Serves 4.

NELLE SAVOYARDE

10 to 12 thin slices cold cooked ham
4 tablespoons butter
4 tablespoons flour
2 cups milk
Salt, freshly ground pepper, nutmeg
¼ pound grated Gruyère and
    Parmesan cheese, mixed
6 eggs, well beaten
Tomato Sauce

Line a charlotte mold with the ham slices. Melt the butter and blend in the flour. Gradually add the milk and cook, stirring, until the sauce is thick and smooth. Season to taste with salt, pepper and a little nutmeg and stir in the cheese. Remove from the heat and stir into the eggs. Pour the sauce over the ham and place foil on the mold, tying it down firmly. Place on a rack over boiling water in a deep kettle and steam for 1¼ hours, replenishing the water when it evaporates too much. Remove mold from steamer and take off the foil. Bake in a 350° oven for 15 to 20 minutes. Unmold and serve with Tomato Sauce. Serves 4.

SOUFFLES

One of the simplest ways to eat well at small cost is to make a habit of serving soufflés. Once you have mastered the basic method (and a soufflé is easy to put together, easy to bake, provided you follow a few rules of procedure), you can make a soufflé with anything you have on hand—cheese, vegetables, leftover chicken, turkey or ham, canned seafood. Having previously set the table, made salad and dessert, you can prepare your soufflé, pop it into the oven and relax over a drink with your family or guests. Then take out the soufflé, puffy, light and beautifully browned, and carry it triumphantly to the table. There is nothing to it.

An average soufflé will serve four, but not four with colossal appetites, so better plan also on having a substantial vegetable and make the dessert fairly hearty.

The secret of making a successful soufflé is in the egg whites. Always have them at room temperature when you beat them, and beat them by hand or in an electric mixer until they are stiff but still moist, not dry. They should be beaten only until they are stiff enough to hold their shape and stand up in peaks when the beater is withdrawn. Finally, always fold the beaten egg whites into the soufflé mixture, using a down, up and over motion; do not stir or mix them in. Fold one half of the egg whites in well, the second half very lightly. Using one more egg white than yolk will give your soufflé additional lightness.

CHEESE SOUFFLE

3 tablespoons butter
3 tablespoons flour
1 cup scalded milk
1 teaspoon salt
½ cup grated sharp cheddar cheese
4 egg yolks
5 egg whites

Melt the butter in the top of a double boiler over hot water and blend in the flour. Gradually stir in the milk, blending until smooth, and then cook, stirring, until the sauce is thick and smooth. Mix in the salt and cheese. Cool the sauce slightly. Beat the egg yolks until they are light and lemon-colored and pour the cream sauce into them. Mix together. Let this stand and cool while you beat the egg whites until stiff but still moist. Fold half the beaten egg whites into the sauce fairly well, then fold the other half in very lightly. Pour the soufflé mixture into a 1½-quart buttered soufflé dish and bake in a 375° oven until puffed up and browned, about 35 minutes. Serve at once. Serves 4.

VARIATIONS

Parmesan-Cheese Soufflé: Substitute 1 cup grated Parmesan cheese for the cheddar cheese.
Swiss-Cheese Soufflé: Substitute ½ pound grated Gruyère cheese for the cheddar.

TUNA SOUFFLE

Prepare the cream sauce as directed above for Cheese Soufflé, but use 1 more tablespoon flour. Cook the sauce until thick and add it to the egg yolks. Stir in a 7-ounce can tuna, drained and flaked, and season with salt and pepper to taste and a squeeze of lemon juice. Fold in the egg whites and bake as directed for Cheese Soufflé.

SALMON-EGG SOUFFLE

As for Tuna Soufflé, make the sauce with 1 extra tablespoon flour, and add to the egg yolks. Drain and flake a 7-ounce can salmon. Add salmon to the sauce–egg-yolk mixture with 2 chopped hard-cooked eggs, ¼ cup chopped parsley, and pepper and salt to taste. Fold in the egg whites and bake as directed for Cheese Soufflé.

CLAM SOUFFLE

Drain a 7-ounce can of minced clams. Measure the liquid and substitute it for part of the milk called for in the sauce for Cheese Soufflé, adding 1 extra tablespoon flour. Cook sauce until thickened, then mix in the clams. Season to taste with salt and pepper and add to the egg yolks. Fold in the egg whites and bake as directed for Cheese Soufflé.

FINNAN HADDIE SOUFFLE

Make the basic cream sauce with 1 extra tablespoon flour. Cook until thickened. Mix in 1 cup poached, flaked finnan haddie, salt to taste and a pinch of nutmeg. Add to the egg yolks. Fold in the egg whites and bake as directed.

CHICKEN SOUFFLE

Prepare the basic cream sauce, adding 1 extra tablespoon flour. Mix in ⅔ cup finely cut chicken and 1 finely chopped pimiento. Season with salt to taste and ½ teaspoon pepper. Mix with egg yolks, fold in egg whites and bake as directed.

HAM SOUFFLE

Follow directions for Chicken Soufflé, substituting 1 cup finely ground ham for the chicken. Add 1 teaspoon dry mustard to seasonings.

SPINACH SOUFFLE

Prepare the basic cream sauce, using 1 extra tablespoon flour. Cook until thickened, season with 1 teaspoon salt and pour sauce into the egg yolks. Stir in 1 cup puréed or finely chopped cooked drained spinach and 2 teaspoons grated onion. Fold in the egg whites and bake as directed for Cheese Soufflé.

ONION-CHEESE SOUFFLE

Sauté 1 cup finely grated or chopped onion in 5 tablespoons beef fat until lightly browned. Stir in 4 tablespoons flour and gradually

add 1 cup beef stock, consommé or bouillon. Stir until thick, season with salt and pepper to taste and mix in ½ cup grated Swiss and Parmesan cheese, mixed. When cheese is melted, pour mixture into 5 slightly beaten egg yolks. Fold in 6 stiffly beaten egg whites and pour into buttered soufflé dish. Bake in a 375° oven for 35 minutes, or until puffy and light. This makes a tasty main course for a quick dinner, with salad and potatoes. It is also an excellent accompaniment to roast beef, mutton or lamb.

QUICHES

In the last few years we have seen an astronomic rise in the popularity of the classic French pie, Quiche Lorraine. Listed by The New York Times as one of its most requested recipes, Quiche Lorraine is served everywhere—as a luncheon or supper entrée, as a first course, or at a cocktail buffet. Actually the cheese, bacon and custard pie most people think of as Quiche Lorraine is not the true, original version. That was made without cheese, or with fresh cream cheese substituting for part of the cream in the custard. Whichever way you make it, Quiche Lorraine is delicious, but it is only one of a number of quiches each of which makes superb and economical eating.

BASIC QUICHE PASTRY

1½ cups flour
⅔ cup butter or shortening (or half butter, half shortening)

1 egg white
¼ teaspoon salt
1 egg yolk, lightly beaten

Sift the flour onto a pastry board or into a large bowl, and make a well in the center. Add the butter—firm, but not ice cold—cut into small pieces; then add the egg white and salt. Blend quickly with the fingers until the mixture forms a smooth ball. Chill for 15 minutes. Roll between two sheets of waxed paper to fit a 9-inch pie tin or 1½-inch-deep flan ring. Strip off one sheet of paper, and invert pastry over pie tin or flan ring set on a cooky sheet. Adjust to fit—do not stretch the pastry, but lift it and allow it to fall into place—and trim off the excess. Crimp the edges. Chill for another 30 minutes, or place in the freezer for 15 or 20 minutes.

Place a piece of aluminum foil, shiny side down, in the pastry shell to form a lining, and cover with dried beans or rice, making certain the beans are distributed against the sides of the shell. These will keep the shell from puffing up in the pre-baking.

Bake in a 425° oven for 15 to 20 minutes, until the bottom is set and the edges are slightly brown. Remove from the oven, take off aluminum foil and brush shell with the egg yolk, then return to the oven for 2 minutes to set the yolk. This will provide a seal for the crust and prevent its soaking up the custard mixture and becoming soggy. Cool the shell slightly before adding the filling.

CLASSIC QUICHE LORRAINE

Pre-baked 9-inch Basic Quiche Pastry shell
6 to 8 slices thickly cut streaky bacon
4 eggs
1½ cups light cream; or 1 cup milk and ½ cup heavy cream
Salt, pepper, nutmeg to taste

Buy bacon that is not flavored with artificial smoke and oversugared, as most brands are today. Genuine bacon can still be found in many farmers' markets and in good pork stores in cities. Try out the bacon until it is cooked through but not crisp. Drain on absorbent paper towels. Arrange the bacon in the pastry shell like the spokes of a wheel, or cut the slices into small pieces and spread evenly. Beat the eggs slightly and combine with the cream or the cream-and-milk mixture. Season to taste with salt, pepper and nutmeg. Pour over the bacon. Bake in a 350° oven for about 30 minutes, or until the custard is set and puffed. Serve hot. This will serve 6 as a first course or 4 as a main dish.

Note: This quiche can also be made in small, individual tart shells, in which case the custard should set in 15 to 18 minutes.

VARIATIONS

1. Substitute 1 cup cream cheese or 1 cup cottage cheese for 1 cup of cream or milk. Beat the eggs with

the remaining cream, combine with the cheese, and sieve before adding to the pastry shell. Otherwise, bake as above.

2. Instead of bacon, use Virginia or country ham of good flavor, cut into small strips—you will need about 1½ cups—and distribute in the shell. Then add the custard and proceed as above.

CHEESE-AND-BACON QUICHE

Pre-baked 9-inch Basic Quiche Pastry shell
6 to 8 slices streaky bacon
1 cup shredded Gruyère cheese
¼ teaspoon nutmeg
4 eggs
1 cup light cream
½ teaspoon salt
½ teaspoon freshly ground black pepper
Dash of Tabasco

Try out the bacon until it is cooked through but not crisp. Leave it in slices or dice. Place in pastry shell, add the Gruyère and the nutmeg. Beat the eggs lightly and blend in the cream. Season with salt, pepper and Tabasco, and pour over the bacon and cheese. Bake in a 350° oven for about 30 minutes. Serve hot. Serves 4 to 6.

VARIATIONS

1. Substitute 1 cup of any of the following cheeses for the Gruyère: cheddar, finely shredded; Roquefort, crumbled; Monterey jack, shredded, mixed with ½ cup finely chopped peeled green chilies; caraway-flavored Swedish or Norwegian cheese, shredded; freshly grated Parmesan or Romano.

2. Substitute ham for the bacon.

SWISS ONION QUICHE

Pre-baked 9-inch Basic Quiche Pastry shell
4 tablespoons butter
4 to 6 onions, peeled and thinly sliced
1 teaspoon salt
1 teaspoon freshly ground black pepper
1 cup shredded Gruyère cheese
2 whole eggs
2 egg yolks
1½ cups heavy cream or 1 cup milk and ½ cup heavy cream, mixed
⅛ teaspoon nutmeg

Melt the butter in a very heavy pan, add the onions, cover tightly and steam over medium-low heat until the onions are soft but not browned, shaking the pan occasionally. Season with salt and pepper. Drain the onions and arrange in the pastry shell and sprinkle with the cheese. Beat the eggs, yolks, cream and nutmeg together and pour into the shell. Bake at 350° for approximately 30 minutes, or until the quiche is set and puffy. Serves 4 to 6. This also makes an excellent accompaniment for steak or roast beef, substituting for a vegetable and potatoes.

VARIATIONS

1. Mix about ½ cup diced cooked bacon with the onions be-

fore putting them into the pastry shell.

2. Mix about ⅔ cup finely chopped ham with the onions.

3. Place 8 blanched pork sausages in the pastry shell before adding the onions, cheese and custard.

4. Steam 14 to 16 green onions lightly in butter and use instead of the sliced onions.

5. Add 14 to 16 pitted black soft olives (Italian or Greek variety) and 12 finely cut anchovy fillets to the onions. Substitute ½ cup grated fresh Parmesan cheese for the Gruyère.

SPINACH QUICHE

Pre-baked 9-inch Basic Quiche Pastry shell
1½ to 2 pounds fresh spinach, cooked, drained and chopped
⅛ teaspoon nutmeg
1 teaspoon dried tarragon, crushed, or 1 tablespoon fresh tarragon, chopped
1 tablespoon lemon juice or wine vinegar
Salt, freshly ground black pepper to taste
2 tablespoons chopped parsley
½ cup Feta cheese, crumbled
4 eggs
¾ cup heavy cream
½ cup yoghurt

The spinach must be thoroughly drained of all liquid for this dish. Combine it with the nutmeg, tarragon, lemon juice, salt, pepper and parsley and arrange in the bottom of the pastry shell. Add the cheese. Beat the eggs lightly, add the cream and yoghurt, and blend well. Pour over the spinach mixture. Bake in a 350° oven for 30 minutes, or until the custard is just set. Serves 4 to 6.

Seafood Quiches

Quiches made with a seafood filling are especially delicate. Below are a number of suggested fillings. In each case a pre-baked 9-inch Basic Quiche Pastry shell is used, and a custard mixture made by blending 1 to 1½ cups heavy cream with 4 eggs and salt and pepper to taste. After placing the seafood in the pastry shell, pour in the custard and bake in a 350° oven until the custard is set, about 30 minutes. Each quiche will serve 4 to 6.

Lobster Quiche: Use 1 to 1½ cups cooked lobster meat—lobster chunks from a freshly cooked or cold-packed lobster, canned lobster, or lobster tails. Season with any of the following: tarragon, cognac and parika, sherry, Madeira.

Crab Quiche: Use about ½ pound cooked, canned or frozen crab lumps or crab legs. Large pieces of crabmeat work best for a quiche, because they do not overcook as readily. Flavor with any of the following: finely chopped onion, parsley and green pepper; fresh dill; tarragon and parsley; chives and parsley; sherry; Madeira.

Shrimp Quiche: Use 1 to 1½ cups cooked shrimp, either small shrimp or larger shrimp cut into pieces. When pre-cooking, be careful not to overcook, since they will get additional baking in the quiche. Flavor with any of the following: fresh dill; fresh or dried tarragon; a touch of curry powder, blended with the custard mixture before baking; 1 teaspoon chili powder; 1 or 2 canned peeled green chilies, chopped; sherry or cognac and paprika; 2 tablespoons lightly sautéed onion, 2 tablespoons tomato paste, 1 small clove garlic, finely grated, and 2 tablespoons chopped parsley.

Finnan Haddie Quiche: Use about 1 to 1½ cups flaked cooked finnan haddie. Flavor with any of the following: freshly ground black pepper and a touch of lemon juice; 3 tablespoons chopped pimiento; 1 teaspoon or more curry powder, to taste.

Scallop Quiche: Use 1 to 1½ cups raw scallops, either whole bay scallops or sea scallops cut in smaller pieces—the baking process will cook the scallops sufficiently. Season with a touch of thyme and 3 tablespoons crumbled crisp bacon; or with chopped fresh dill, a bit of onion juice and 2 tablespoons chopped parsley.

OMELETS

Few people except the most accomplished professionals seem to be able to make a good omelet, yet nothing is simpler or quicker, and few dishes are more versatile. The secret of a good omelet is first to have a heavy pan of iron or cast aluminum that is used for nothing else and is never washed, merely wiped out with a paper towel after use, or else one of the heavy Teflon-lined enameled-iron pans. The rest of the secret is plenty of butter, fresh eggs and just a little water added to the beaten-egg mixture. It is better to make a series of individual omelets than to make one big one that must be cut and served. You can't make a good omelet if you have too much egg mixture in the pan.

BASIC OMELET

For each omelet allow 2 or 3 eggs per person (depending on their size), beaten up with 1 or 2 teaspoons water, a scant ½ teaspoon salt and a dash of Tabasco.

Melt a good-sized piece of butter (about 2 tablespoons) in your omelet pan and let it get bubbly hot, but not brown or smoking. Pour in the egg mixture and, holding the pan handle with one hand and a fork with the other, shake the pan and stir briskly with the fork for just a minute or two. When the egg mixture begins to settle and to firm in the center of the pan (it should still be runny and creamy on top), slip the fork or a spatula under one edge and roll it over, folding it onto a hot plate. Serve at once.

If you have a filling for the omelet, fold part of it in just before you fold the omelet and remove it from the pan. Pour the rest of it around the omelet after it has been put on the plate. Certain flavorings or foods, such as chopped herbs, watercress or sautéed green onions, are often mixed into the beaten egg and cooked in the omelet.

FILLINGS FOR OMELETS

1. Croutons fried in olive oil, with or without garlic.
2. Potatoes, ham and onion cooked together—a farmer's omelet.
3. Spanish or creole sauce—a Spanish omelet.
4. Creamed chicken or turkey; or creamed fish.
5. Fresh asparagus tips with butter.
6. Crisp bacon, crumbled.
7. Onions sautéed in butter and covered with grated cheese.
8. Sautéed fresh tomatoes.
9. Grated cheddar, Swiss or Parmesan cheese.
10. Buttered cooked spinach.
11. Strips of frizzled ham.
12. Sautéed lamb kidneys cut in small bits and seasoned with a little onion and prepared mustard.
13. Sautéed or creamed mushrooms.
14. Creamed dried beef.

OMELETTE SAVOYARDE

For each serving you will need a good slice of ham that has been broiled or frizzled in a skillet. Make a 2-egg omelet as directed for the Basic Omelet, but do not roll it. Instead, slip it, pancake fashion, onto the ham. Sprinkle liberally with grated cheddar, Emmenthal or American Swiss cheese and put under the broiler until the cheese melts. Omelette Savoyarde makes a wonderful Sunday-breakfast dish or a fine supper dish when there are not too many to be served.

Another versatile way to use eggs is in a frittata, an Italian version of the omelet in which the eggs are cooked until set.

ZUCCHINI FRITTATA

6 to 8 small zucchini
3 tablespoons olive oil
2 tablespoons butter
8 eggs
1 teaspoon salt
½ teaspoon freshly ground black pepper
½ cup grated Parmesan cheese

Wash but do not peel the zucchini. Cut into ¼-inch slices and cook slowly in a skillet in the oil and butter until just tender. Beat the eggs with the salt and pepper and pour gently over the zucchini. Cook until just set. Sprinkle the cheese on top and put under the broiler to brown lightly. Let the frittata stand for a minute or two, then cut into wedges and serve. Serves 4 to 6.

FRITTATA OF ARTICHOKE HEARTS

For the zucchini, substitute 2 packages frozen artichoke hearts. Thaw the artichoke hearts and toss them in ⅓ cup hot oil in which 1 chopped garlic clove has been cooked for 3 or 4 minutes. When the artichoke hearts are thoroughly heated through pour the egg mixture over them and proceed as for Zucchini Frittata.

FRANKFURTER FRITTATA

6 tablespoons butter
1 medium onion, thinly sliced
½ green pepper, chopped fine
4 to 5 frankfurters, cut in shreds
6 eggs, beaten
½ cup grated Parmesan cheese
¼ cup chopped parsley
1 teaspoon salt
¼ teaspoon Tabasco

Melt the butter in a skillet and cook the onion and green pepper until the onions are just golden. Add the frankfurters and cook until delicately browned and cooked through—about 5 minutes. Pour over them the eggs mixed with the cheese, parsley and seasonings and cook until eggs are just set. Put under the broiler for 3 to 4 minutes to brown the top a little. Serve cut into wedges with potato salad or Cole Slaw. Serves 4.

Note: You may substitute thinly sliced salami, summer sausage or knackwurst for the frankfurters.

Eggs, rice and vegetables are combined in this unusual Provençal dish:

TIAN VENÇOIS

2 pounds spinach, washed and finely chopped
Olive oil
Salt, freshly ground black pepper
2 pounds Swiss chard, washed and finely chopped
2 pounds zucchini, diced
3 cloves garlic, chopped
1 cup cooked rice
6 eggs
¾ cup fine dry bread crumbs
¾ cup grated Parmesan cheese

Cook the spinach in a skillet in 1 tablespoon or more oil until just wilted. Season with salt and pepper to taste. Cook the Swiss chard and the zucchini in the same way, in separate skillets. Combine the three vegetables with the garlic and rice. Oil a flattish baking dish well, put in the rice-vegetable mixture and sprinkle with oil. Bake in a 300° oven for about 20 minutes. Beat the eggs slightly and pour over the vegetable mixture. Sprinkle with the crumbs and cheese, mixed. Return to the oven and bake just until the eggs are set. Serve hot or cold. Serves 8.

This Basque specialty, a delicious mixture of vegetables with lightly scrambled eggs, makes a good brunch or supper dish.

PIPERADE BASQUAISE

4 tablespoons olive oil
3 sweet red or green peppers, seeded and cut into strips
1 small hot red pepper, seeded and finely chopped, or ½ teaspoon Tabasco
1 large onion, coarsely chopped
1 clove garlic, finely chopped

4 medium tomatoes, peeled, seeded
and coarsely chopped
½ teaspoon thyme
Salt, freshly ground black pepper
5 tablespoons butter
6 eggs, slightly beaten
2 tablespoons chopped parsley

Heat oil in a skillet. Add sweet and
hot peppers, onion, garlic, tomatoes, thyme, and salt and pepper
to taste. Cook over medium heat,
stirring, until lightly sautéed but
not reduced to a purée. Melt butter
in another skillet, add eggs and set
over medium to medium-low heat.
Spoon in vegetable mixture and stir
vegetables and eggs constantly with
a wooden spoon until the vegetables are mixed in and the eggs
have formed small soft lumps.
Serve immediately, sprinkled with
parsley. Serves 4.

Scrambled eggs provide the filling for this unusual luncheon dish:

SPINACH ROLL WITH SCRAMBLED EGGS

3 pounds fresh spinach or
3 packages frozen spinach
9 tablespoons butter
Salt, pepper, nutmeg
4 eggs, separated
½ cup dry bread crumbs
4 or more tablespoons grated
Parmesan cheese
Scrambled eggs flavored with
Tabasco

If you are using fresh spinach, wash
it well in lukewarm water (this re-
moves the dirt more easily) and remove the stems. Place in a large
saucepan without any water except
that clinging to the leaves, cover
tightly and wilt down over heat;
this will take a very few minutes.
Drain well and chop coarsely. If
you are using frozen chopped
spinach, thaw it over low heat and
dry well. Frozen leaf spinach will
need to be chopped also. Put
drained spinach in a bowl and mix
with 6 tablespoons of butter,
melted, and salt, pepper and nutmeg to taste. Beat in the egg yolks,
one by one. Line an 11-by-15-by-½-
inch jelly-roll pan with heavy
waxed paper and butter it well with
the remaining 3 tablespoons butter.
Sprinkle with the bread crumbs.
Beat egg whites until they hold soft
peaks, and fold into the spinach
mixture. Immediately turn mixture
into the prepared pan and spread
evenly with a rubber spatula.
Sprinkle top with the grated Parmesan. Put immediately into a preheated 350° oven and bake for 12
to 16 minutes, or until center feels
barely firm when lightly touched
with a fingertip. Remove from oven
and cover top of roll with buttered
waxed paper or foil and invert onto
a warm platter. Remove lining
paper adhering to roll, spread roll
with scrambled eggs and roll up
gently with the aid of paper. Add a
dash more grated cheese. Serves 4.

CREPES

If you can become adept at making
a crêpe (a thin French pancake),
you have the foundation for many
inexpensive and delicious dishes—
first course, entrée or dessert.

BASIC CREPE MIXTURE

⅞ cup flour
⅛ teaspoon salt
3 eggs
2 tablespoons cognac or rum
1 teaspoon grated lemon rind
2 tablespoons melted butter
1 to 1½ cups milk

Sift the dry ingredients together. Add the eggs, one at a time, mixing well after each addition and until there are no lumps; an electric mixer set at low speed is ideal for this. Add cognac, lemon rind and melted butter. Gradually stir in the milk—enough to give the batter the consistency of thin cream. Let the batter rest for an hour or two before using.

To make the crêpes you need a 6-inch pan with rounded sides, well greased with butter, set over fairly brisk heat. Pour a little of the batter into the pan, tilting the pan so that it coats the surface evenly. If there is excess batter, pour it back into the bowl of batter. Cook the crêpe until lightly browned on the underside, turn and brown lightly on the other side. Remove. Keep warm in a low oven, with foil over the top of the dish, until ready to use. This amount of batter makes about 18 crêpes.

For Dessert Crêpes, add sweetening to the batter. See page 197.

When you are ready to serve, fill the crêpes with any of the fillings that follow. Roll up and arrange in a shallow baking dish. Proceed according to directions.

FILLINGS FOR CREPES

1. Fill with creamed chicken or turkey. Arrange in individual serving dishes or in a large baking dish. Sprinkle with grated Parmesan cheese and put under the broiler for a few minutes to glaze.
2. Fill with creamed shrimp or lobster flavored with lemon juice. Top with chopped parsley and paprika. Serve at once.
3. Fill with creamed tuna fish mixed with finely chopped pimiento and capers. Top with chopped hard-cooked egg.
4. Fill with curried shrimp. Top with chopped hard-cooked egg or grated coconut or chopped buttered peanuts. Serve with chutney or pickles.
5. Fill with ground leftover meat soaked with Tomato Sauce. Top with grated Swiss cheese and put under the broiler to melt the cheese.

You can fill crêpes with almost anything you might normally serve on toast, in patty shells or over rice. Crêpes just make it taste different and more delicious, and the cost is next to nothing. Here are some further suggestions for using crêpes:

CURRIED CRABMEAT CREPES

6 tablespoons butter
2 tablespoons oil
1 small onion or 6 shallots, chopped
2 pimientos, chopped

2 pounds frozen crabmeat, thawed
4 tablespoons flour
2 teaspoons curry powder
1 cup milk
¼ cup cognac
2 tablespoons chopped parsley
12 crêpes (unsweetened)

Heat the butter and oil in a skillet and sauté the onion until golden brown. Add the pimientos and crabmeat and cook 2 to 3 minutes, or until heated through. Drain, reserving 1 cup of the liquid from the cooked mixture.

Melt the remaining 4 tablespoons butter in a saucepan, add the flour and curry powder and blend well. Gradually stir in the milk, the reserved crabmeat liquid and the cognac. Cook until smooth. Add the parsley and the crabmeat mixture. Spoon onto crêpes and roll up.

CANNELLONI

6 to 8 crêpes (unsweetened)
6 Italian sausages
1 pound Ricotta cheese
Grated Parmesan cheese
Tomato Sauce or Béchamel Sauce
(see below)
Freshly ground pepper

Prepare 2 crêpes for each person, making them rather large. Poach the sausages in water for 10 minutes. Remove and drain. When they are cool enough to handle, peel off the skin and cut the sausages into large shreds or slices.

Spread the crêpes with a layer of Ricotta cheese, sprinkle with Parmesan cheese and add a few pieces of sausage. Roll and arrange in a shallow baking dish or individual baking dishes. Cover with Tomato Sauce or Béchamel Sauce. Sprinkle with a little additional Parmesan cheese and some freshly ground black pepper. Heat in a 375° oven until bubbly and, if the Béchamel is used, slightly browned on top.

VARIATIONS

Bits of leftover chicken, cold meat, ham, or cooked vegetables may be used for filling, instead of the sausage.

TOMATO SAUCE

2 tablespoons olive oil
1 clove garlic, finely chopped
1 small onion, finely chopped
1½ cups solid-pack tomatoes
½ teaspoon dried basil
1 six-ounce can tomato paste

Heat the olive oil and sauté the garlic and onion lightly. Add the tomatoes and basil and simmer 30 to 40 minutes. Add the tomato paste and simmer 15 minutes longer. Strain. If the mixture is not thick enough, reduce over brisk heat for several minutes, stirring frequently and being careful that the sauce does not scorch.

BECHAMEL SAUCE

3 tablespoons butter
3 tablespoons flour
Salt, pepper, nutmeg
1½ cups light cream

Melt the butter in a saucepan, blend in the flour and seasonings. Gradually stir in the cream and cook, stirring, until the sauce thickens.

9

PASTA, RICE
and
GRAIN DISHES

Any cook with an eye to economy and a taste for good food would do well to keep her shelf stocked with different types of pasta and rice. With a package of either, and any whit of ingenuity, it is possible to have a distinctive and delicious meal on the table in no time flat. Pasta, rice and also hominy and cornmeal belong in the invaluable category of food stretchers. A minimum of fish, meat or poultry, leftovers, vegetables and cheese combined with these expansive starch products make a nourishing, satisfying meal. It is no secret that the regional cooking of many countries around the world—especially Italy—leans heavily on pasta and rice to assuage appetites sharpened by long hours of work in the fresh air, and we in turn have borrowed many of their most interesting dishes to bolster our menus.

PASTA

The variety of things you can make from a 1-pound package of fettuccine, spaghetti or macaroni seems almost endless, from a simple dish of spaghetti dressed with oil and garlic or butter and grated cheese to something as rich and unctuous as Spaghettini alla Carbonara. Like cheese and egg dishes, you could serve a pasta a day for a year without beginning to exhaust the possibilities. Count on 4 ounces of pasta per person, unless you are serving it not as a main dish but as a pasta course before the entrée.

SPAGHETTI CON AGLIO E OLIO
(Spaghetti with Garlic and Oil)

1 pound spaghetti
2 or 3 cloves garlic per person, coarsely chopped
6 tablespoons olive oil
Coarsely ground black pepper

Cook the spaghetti in plenty of boiling salted water in a large pot, so that the strings do not stick together. Cook until just tender but still bitey—what the Italians call *al dente.* Drain.

Meanwhile cook the garlic in the oil without letting it brown. For 4 servings, you will need 8 to 12 cloves garlic; this may sound like a lot, but the garlic is what makes the dish. Pour the garlic and oil over the cooked spaghetti. Grate pepper over the top. Do not serve cheese with this. Serves 4.

SPAGHETTI CON TONNO
(Spaghetti with Tuna)

1 small onion, chopped
1 clove garlic, chopped
4 tablespoons oil
1 eight-ounce can tomato sauce
1 teaspoon basil
Salt, freshly ground black pepper
1 seven-ounce can tuna in oil
1 pound spaghetti
Chopped parsley
Grated Parmesan cheese

Sauté the onion and garlic in the oil until just tender. Add the tomato sauce and bring to a boil. Reduce heat to a simmer, add the basil and salt and pepper to taste and cook until the flavors are well blended, about 10 minutes. Add the tuna, broken into fairly small pieces, with the oil from the can. Simmer until fish is just heated through.

Cook the spaghetti until just tender, drain it and pour the sauce over it. Serve sprinkled with parsley and cheese. Serves 4.

SPAGHETTI WITH CLAMS

3 cloves garlic, finely chopped
6 tablespoons olive oil
¼ teaspoon basil or thyme
2 seven-ounce cans minced clams
¼ cup chopped parsley
1 pound spaghetti
Grated Parmesan cheese

Sauté the garlic in the oil until just tender. Add the basil or thyme and the clams with a little of their juice. Blend well, cook for about 4 minutes, then add the parsley. Cook the spaghetti until just tender, drain it and pour the clam sauce over it. Serve with grated Parmesan. Serves 4.

SPAGHETTINI ALLA CARBONARA

¼ pound ham or bacon, cut into short matchstick lengths
2 tablespoons butter
½ pound spaghettini
2 eggs, beaten
Grated Parmesan cheese

Fry the ham or bacon gently in the butter. Cook the spaghettini until just tender, drain and put into a heated dish. Add the eggs to the bacon and fat and stir as you would for scrambled eggs, pouring the whole mixture onto the spaghettini at the precise moment when the eggs are beginning to thicken, so that they present a slightly granulated appearance without being as thick as scrambled eggs. Stir with a wooden spoon so that the bacon-egg mixture is evenly distributed. Add some grated Parmesan and serve with more Parmesan. Serves 4.

MACCHERONI CON QUATRO FORMAGGI
(Macaroni with Four Cheeses)

2 pounds macaroni
½ pound butter
¼ pound Bel Paese cheese, grated
¼ pound Gruyère cheese, grated

¾ cup grated Parmesan cheese
¾ cup grated Romano cheese
Freshly ground black pepper

Cook the macaroni in boiling salted water until just tender. Meanwhile, melt the butter in the top of a double boiler and keep warm. Drain the cooked macaroni well and keep hot over hot water while you mix into it the first three cheeses, one by one, turning thoroughly and spooning in the butter as you go. Serve very hot with the grated Romano and pepper. Serves 8.

CREAMED CABBAGE WITH NOODLES

A 2- to 3-pound head cabbage
5 tablespoons bacon or chicken fat
2 tablespoons flour
Salt, freshly ground black pepper
½ to ¾ cup evaporated milk or light cream
1 pound noodles

Slice the cabbage thin and wash thoroughly. Melt the fat in a large skillet and brown the cabbage. Cover and simmer for 10 minutes. Sprinkle with the flour, salt and pepper to taste and add the milk or cream. Simmer until sauce is thickened.

Meanwhile, boil the noodles until just tender, drain and combine with the cabbage, mixing thoroughly. Taste for seasoning. Serves 4.

NOODLES AND POTATOES AL PESTO

6 potatoes, unpeeled
½ pound noodles
¾ cup Pesto

Cook the potatoes in boiling salted water until just pierceable with the point of a paring knife. Meanwhile cook the noodles in boiling salted water until just tender. Drain both well and slice the potatoes thin. Combine potatoes and noodles and mix in the Pesto. Serve hot as a pasta course, Italian style, or with broiled chicken. Serves 6.

Note: Pesto is delicious served on cooked pasta such as fettuccine or spaghetti. If you don't have Pesto, here is another recipe that calls for basil, either fresh or dried.

GREEN NOODLES WITH BASIL

1 pound green noodles
4 tablespoons butter
2 cloves garlic, coarsely chopped
1½ tablespoons fresh basil, shredded, or 1 teaspoon dried basil
Salt, freshly ground black pepper
Grated Parmesan or Gruyère cheese

Boil the noodles in salted water until just tender. Drain well and return to the pan with the butter, garlic and basil. Season with salt to taste and plenty of freshly ground pepper. Mix well and pour into a serving dish. Top with grated cheese. Serves 4.

If you want a remarkably good and different buffet dish, try making Lasagna—the Italian name for the very broad noodle.

LASAGNA

6 tablespoons olive oil
3 to 4 cloves garlic, finely chopped

1 medium onion, chopped
1 twenty-nine-ounce can Italian
   plum tomatoes
1 six-ounce can Italian tomato paste
1 cup red wine or beer
1 tablespoon basil
1 teaspoon salt
1 teaspoon freshly ground black
   pepper
¾ pound lasagne
1 pound Italian sausages, sliced, or
   1 pound ground beef and pork
   browned quickly in 3 tablespoons
   butter
¾ pound mozzarella cheese, thinly
   sliced
¾ pound ricotta cheese
Grated Parmesan cheese.

First make a rich tomato sauce:
Heat the oil in a skillet and sauté
the garlic and onion until golden.
Add the tomatoes, tomato paste,
red wine or beer and seasonings,
and simmer for 2 hours. Strain and
keep warm.

Cook the lasagne in plenty of
boiling salted water until just tender. Be sure not to overcook—it
should be definitely al dente. Remove and place on paper towels to
absorb the moisture and so that
the pieces do not stick together.

Oil a straight-sided casserole or
baking dish (a square pan or dish
is best) and line the bottom with
lasagne. Cover with a layer of meat,
then a layer of sauce, then a layer
of mozzarella and a layer of ricotta cheese. Alternate layers until
everything but half the sauce has
been used. Sprinkle liberally with
grated Parmesan and bake in a
350° oven for about 20 minutes.
Serve cut into squares and topped
with the remaining sauce. Serves 6.

This is a really heavy dish, and all
you need in addition is a salad and
some fresh fruit. Either a good red
wine or beer is the perfect accompaniment.

SPEEDY SPAGHETTI SAUCE

1 cup leftover meat or chicken or
   ½ pound hamburger
3 cloves garlic, finely chopped
2 tablespoons butter
12-ounce jar spaghetti sauce
1 teaspoon basil or thyme
1 bay leaf
¼ cup chopped parsley
Salt, freshly ground black pepper

Grind the leftover meat or chicken.
If using hamburger, brown it
lightly in a skillet, breaking it up
with a fork. Set aside.

Sauté the garlic in the butter for
a minute or two, then add the tomato soup, the basil or thyme and
the bay leaf. Simmer for 1 minute.
If the mixture seems too thick, add
about ½ cup tomato juice or water.
Mix in the meat or chicken and the
parsley, season with salt and pepper
to taste and simmer 10 minutes.
Serve on cooked drained spaghetti
with grated Parmesan.

RICE

Rice is one of those kitchen-
cabinet staples that is really a cook's
lifesaver. Plain Steamed Rice or a
Rice Pilaf goes with almost any kind
of entrée; and with the addition of
meat, shellfish or vegetables, rice
becomes a delicious main dish. If
you use converted rice it needs no

washing, but if you use Italian, long-grain, Carolina or Patna rice it should be thoroughly washed before it is cooked.

STEAMED RICE

1 cup rice
Butter
½ teaspoon salt
Water or stock

Wash the rice. Lightly grease a heavy skillet with butter and add the rice, salt and enough water or stock to come 1½ inches above the rice. Cover tightly and quickly bring to a rapid boil. Lower the heat and cook the rice very slowly until all the liquid is absorbed, about 15 to 20 minutes. Do not remove cover while rice is cooking. Fluff up rice with a fork and serve. Serves 4.

VARIATIONS

1. Substitute chicken broth for the water or stock if you are using it with a chicken dinner.
2. Mix the steamed rice with sautéed mushrooms.
3. Mix the steamed rice with chopped, sautéed onion and crisp bacon bits.
4. Steam the rice in a rich broth. When cooked, toss with toasted buttered almonds and melted butter.

RICE PILAF

1 cup rice
1 large onion, sliced

4 tablespoons butter
2 cups (approximately) stock, broth or bouillon, heated to boiling

Wash the rice. Brown the onion lightly in the butter and add the rice. Cook it over low heat for about 4 or 5 minutes, stirring it frequently, until lightly and evenly colored. Pour the boiling liquid over the rice—it should come a good 1½ inches above it. Cover the pan tightly and bake in a 350° oven for 25 to 30 minutes, or until all the liquid is absorbed, or cook on top of the stove over very low heat. Serve with a generous amount of butter. Serves 4.

VARIATIONS

1. Sauté ½ pound sliced mushrooms with the onion and cook with the rice.
2. Add a pinch of saffron to color and flavor the pilaf.
3. Sauté blanched slivered almonds with the onion and cook with the rice.
4. Add a pinch of thyme or oregano to the liquid.
5. Use tomato juice in place of the stock.

RISOTTO ALLA MILANESE

5 to 6 tablespoons butter
1 small onion, finely chopped
2 cups rice
½ cup dry white wine
3 or more cups boiling stock
1 teaspoon salt
Pinch of saffron
Grated Parmesan cheese

Melt 3 tablespoons butter in a heavy skillet. When it bubbles, add the onion and cook for 2 to 3 minutes, until golden; do not allow it to brown. Add the rice and stir well with a wooden spoon; do not let it color. Stir until rice and onion are well coated with butter. Add the wine and let it almost cook away. Start to add the boiling stock, a cup at a time. Let each cup of stock cook away before adding more. As the rice absorbs the stock and becomes tender, stir it with a fork to keep it from sticking to the pan. Add the salt and saffron. When the rice is done, stir in the remaining butter and a little grated Parmesan. Serve at once with Parmesan cheese as a first course, Italian style, with an entrée or as a main course at luncheon. Serves 4 as a main course.

VARIATIONS

1. Before adding the wine, add 4 to 5 slices poached marrow.
2. Add a little dry sherry, about ⅓ cup, to the Risotto when you add the stock.
3. If you are serving the Risotto with veal or chicken, use hot tomato juice instead of stock, and a little chopped fresh basil.

RISI E BISI

1 small onion, finely chopped
5 tablespoons butter
½ cup shredded smoked ham
1 package frozen peas, thawed

3 to 4 cups chicken or beef stock, heated to boiling
1½ cups rice
3 tablespoons grated Parmesan cheese

Sauté the onion in 2 tablespoons butter until golden. Add the ham and peas. Mix in 1 cup stock and bring to a boil, then add the rice. Add 2 cups more hot stock and cook until all the liquid is absorbed. If more liquid is needed, add another cup of hot stock, little by little. The cooked rice should be just dry but not too soft. Stir in the remaining butter and the cheese. Serve at once. Serves 4.

BAKED MEXICAN RICE

1 onion, finely chopped
1 clove garlic, finely chopped
⅓ cup olive oil
1 cup rice
1 teaspoon salt
1 teaspoon freshly ground black pepper
1 tablespoon chili powder
1 four-ounce jar button mushrooms
8 to 12 slices chorizo (Spanish sausage) or garlic sausage
1½ cups (approximately) stock, heated to boiling
Grated Parmesan cheese

Sauté the onion and garlic in the oil until just soft. Add the rice and seasonings and brown the rice lightly. Add the mushrooms, sausage and enough boiling stock to come 1 inch above the rice. Cover with a tight lid and bake in a 350° oven until the liquid is completely absorbed, about 30 to 35 minutes.

To serve, sprinkle with the cheese. Serves 4.

FRIED RICE ORIENTALE

⅓ cup peanut oil
½ cup finely sliced green onions
1 cup julienne strips meat—country ham, pork, chicken or turkey
3 cups cooked rice
½ cup sliced water chestnuts
2 eggs, slightly beaten
3 tablespoons soy sauce
Chopped Chinese parsley (cilantro)

Heat the oil and sauté the onions and meat lightly. (Use all one meat, or a combination of chicken or turkey with ham.) Blend in the rice and water chestnuts. Stir in the eggs and soy sauce and cook until the eggs are thoroughly mixed with the rice and other ingredients. Taste for seasoning; the soy sauce will probably have made this salty enough.

Pack the mixture into a bowl or a charlotte mold, pressing it down well with the back of a spoon. Unmold onto a hot platter and garnish with chopped Chinese parsley (if not available, use ordinary parsley and a few shredded green onions). Serves 4 to 6 as a main course.

RICE TRIANON

2 cups cooked rice
2 cups cooked elbow macaroni
1 cup peas
1 cup buttered sliced beans
1½ cups diced ham
1 cup diced tongue
1 cup Tomato Sauce
Parmesan cheese

Combine the rice, macaroni, peas, beans, ham, tongue and Tomato Sauce in a casserole and sprinkle with Parmesan cheese. Bake in a 350° oven for 25 minutes or until heated through. Serves 6 to 8.

POLENTA

Another good accompaniment to meats, especially pork, game, chicken and spicy Mexican foods such as Turkey Mole, is the Italian cornmeal Polenta. It can also be turned into tasty casserole dishes.

POLENTA

1½ cups cornmeal
4½ cups water
1 teaspoon salt
2 ounces butter
Grated Parmesan cheese

Put the cornmeal in the top of a double boiler and stir in 1 cup of the water. Bring the rest of the water to a boil in a separate pan. When the cornmeal is well mixed, stir in the boiling water and cook over very low heat, stirring constantly, until the mixture comes to a boil. Add the salt. Place over hot water and steam for 1 to 1½ hours.

Add the butter and a lavish sprinkling of Parmesan; or grate the cheese over the Polenta just before serving. Serves 4.

Note: Leftover Polenta may be sliced, brushed liberally with melted butter, sprinkled with grated cheese and browned under the broiler.

POLENTA WITH SAUSAGES

1½ pounds hot Italian sausages
1 recipe Polenta
Tomato Sauce
Grated Parmesan cheese

Cover the sausages with water, bring to a boil and simmer for 12 minutes. Drain thoroughly and return to the pan to brown. Turn the sausages once or twice to be sure they brown evenly on all sides.

Oil an oval ovenproof serving dish and pour in the Polenta. Top with the sausages and bake in a 375° oven for 15 minutes. Spoon a little Tomato Sauce over the sausages and Polenta and sprinkle with grated Parmesan cheese. Serve with additional Tomato Sauce and cheese. Serves 6.

POLENTA WITH SPINACH

2 packages frozen spinach
1 clove garlic, chopped
Juice of ½ lemon
½ teaspoon salt
4 tablespoons olive oil
1 recipe Polenta
Butter
Grated Parmesan cheese

Cut the frozen blocks of spinach into small pieces and place in a heavy skillet without water. Cover the pan and heat the spinach just until it is thoroughly thawed. Drain and chop very fine. Blend the chopped spinach with the garlic, lemon juice, salt and olive oil. Oil an oval or square baking dish and put the spinach in the bottom. Top with Polenta, dot with butter and sprinkle with grated Parmesan cheese. Bake in a 375° oven for 15 to 20 minutes, or until the Polenta is delicately brown. Serve as an accompaniment to beef, veal or pork dishes. Serves 6.

POLENTA WITH SALT CODFISH

2 pounds filleted salt codfish
2 tablespoons olive oil
1 clove garlic, chopped
1 small onion, chopped
1½ cups drained solid-pack tomatoes (or 1½ pounds ripe tomatoes, peeled, seeded and chopped)
1 tablespoon dried basil (or a few leaves of fresh basil)
1 six-ounce can tomato paste
Salt, pepper
1 recipe Polenta
Grated Parmesan cheese

Soak the codfish in cold water to cover for 8 hours, changing the water once during the soaking. Drain and cover with fresh water, bring to a boil, lower the heat and simmer until the fish is tender.

Heat the olive oil and sauté the garlic and onion. Add the tomatoes and basil and simmer for 30 to 40 minutes. Add the tomato paste and simmer for 15 minutes. Season to taste with salt and pepper. The sauce should be quite thick. If it is not, reduce it over a brisk flame, stirring constantly.

Pour Polenta into an oiled casserole or baking dish and top with the codfish. Cover with the tomato sauce, sprinkle with grated Parmesan cheese and put under the broiler flame for a minute or two, until the top is glazed. Serves 6.

VARIATION

For a Mexican version, chop 2 canned peeled green chilies and add them to the Polenta with ½ cup grated Gruyère cheese. Add 1 tablespoon chili powder to the tomato sauce and simmer until thick.

10

DESSERTS

Although the trend to calorie counting has brought about a change in American eating habits in the last few years, there will always be a place on the menu for a really good dessert, either to bring a dinner party to a splendid conclusion or to satisfy the craving for something sweet that we all have from time to time. There is a hidden economy in serving dessert. A properly chosen dessert can unobtrusively pad out a slim meal—a fruit tart after a dinner of broiled chicken and salad, for instance, or a rich creamy cheesecake following a soup and salad luncheon, or a luscious chocolate roll or a steamed pudding in winter when appetites are sharpened by icy air. Even when the main course has been fairly substantial, a few spoonfuls of a granita or a strawberry sorbet will be welcome, clearing the palate and soothing the taste buds. The desserts in this chapter qualify on two counts. First, they do not involve the cook in a great outlay of time or money. Second, they are special and tempting enough to be served at the finest dinner. Some of them also illustrate the theory that a strategic dash of wine, liquor or liqueur can do wonders for the simplest dish; the amount is seldom more than would be consumed in a before- or after-dinner drink, but it goes a great deal farther.

Of all the French desserts, the ones I like the best—probably because they are not excessively sweet and rich—are Baba au Rhum and Savarin. They are made with the same dough, and both are drenched with a rum syrup. The difference is that one is small and the other is baked in a large ring mold.

BABA AU RHUM

1 package yeast
½ cup lukewarm milk
Sugar
2 cups all-purpose flour
4 eggs, slightly beaten
½ teaspoon salt
⅔ cup softened shortening
Rum syrup (see below)

Dissolve the yeast in the lukewarm milk with a pinch of sugar. Sift the flour into the center of a large mixing bowl or an electric mixer with a dough attachment. Add the eggs, salt, 1 tablespoon sugar, and the yeast mixture. Beat until it forms a soft sticky dough; you may have to add a little more milk to get the right consistency. When it is mixed, beat for 2 minutes with your hands. Pull up the dough and let it drop back in the bowl. Cover the bowl lightly and let it stand in a warm place for ¾ hour, or until doubled in bulk.

Stir the dough down and add the softened shortening, in small bits, beating it into the dough with your hands for about 4 minutes. Turn the dough into well-buttered muffin tins or popover molds. Let it rise again, up to the top of the molds. Bake in a 450° oven for 10 minutes, then reduce the heat to 350° and continue baking until it is nicely browned, about 20 minutes. Test with a cake tester or a skewer; the babas are done if it comes out clean. Unmold babas and let them cool slightly.

Make the rum syrup by cooking 1 cup sugar with 1½ cups water and ½ cup rum for 20 to 25 minutes. Pour the hot syrup over the slightly cooled babas. Serve with more rum poured over them, and topped with whipped cream. Or reheat them in a little rum syrup before serving, pour a little heated rum over each serving and blaze at the table; serve with whipped cream. Makes about 12 babas.

SAVARIN

Use the same dough as for Baba au Rhum, but pour it into a well-buttered 8-cup ring mold. Bake as directed for Baba au Rhum. When it is baked, remove from ring. When it is partly cool, pour rum syrup over the ring. Cool.

To serve cooled Savarin, fill the center with whipped cream or with brandied fruits mixed with whipped cream, and add a little more rum to the cake. It should be very moist. Serves 6 to 8.

VARIATIONS

1. Glaze the Savarin with apricot purée. (To make, bring contents of a 1-pound jar of apricot jam to a boil in a saucepan. Reduce heat and cook 2 minutes. Force through a fine sieve.) Fill the center with whipped cream and chopped nuts.

2. Fill the center with a layer of macaroons that have been soaked in sherry, then a layer of raspberry jam, and a final layer of whipped cream and chopped nuts. Chill thoroughly and serve.

CHOCOLATE DESSERTS

Chocolate is not only sweet-tooth America's favorite flavor, it also makes wonderfully rich, satisfying but low-cost desserts for company dinners or family meals.

CHOCOLATE FUDGE PUDDING

1¼ cups flour
1¼ cups granulated sugar
2 teaspoons baking powder
¼ teaspoon salt
1 ounce semisweet chocolate
2 tablespoons butter
½ cup chopped nut meats
½ cup milk
1 teaspoon vanilla
½ cup brown sugar
2 tablespoons cocoa
1 cup boiling water
1 quart vanilla ice cream
Chocolate Sauce (see below) or
  whipped cream

Sift the flour, ¾ cup granulated sugar, baking powder and salt together three times. Melt the chocolate and butter in the top of a double boiler over hot water, then mix with the nuts, milk and vanilla. Add to the flour mixture, beating well. Pour into a greased 8-cup ring mold. Mix the brown sugar, the remaining ½ cup granulated sugar and the cocoa and sprinkle over the top of the pudding. Pour the boiling water over the pudding. Bake in a 350° oven for 40 to 50 minutes. Serve warm with the ice cream mounded in the center of the ring. Serve with chocolate sauce poured over the ice cream in dribbles, or with whipped cream. Serves 8 to 10.

CHOCOLATE SAUCE

In a double boiler over medium heat melt 12 ounces chocolate chips, 2 squares bitter chocolate and 1 tablespoon instant coffee. Stir until smooth and blend in 1 cup heavy cream and 2 tablespoons cognac.

CHOCOLATE RING

8 ounces semisweet chocolate bits
½ pound butter
2 teaspoons vegetable shortening
8 ounces (1⅛ cups) sugar
8 eggs, separated
¼ teaspoon salt
1 teaspoon vanilla

Melt the chocolate with the butter and vegetable shortening in the top of a double boiler over hot water. Add the sugar and remove from the heat. Beat in the egg yolks and cool for a few minutes. Turn into a bowl and fold in the egg whites, stiffly beaten. Pour into a buttered and sugared 8-cup ring mold and bake in a 300° oven for 2½ hours. Serves 6. Serve with whipped cream.

CHOCOLATE ROLL

This chocolate dessert has the light texture of a soufflé. It is very easy to make, and if you like it as much as I do it may become your standard dessert.

5 large eggs, separated
½ cup sugar
6 ounces semisweet chocolate
3 tablespoons strong coffee
Cocoa
1½ cups heavy cream, whipped
  and sweetened

Butter a 10-by-15-inch jelly-roll pan, line it with waxed paper and butter the paper.

Beat the egg yolks until they are light and lemon-colored. Gradually beat in the sugar until mixture is light and creamy. Melt the chocolate in the coffee in the top of a double boiler over hot water. Let cool slightly, then beat it into the egg-sugar mixture. Beat the egg whites until stiff enough to form peaks when you remove the whisk or beater, but not dry. Fold them into the chocolate mixture.

Pour the batter into the greased pan and spread evenly with a spatula. Bake in a 350° oven for about 15 minutes, or until a knife inserted into the center comes out clean. Remove from the oven, cover with a slightly damp towel and let stand for about 20 minutes, until cool.

Arrange two 18-inch lengths of waxed paper on a work table, side by side and slightly overlapping. Sprinkle with cocoa. Run a spatula around the edges of the cake and invert it onto the waxed paper—it should come out easily. Carefully remove the paper from the bottom of the cake. Spread the roll with the sweetened whipped cream. Then, by lifting the long edge of waxed paper under the side of the cake nearest to you, start the cake rolling up like a jelly roll. Continue lifting the waxed paper, gently but quickly, until cake is completely rolled. If the surface breaks a little, don't worry, you can cover the marks with a light dusting of cocoa. To serve, arrange on a long board or platter and cut in crosswise slices. This makes 8 to 10 servings.

DESSERT CREPES

The most delicious, inexpensive and elegant desserts are those made with crêpes, the very thin pancakes of French cuisine. You can get a head start on dinner by preparing the crêpes ahead of time and gently reheating them in butter when you are ready to serve. Crêpes also keep well: you can wrap them tightly in foil and hold them in the refrigerator for several days or in the freezer for a month or so. Endlessly versatile, they can be rolled around all manner of fillings.

BASIC RECIPE FOR DESSERT CREPES

⅞ cup flour
1 tablespoon sugar
3 eggs
2 tablespoons melted butter
⅛ teaspoon salt
1 teaspoon vanilla
2 tablespoons cognac
1½ cups (approximately) milk

Sift together the flour and sugar. Add the eggs, one at a time, mixing well until there are no lumps (an electric mixer at low speed is excellent for this). Add the melted butter, salt, vanilla and cognac. Gradually stir in the milk—just enough to give the batter the consistency of heavy cream. Let the batter rest for an hour or two before making the crêpes.

To make crêpes, heat a 6-inch crêpe pan over a fairly brisk heat and butter it well. Pour a small amount of the batter (about 1½ tablespoons) into the pan and tip the pan so that the batter spreads all over the bottom of the pan in a thin film. Pour any excess batter back into the bowl. Bake crêpe until it can be shaken loose from the bottom of the pan. Turn with fingers or a spatula and brown lightly on the reverse side. As you make the crêpes, keep them warm in a low oven or over hot water, wrapped in foil, until ready to use. Here are ways to use the crêpes.

Banana crêpes: Bake bananas in their skins in a 350° oven for 18 minutes. Remove skins. Sprinkle crêpes lightly with sugar, wrap bananas in the crêpes, pour over 3 or 4 tablespoons of heated rum and flame.

Jam crêpes: Spread baked crêpes with any good jam—raspberry, apricot, strawberry. Sprinkle with confectioner's sugar and keep hot.

Strawberry crêpes: Slice strawberries and marinate in sugar and kirsch. Roll in baked crêpes and flambé with kirsch. Serve with whipped cream.

Pineapple crêpes: Open 1 package or can of frozen pineapple and heat it with 4 tablespoons butter until the pineapple is almost browned. Add ⅓ cup rum and 12 crêpes, folded in quarters. Heat them in the liquid, turning often. At the last minute, add another ⅓ cup rum and blaze. Serve at once.

Apple crêpes: Grate ½ cup apple very fine and add it to the crêpe batter. Cook as directed. Spread with applesauce and roll. Reheat in a sauté pan with a little butter and some applejack or rum. Sprinkle with sugar, add warm rum and ignite just before bringing to the table.

Peach crêpes: Flavor thinly sliced peaches with sugar and bourbon. Make crêpes and place a layer of peaches on each, arranging them in a stack of 8 or 10 crêpes, topped with a plain crêpe. Heat and flame with bourbon. Serve cut in wedges, with whipped cream.

Chocolate crêpes: Stack about 14 to 16 crêpes as you make them, sprinkling a small amount of grated chocolate on each crêpe and keeping them warm. When they are stacked, pour Chocolate Sauce (see recipe on page 196) over them and serve cut in wedges, with sweetened whipped cream spiked with a little cognac. Garnish with chopped pistachio nuts.

Crêpes suzette: Rub 12 lumps of sugar over 2 large oranges to let them absorb the oil from the rind. Cream ⅓ cup butter. Squeeze the juice from the oranges and pour it over the sugar. Mix the juice, sugar and butter in a skillet and heat. Add ¼ cup Grand Marnier or Cointreau. When the sauce is hot and bubbling, add 12 crêpes, folded in quarters. Heat them through in the sauce, turning frequently. At the last minute add a good slug of cognac, whiskey or rum to the pan, let it warm up and then ignite. Carry the blazing skillet to the table and serve. Serves 4.

This classic dessert would cost you about three dollars a person in a restaurant. You can make enough for four at home for much less.

CREAM CHEESE DESSERTS

The simplest possible cream cheese dessert is also one of the most delicious and tempting.

CREAM CHEESE WITH FRUIT

Thin 8 ounces cream cheese with heavy cream and beat until light and fluffy. Serve as a dessert with hot toast and rich preserves or tiny crêpes and preserves. Or add chopped raisins and nuts to the cheese mixture and heap on tiny crêpes.

ICEBOX CHEESECAKE

1 package zwieback
½ cup softened butter
¾ cup sugar
Cinnamon
3 eggs, separated
½ cup milk
2 tablespoons unflavored gelatin
½ cup water
1 pound cream cheese
1 teaspoon lemon juice
Grated rind of 1 lemon
1 teaspoon vanilla
1 cup heavy cream

Roll the zwieback into crumbs and mix with the softened butter, ¼ cup sugar and a dash of cinnamon. Press ¾ of the mixture into a 9-inch spring-form pan with your hand to make a nice firm crust. Bake for 10 minutes in a 400° oven. Cool. Reserve remaining crumb mixture for the topping.

Prepare a custard with the 3 egg yolks, ½ cup milk and the remaining ½ cup sugar. Stir constantly until thickened, but do not let it come to a boil. Soften the gelatin in the ½ cup water and stir into the custard until thoroughly dissolved. Gradually stir the thickened custard into the cream cheese. Put it through a sieve or a food mill. Flavor with the lemon juice and rind and vanilla. Lightly whip the heavy cream and stiffly beat the egg whites. Mix first the whipped cream and then the beaten egg whites into the cream-cheese mixture, blend well and pour into the baked crust. Top with the reserved crumb mixture and chill in the refrigerator until set. Makes 8 to 10 servings.

This cheesecake has an elegant taste, not too sweet, and a wonderful texture, and is not at all difficult to make. If you bought it in one of the fine bakeshops in New York it would cost at least seven or eight dollars. This version costs a fraction of that amount.

No cream cheese, just sweetened condensed milk, makes this

MOCK CHEESE TORTE

⅔ box graham cracker crumbs
¼ pound butter, melted
6 eggs, separated
2 cans sweetened condensed milk
Juice of 3 lemons
Grated rind of 2 lemons

Line a spring-form pan with the crumbs mixed with the butter. Beat the egg yolks until they are light and lemon-colored, then mix in the evaporated milk, lemon juice and rind and, lastly, the egg whites, stiffly beaten. Pour into the lined spring-form pan and bake in a 350° oven for 35 minutes. Serves 6 to 8.

DESSERT SOUFFLES

The soufflé is a dramatic dessert featured on the menus of the best French restaurants, yet it takes far less work and money to produce than many other less impressive sweet dishes. The secret here is the timing, for a soufflé should be served at its peak of perfection, the minute it comes out of the oven. This isn't as difficult to achieve as you might think. You can prepare the basic batter mixture hours ahead of time. Keep the egg whites in a bowl, unbeaten—they should stand at room temperature for about an hour before being beaten. Put the soufflé together at the last minute and pop it in a preheated oven to bake while you are eating dinner. It will be ready when you are, and should be eaten right away.

BASIC DESSERT SOUFFLE

3 tablespoons butter
3 tablespoons flour
¾ cup milk
4 eggs, separated
½ cup sugar
2 teaspoons vanilla

Melt the butter in a saucepan and blend in the flour. Remove the pan from the heat (or cook the mixture in the top of a double boiler over hot water) and gradually stir in the milk, mixing until smooth. Return to the heat and cook, stirring until thick and smooth. Cool slightly.

Beat the egg yolks until they are light and lemon-colored and pour the cream-sauce mixture over them. Mix thoroughly. Add the sugar and vanilla and blend in.

Beat the egg whites until they are stiff but still moist. (If you want a lighter, puffier soufflé, use 1 or 2 extra egg whites.) Fold half of the beaten egg whites into the batter mixture fairly well. Then fold the other half in very lightly. Pour the mixture into a buttered and sugared soufflé dish and bake in a 375° oven for 25 to 35 minutes, or until the soufflé has puffed up and is lightly browned on top. Baking time depends on your preference. Some people prefer a soufflé that is still slightly runny in the center, what is known as a French soufflé, while others like them thoroughly cooked, almost dry. Experiment to find the exact length of cooking time it takes to get the soufflé you like. Serve at once.

If you like a very high soufflé, make a collar of paper to go around the top of your soufflé dish that the mixture can cling to as it rises. Fasten it with paper clips or Scotch Tape. When the soufflé is done, remove the collar.

Chocolate Soufflé: Melt a 5-ounce package of semisweet chocolate with a little hot strong coffee (about 2 tablespoons) and mix into the cream sauce before you add the egg yolks.

Ginger Soufflé: Add ½ cup shredded preserved or candied ginger to the cream sauce. You may use the ginger syrup for sweetening in place of the sugar.

Coffee Soufflé: Add 1 teaspoon or more instant coffee, according to taste, to the cream sauce.

Orange Soufflé: Add 2 teaspoons grated orange rind and 4 tablespoons concentrated undiluted frozen orange juice to the cream sauce.

Lemon Soufflé: Add the grated rind of 1 lemon and 3 tablespoons lemon juice to the cream sauce.

Liqueur Soufflé: Add ½ cup of any liqueur you like to the cream sauce; Cointreau, Benedictine, Grand Marnier, Cherry Heering are all good choices. Pour additional liqueur over the soufflé when you serve it, if you like.

Fruit Soufflés: Use 1 cup puréed fruit—fresh berries, peaches, plums or other suitable fruits, canned or frozen fruit, whatever you like. Taste the purée for sweetness and, if necessary, add a tablespoon or two of sugar, heating the purée and sugar until well blended. Or you may use 1 cup pure fruit preserves (without pectin), heated gently until dissolved. (This will not need sugar.) Cool purée or preserves slightly and flavor to taste with liqueur, rum or whiskey. Beat 4 egg whites until they hold soft peaks, then gradually beat in 5 tablespoons sugar and continue beating until stiff. Fold in the cooled fruit purée and pour into a buttered and sugared soufflé dish. Bake in a 375° oven for about 30 minutes. Serve with whipped cream.

PUDDINGS

BREAD-AND-BUTTER PUDDING

Softened butter (about 1 cup)
8 to 9 thickish slices bread, homemade if possible
1 cup raisins soaked in cognac or
   sherry for 30 minutes
4 eggs
½ cup sugar
Pinch of salt
1 quart half-and-half
1 teaspoon vanilla

Butter a 2½-quart pudding dish or soufflé dish. Trim the crusts from the bread, and butter the slices well. Arrange them in the dish, buttered side down, in layers, sprinkling each layer with some of the raisins.

Lightly beat the eggs and add the sugar, salt, half-and-half and vanilla. Pour through a strainer over the bread and let stand for 30 minutes. Cover with foil and bake in a 350° oven for 35 minutes. Remove the foil and continue baking until the pudding is lightly browned and set, about 30 to 35 minutes. Serve warm with cream. Serves 8.

APPLE CHARLOTTE

*12 to 14 apples, washed, quartered
    and cored, but not peeled
1½ cups boiling water
Sugar
Vanilla
Thinly sliced toasted bread
Melted butter
Whipped cream*

Cook the apples in the boiling water until soft and then force them through a sieve. Add an equal amount of sugar and a touch of vanilla and return to the pan to cook down for about 15 minutes, until they form a very thick sauce.

Meanwhile, cut the crusts from the toasted bread, dip each piece in melted butter and brown quickly in a skillet. You will need enough pieces to line a mold. Cut part of the browned bread into triangles and fit these tightly over the bottom of the mold. Line the sides of the mold with long fingers of the browned bread, overlapping them slightly. The mold must be thoroughly lined or the applesauce

will break through. Fill the center of the lined mold with the applesauce and cover the top completely with more of the browned bread. Place the mold in a pan of hot water and bake in a 350° oven for 30 to 35 minutes, or until the toast lining is solid enough to contain the apple filling. Unmold carefully and serve warm or cold with whipped cream. Serves 6 to 8.

FRUIT DESSERTS

Fresh or cooked fruit is always a delightful dessert, light and flavorful, yet inexpensive, especially when in season. It is especially fitting as the end of a rich, heavy dinner. Certain fruits make excellent combinations, and fruits with liqueurs or wines have an elegant quality. If you buy a bottle of domestic kirsch or cherry brandy, which keeps month in and month out, you can add a dash of it to your fruit mixtures and turn them into Continental party fare. Or keep a little bottle of cognac on hand for this purpose. Other liquors that go well with fruit are rum and bourbon. All these give fruit a delightful flavor. Here are some suggestions:

Apples

BAKED APPLES

Serve hot, spicy baked apples with a slug of applejack, rum or whiskey poured over them and blaze them. Pass sour cream with these.

APPLE DUMPLINGS

Make your favorite pastry and roll it out ⅛-inch thick. Cut into 5-inch squares. Place a peeled, cored cooking apple on each one. Fill the core with sugar, dot with butter and sprinkle with cinnamon, nutmeg and a tiny pinch of salt. Fold the corners of the pastry over the apples and pinch the edges together. Arrange dumplings on a baking sheet, brush with beaten egg and sprinkle with chopped almonds and sugar. Bake in a 450° oven for 10 minutes, then reduce the heat to 350° and continue baking until the apples are cooked through and the pastry is nicely browned, about 40 to 45 minutes. Serve hot with heavy cream.

Apricots

FRESH APRICOTS

1. Peel and slice fresh apricots and drench them with sugar and sour cream.

2. Combine fresh apricots with fresh strawberries. Sugar them and lace them with kirsch or brandy.

FLAMBEED APRICOTS

Peel apricots and poach them for about 10 minutes in a syrup made of equal parts of sugar and water flavored with a little vanilla. Serve hot with rum, brandy or bourbon whiskey poured over them, and blaze them as you bring them to the table.

Bananas

FRESH BANANAS

Combine sliced bananas, fresh or frozen strawberries and sugar to taste. Add a little squirt of lemon or lime juice to give them zip.

BAKED BANANAS

Cut bananas in half the long way, sprinkle with brown sugar, add a squeeze of lemon juice and dot with butter. Bake them for 15 minutes in a 375° oven. Serve with toasted coconut, or pour rum over them and blaze it.

Cherries

CHERRIES JUBILEE

This famous dessert can be made with fresh cherries that have been poached in a sugar-and-water syrup or with canned cherries. Pour off a little of the juice and heat the cherries. Add a little brandy or kirsch to the cherries while they are heating. (You can do this at the table in a chafing dish if you have one.) When you are ready to serve, pour a little more liquor over the cherries and blaze it. Dish up the blazing fruit over ice cream. Or serve it plain.

BRANDIED CHERRIES

Serve canned or poached cherries chilled, with a little brandy or kirsch poured over them. Sprinkle with chopped toasted almonds.

Figs

FRESH FIGS

Select perfectly ripe fresh figs. Slice them very thin and serve with sugar and heavy cream.

BRANDIED FIGS

Add a little brandy or whiskey to canned figs and chill them thoroughly.

Gooseberries

GOOSEBERRY FOOL

One of the wonderful old-fashioned dishes that is neglected these days. Wash and clean 1 quart of gooseberries. Cook them very slowly with ½ cup of sugar and ¼ cup of water until they are tender enough to mash. Put them through a sieve or a food mill and taste for sweetness. Combine 1 cup of heavy cream with 1 cup of milk or use 2 cups of undiluted evaporated milk. Blend with the gooseberry pulp. Chill thoroughly, for several hours if possible.

Melons

MELON WITH WINE

Cut ripe cantaloupe in halves and add 2 to 3 tablespoons of port wine to each half. Let them stand in the refrigerator or a cool place for an hour or so before serving.

MELON SURPRISE

An attractive and delicious dessert for a summer evening. Choose a large, perfect melon for this. Cut a circular piece, about 7 inches in diameter, from the top. Carefully remove all the seeds and stringy parts and then scoop out all the meat with a ball cutter. Combine with any other fruit or with melon balls cut from other melons. Flavor with brandy, whiskey or rum, and put the fruit back into the melon. Attach the top piece, fix it securely and chill the melon thoroughly. Arrange the melon on a large platter and surround it with decorative leaves.

MELON ALASKA

A version of the famous baked Alaska. Peel the melon and then fix it as above (Melon Surprise), leaving just enough of the meat to hold the fruit securely. Be sure that it is tightly packed with brandied fruit. Chill the melon thoroughly. When you are ready to serve, cover the melon with a meringue, place it on a board or a baking sheet and bake at 500° for about 5 minutes, or until the meringue is slightly browned.

VARIATION

Fill part of the melon with ice cream and the rest with brandied melon balls. Be sure the ice cream is very firm.

DRUNKEN WATERMELON

This makes an amusing first course or light dessert. Cut a deep plug about 2 inches square out of the top of a ripe watermelon. Remove plug and slowly pour in light rum, brandy or champagne—as much as the melon will absorb. Replace plug and seal with tape. Refrigerate watermelon for 24 hours, turning 4 or 5 times to allow the liquor or wine to permeate the melon pulp. Serve just like any other watermelon.

Nectarines

Make a syrup of equal parts of water and sugar flavored with vanilla. Poach nectarines, whole or halved, until they are just tender. Add brandy or not as you choose.

Peaches

FRESH PEACHES

1. Add maple syrup to sliced peaches for sweetening. Serve with sour cream or heavy cream.
2. Add cognac or bourbon to fresh or stewed peaches.
3. Blanch ripe peaches in boiling water for 5 minutes. Peel and arrange in a serving dish. Sprinkle lightly with sugar. Purée a package of frozen raspberries in the blender, first pouring off some of the liquid. Flavor lightly with kirsch. Spoon purée over peaches and serve very cold with ice cream or whipped cream.

PEACH MELBA

This is probably the most famous of all desserts, but it is seldom made correctly. Poach fresh peach halves in vanilla-flavored syrup. Arrange them in a glass or silver bowl. Top with a scoop of vanilla ice cream for each 2 peach halves and cover with the raspberry purée given in No. 3, or with bottled sauce Melba.

FLAMBEED PEACHES

Halve fresh peaches and arrange halves on a baking sheet. Heap 1 tablespoon brown sugar in the center of each and dot with ½ tablespoon butter. Sprinkle with cinnamon. Place about 4 inches from the broiler and broil for 5 minutes, or until the sugar is melted and the peaches slightly browned. Arrange on a flameproof serving dish. Warm bourbon (about 1½ tablespoons for each peach half) and pour over the peach halves. Ignite and serve flaming.

Note: If you take the trouble to can or freeze peaches when they are in season, you will have a good supply for desserts all winter long.

Pears

FRESH PEARS

1. Serve ripe juicy pears with a good cheese for dessert after a heavy meal. Try them with Camembert or Roquefort, or with that most

superb of Italian accompaniments to fruit, Taleggio.

2. Core whole pears and stuff them with cream cheese. Pour a little melted currant jelly over them before serving.

3. Slice pears and sprinkle them with maple sugar. Serve with heavy cream. (These are delicious for Sunday breakfast.)

POACHED PEARS

Peel whole pears and poach them in a syrup of equal parts of sugar and water. Cook them for about 15 minutes, or until they are tender. Cool them in the syrup.

VARIATIONS

1. Add ½ cup of finely cut preserved or candied ginger, or a few shreds of fresh ginger, to the syrup.

2. Add 1 cup of port wine to the syrup after it has partly cooled.

3. Add ½ cup of green crème de menthe after the pears have cooled. Turn the fruit about several times to mix the flavors thoroughly.

PEAR HELENE

Arrange poached vanilla-flavored pear halves in a bowl and add a scoop of vanilla ice cream for each two pear halves. Serve with hot Chocolate Sauce.

Pineapple

FRESH PINEAPPLE

Cut a small pineapple into quarters, or a large one into 6 sections. Cut lengthwise, from top to bottom, and be sure you cut right through the green top. Using a very sharp knife or a grapefruit knife, cut between the flesh and the skin of the pineapple. Then slice the fruit across in thin slices. With your fingers, slide the slices out a little, pushing alternate slices toward opposite sides of the shell. This will fan out the wedges, making an attractive pattern and making them easy to pick up for eating. Now sprinkle the tops of the wedges with sugar and add about 1 ounce of rum to each serving. Chill thoroughly and serve 1 section (a quarter or a sixth of a pineapple) to each person.

PINEAPPLE WITH ICE CREAM

Here is an impressive dessert of stuffed pineapple. Serve it to a large group of people; it's much more spectacular when made with one of the very big pineapples. Cut off the top of the pineapple and scoop out most of the fruit. Cut it into bite-size pieces and sugar it. Let it stand for 3 hours. Chill the shell thoroughly. When ready to serve, put several scoops of ice cream into the shell, add some fruit, then more ice cream and more fruit, until the shell is full. Place the top back on and serve on a large platter.

PINEAPPLE WITH RASPBERRIES

1. Arrange sugared pineapple in a bowl. Top with 1 box frozen

raspberries. Let the raspberries thaw out and melt down over the pineapple.

2. Using a large pineapple, fix it for stuffing (as in Pineapple with Ice Cream above), but combine the pineapple with frozen raspberries (thawed out) before you put them back into the shell with the ice cream.

BROILED PINEAPPLE

This unusual broiled pineapple dessert comes from the West Indies and South America. It is best when made with the small sugar pineapples. These are in the markets a good part of the year.

Cut each pineapple in half. Then cut the flesh loose from the skin and slice it down (see Fresh Pineapple, above). Sprinkle each half with brown sugar and dot with butter. Place the halves on the broiler rack about 4 inches below the heat and broil for 10 minutes, or until the sugar is melted and the fruit delicately browned. Add a bit of rum to each half just before serving, if you wish.

Quince

Quince are usually used only to make jelly or preserves. Actually, they have a delicate, exotic flavor and can be especially delicious when baked. Peel and core the quince. Arrange them in a baking dish and pour over them a syrup made from 2 cups of sugar boiled for 15 minutes with 2 cups of water. Add 1 clove and a bit of vanilla. Bake in a 350° oven, basting the fruit often with the sauce. Cook until the quince are tender and have turned a little pink. Serve with heavy cream.

Rhubarb

Cut fresh rhubarb into 4-inch lengths and put it in a baking dish with brown sugar to taste. Add no water. Cover and bake in a 300° oven until just tender. Cool and combine with sliced or whole fresh strawberries. Taste for sweetness. Sprinkle with pecan halves just before serving.

Strawberries

FRESH STRAWBERRIES

1. Here is an elegant change from the usual strawberries and cream. Wash and hull the strawberries, sprinkle with sugar to taste and add the juice of 2 oranges. Let the berries stand for 2 hours and then add ½ cup of port wine and, if you like, a little Grand Marnier or Cointreau. Mix heavy cream, whipped very stiff, with the berries just before serving.

2. Wash and hull strawberries and sugar them to taste. Just before serving add a little kirsch.

STRAWBERRIES SUPREME

This is another of those famous dishes that we all hear about. Wash, hull and slice 1 quart of fresh strawberries. Add 2 cups of sugar and let the berries stand for 1 hour. Place in a saucepan and bring slowly to a boil. Boil for 1 minute. Remove from the fire and cool thoroughly. Serve with vanilla ice cream and with whipped cream flavored with a little cognac or Cointreau.

FRUIT TARTS

These delicious desserts, as good to eat as to look at, are strangely neglected in this country, although they are standard fare in European countries, especially France. Anyone who can make a pie can easily turn out a fruit tart. The following pastry is excellent for making the tart shells, and far superior to any of the mixes on the market. (However, if you do use a mix, add 2 tablespoons butter and 1 egg yolk to it to make a richer dough.)

RICH SWEET PASTRY

2 cups unsifted flour
3 tablespoons sugar
3 hard-cooked egg yolks, mashed
2 raw egg yolks
¾ cup butter, or ½ cup butter and ¼ cup vegetable shortening, firm but not icy
1 teaspoon grated lemon rind
½ teaspoon salt

Put the flour on a marble work table or a wooden table or in a bowl, and make a well in the center. Working quickly with your fingertips, mix the flour with all the other ingredients. When the dough is well blended, break off small bits and rub them on the table top with the heel of your hand. This mixes

the dough thoroughly. Press the dough pieces into a ball and chill for at least ½ hour before using. Roll it out between 2 sheets of waxed paper. Roll it away from you and then toward you; turn the dough, loosen the paper and roll again. Repeat this process until the dough is the size you need. Line a 9-inch flan ring or pie pan with the rolled-out pastry. Cover the dough with a piece of waxed paper or foil, fitting it in loosely. Fill it with raw rice or dry beans so that the shell will not puff up during baking. Bake in a 425° oven for 10 to 15 minutes, or until the shell is just baked and delicately browned. Remove the paper or foil and the rice or beans (save them and use again for the same purpose). Cool the shell.

CREME PATISSIERE
(Pastry Cream)

This is the cream used in French pastry shops to fill eclairs, cream puffs, and shells for fruit tarts.

4 cups milk
1 inch vanilla bean or 1 teaspoon vanilla
¾ cup flour
1 teaspoon cornstarch
1 cup sugar
8 egg yolks

Heat the milk with the vanilla bean or essence. Combine the flour, cornstarch, sugar and egg yolks in a heavy saucepan and beat thoroughly. Gradually stir in the hot milk and continue stirring briskly over a very low flame until the mixture is thickened and smooth like mayonnaise. Do not let it boil, or the egg yolks will curdle. Cool before using.

APRICOT AND CURRANT GLAZES

Most fruit tarts taste much better if you glaze the fruit lightly. To make a glaze, heat the contents of a 1-pound jar of apricot jam or currant jelly over medium heat and boil down for 2 minutes. Use the Apricot Glaze for light fruits, the Currant Glaze for the darker ones.

STRAWBERRY TART

Half fill baked Rich Sweet Pastry tart shell with Crème Pâtissière and arrange fine ripe strawberries on top. Brush heavily with Apricot or Currant Glaze. You may serve with whipped cream, but it is not necessary.

RASPBERRY TART

Make this as you would Strawberry Tart, using a Currant Glaze.

APRICOT TART

Half fill baked Rich Sweet Pastry tart shell with Crème Pâtissière. Poach apricot halves in a sugar-and-water syrup until just tender; or use canned apricot halves. Arrange them on top of the Crème Pâtissière and brush with Apricot Glaze.

PEACH TART

Half fill baked Rich Sweet Pastry tart shell with Crème Pâtissière and arrange fine ripe juicy peach halves on top. Brush with Apricot Glaze. Serve decorated with whipped cream.

COOKED FRUIT TART

Line a tart pan or pie tin with Rich Sweet Pastry. Sprinkle it with ½ cup sugar and arrange fresh apricot halves, cut side down, in a spiral pattern on the shell. Sprinkle them lightly with sugar and bake in a 375° oven for about 40 minutes, or until the crust is brown and the fruit cooked through. Cover with an Apricot Glaze.

COUNTRY-STYLE CHERRY TART

This tart is beautiful to look at and delicious to eat. Line a tart pan or pie tin with Rich Sweet Pastry and cover with 2 cups sweet cherries. Blend together 1 egg beaten with 3 tablespoons flour, ½ cup heavy cream, 2 tablespoons sugar and a pinch of salt. Pour this over the cherries. Bake in a 375° oven for 30 to 35 minutes, or until the top is delicately browned.

FROZEN DESSERTS

If you have had a fairly heavy meal, such as a Poule au Pot, but would still like a taste of something sweet to finish with, there is nothing better than a granita—the Italian water ice, or sorbet.

GRANITA DI CAFFE

8 tablespoons Italian-roast coffee, ground for espresso
Sugar to taste
4 cups boiling water

Combine the coffee, sugar to taste (according to how sweet you like your sorbet) and boiling water in a glass or pottery coffee maker and steep for 30 to 40 minutes. Let cool and strain through filter paper (the type used for drip pots). Freeze in ice trays, stirring several times during the process. Serve in sherbet glasses, topped, if you wish, with whipped cream.

GRANITA DI LIMONE

Make a syrup by boiling 1 cup water with ½ cup sugar for 5 minutes. Cool. Mix in ⅓ to ½ cup lemon juice, depending on how tart you like it, and freeze in ice trays, stirring several times during the process. Serve in sherbet glasses.

The following sherbets or sorbets, while a little richer, are also a refreshing end to a meal.

ORANGE SHERBET

This should be served softly frozen, not hard. Freezing will take about 20 minutes in an ice-cream freezer and 2 to 3 hours if you use ice trays in the refrigerator freezing compartment.

1 cup water
1 cup sugar
½ cup lemon juice
4 cups frozen orange juice, thawed but undiluted
½ cup bitter orange marmalade
½ cup Grand Marnier

Cook 1 cup water and the sugar together until they come to a boil. Add the lemon juice and combine with the thawed orange juice. Fold in the marmalade and the Grand Marnier and freeze in an ice-cream freezer or in ice trays.

If you are using ice trays, remove the sherbet when barely frozen, beat well with a fork and return to the freezing compartment. Repeating this process will improve the sherbet, or you may prefer to incorporate 2 to 3 tablespoons of heavy cream to give it a smoother texture. Serves 8.

STRAWBERRY SORBET

3 pints strawberries or 3 packages frozen strawberries
2 cups sugar
1½ cups orange juice
¾ cup lemon juice
⅓ cup Grand Marnier

Wash and hull the fresh strawberries or slightly thaw the frozen strawberries. Combine in a bowl the fresh or frozen strawberries, sugar, orange and lemon juice, and let stand 2 to 3 hours. Put the mixture through a sieve or a food mill, or purée in an electric blender. Stir in the Grand Marnier and pour into 2 large freezing trays. Freeze until about 1 inch of the mixture is frozen on all sides of the tray. Remove and beat mixture until mushy. Return to trays and freeze until firm. For a more delicate sorbet, beat the mixture up twice, freezing slightly in between. You may also freeze it in an ice-cream freezer. Serves 8.

11

THE INSTANT MEAL:
A Guide
to Impromptu Cooking

It's bound to happen, usually when you least expect it and always when you are unprepared. Friends drop in for a quick drink and a chat and stay on until dinnertime. An unexpected guest or relative arrives from out of town. Your husband calls up at the last minute to say he is bringing his old college or army chum or, even worse, the boss back for dinner. The children collect a couple of friends on the way home from school. Or you are delayed in town and can't get home in time to shop or to prepare a regular meal. These are common situations that challenge the patience, fortitude and ingenuity of the person who has to do the cooking—you.

This chapter is planned to help you face such emergencies with confidence and calm. It includes quickie recipes that can be whipped up in half an hour or less, suggestions for stretching or dressing up simple family fare or end-of-the-week leftovers to feed the sudden guest, and shortcut yet delicious dishes that can be whipped up from the supply of reserve foods on your kitchen shelf—all those canned and bottled, packaged and dehydrated products that the food industry is turning out in greater volume every year. And if you have a blender (and we hope you do, for it is one of the best investments a busy cook can make), you are even farther ahead in the gourmet-meal race, for in no time at all you can have a super sauce like Hollandaise, a smooth and perfect soup or a frozen dessert ready to put on the table.

Capitalize on Mixes

Despite the dark mutterings of the food purists, we are lucky today to have a battery of foods at our fingertips—mixes, refrigerated and frozen foods—that remove many of the time-consuming processes from meal-making and usually cost no more than if you had started from scratch (and, dare I say it, the end result is often as good as or even better than what you might have produced yourself).

Mixes are probably the best friend a hurried cook and hostess can have.

One of their main advantages is the many ways they can be used, not just as directed on the package, but as substitutes or shortcuts in all kinds of recipes. In the last few years they have been supplemented by products that go even farther, refrigerated bake-and-serve foods—rolls, biscuits, cookies, pastries—that are even more versatile and simple to use. Dinner rolls can be used to top meat pies and baked fruit desserts. Flaky crescent rolls (our old friend the croissant under an American name) make great roll-ups for little sausages or fingers of cheese as an hors d'oeuvre, and the cooky doughs are ideal for making crusts for fruit tarts and cheesecake. Look around the supermarket shelves and in the refrigerated cases and you'll find all kinds of things to experiment with.

Count on Canned Goods

Even familiar old canned goods should not be underestimated. Deviled ham, for instance, can be used in recipes calling for a small amount of ground ham; canned fish are great for stretching casseroles and soups or for making pasta sauces and omelet fillings; and every shelf should have a full range of tomato products—paste, sauce and the whole peeled tomatoes. These, especially the Italian plum type, are vastly superior to the pale flavorless fresh ones we are restricted to in winter—and cheaper too. Also, don't overlook canned baby foods, if you happen to have them in the house. In a pinch, they make an excellent quick substitute for purées in soufflés.

While it may be true that today, with telephones, refrigerators and freezers and all the modern conveniences and services, we have no need to keep an enormous supply of canned and packaged foods on hand, how often have you found yourself at a loss for something to cook for dinner and making a hurried call to the meat department for a quick-cooking and expensive item like lamb chops or a steak? The refrigerator may be at the week's low point of supply and the roast in the freezer will take hours to defrost. If you took the advice we gave you at the beginning of this book, you should have some dishes already prepared and frozen for just such a contingency. But somehow it is often more fun to go to the kitchen shelf and let your creativity swing into high gear. There are few satisfactions equal to being able to turn out a really divine meal in nothing flat to the pleasure and admiration of your family and friends.

Stock an Emergency Shelf

What constitutes a well-stocked emergency shelf? It all depends on your space and location. The woman living in a big house in Grand Falls, Nebraska, may have room for cases and cases of supplies, while the cave dweller in New York may not be able—or need—to give up more than a few feet of cabinet space. The following list is to be regarded merely as a check for things to have on hand. It includes the foods I like to keep on my shelves and have found most useful. Add to or subtract from it according to your taste, budget and storage space.

MEATS

Chili con carne	2 cans
Chili with beans	2 cans
Corned beef	4 cans
Corned-beef hash	2 cans
Ham, deviled	2 cans
whole	2 cans
Tongue	1 can

You should also have on hand a selection of dried sausages, such as salami, cervelat, and summer sausage, that will keep indefinitely. Snack sausages like pepperoni and the Spanish chorizo are also good to stock in the refrigerator and can be used in cooking.

FISH

Anchovy fillets	6 cans
Caviar, red	2 jars
Clams, minced	4 cans
Crabmeat	4 cans
Gefilte fish	4 jars
Lobster meat	2 cans
Mussels	2 cans
Salmon	4 cans
Sardines	6 cans
Shrimp, medium	4 cans
small	4 cans
Tuna	6 cans

VEGETABLES

Artichoke hearts	2 cans
Beans, baked	6 cans
cannellini	2 cans
kidney	4 cans
Beets, whole	2 cans
Chick-peas	2 cans
Corn, whole kernel	2 cans
Mushrooms, broiled in butter	4 cans
dried	½ pound
Onions, small white	2 jars
Peas, tiny French	4 cans
Pimientos	4 cans
Potatoes, small white	2 cans
Tomatoes, baby, sliced	2 cans
peeled, whole	6 cans

GRAVIES, JUICES, SAUCES

Applesauce	2 jars
Beef gravy	4 cans
Catsup	1 bottle
Chili sauce	1 bottle
Clam broth	4 bottles
Soy sauce	1 bottle
Steak sauce	1 bottle
Tabasco sauce	1 bottle
Tomato juice	4 cans
paste	2 cans
sauce	4 cans
Worcestershire sauce	1 bottle

CANNED SOUPS

Black bean	2 cans
Broth, beef	2 cans
chicken	4 cans
Consommé	2 cans
Cream of celery	2 cans
of chicken	2 cans
of mushroom	2 cans
of tomato	2 cans

MISCELLANEOUS

Bread crumbs, dry	1 package
Capers	1 bottle
Chili powder	1 jar
Chutney	1 bottle
Cornstarch	1 box
Curry powder	1 can
Evaporated milk	6 cans
Kitchen Bouquet	1 bottle
Liver pâté or purée	3 cans
Mustard, dry	1 can
French	1 jar
Nuts, almonds	1 can
peanuts	1 can
walnuts	1 can
Oil, olive	1 bottle
peanut or vege-	1 bottle
table	
Olives, small green	1 jar
black	1 can
Pickles, assorted	3 jars
Preserves, apricot	1 jar
black-currant jelly	1 jar
Relishes, assorted	3 jars
Tortillas, canned	3 cans
Vinegar, cider	1 bottle
wine	2 bottles

PASTA AND GRAIN

Cracked wheat (bulghur)	1 pound
Noodles	2 pounds
Rice, long grain	2 pounds
short grain	2 pounds
Spaghetti	2 pounds

FRUITS

Apricots, dried	1 box
Cherries, bing, canned	1 can
Peaches, canned	1 can
Pineapple, canned	2 cans
Prunes, dried	1 box

DEHYDRATED PRODUCTS AND MIXES

Biscuit mix	2 boxes
Brownie mix	1 box
Brown gravy mix	1 box
Cornbread mix	2 boxes
Hot roll mix	2 boxes
Piecrust mix	2 boxes
Potato pancake mix	1 box
Soup mixes: leek, mushroom onion, pea, vege- table	1 box each
Dehydrated shallots	2 jars
Instant minced onion	2 jars
Instant mashed po- tato	2 boxes

WINES AND LIQUORS

Brandy
Sherry, dry and sweet
Vermouth, dry white
Wine
    Red, California, jug-type
    White, California jug-type
Plus an assortment of liqueurs in small bottles or miniatures for flavoring.

In addition to this I assume that you always have on hand plenty of staples such as flour, sugar, an assortment of herbs and spices, basic vegetables and fresh fruits, and that your refrigerator is well supplied with dairy produce and salad greens. Given all this, there is just about no culinary emergency that can faze you.

And now for some of our favorite impromptu dishes, based on the supplies on the emergency shelf.

First, a quick version of a famous French dish called Gratin Savoyard that is made with potatoes and sausages.

QUICK GRATIN SAVOYARD

Butter a casserole; place a layer of sliced potatoes on the bottom, then a layer of sausage of any sort, then more potatoes, more sausage, and top with potatoes. Sprinkle with salt and black pepper and dot well with butter or margarine. Mix ½ cup of milk with 1 can of condensed cream of celery soup and pour over the dish. Top it with grated cheese—Parmesan, Swiss, or whatever you have. Cover and bake in a 375° oven for 30 minutes, or until the potatoes are tender. Uncover for the last 10 minutes and add a little more cheese to make the top crusty and brown. Serves 4.

Together with a salad and perhaps fruit or whatever you may have in the house for dessert, this makes a hearty flavorful dinner in little time and for low cost.

Here is a quick version of coq au vin (chicken in wine) which is something special. It might make Escoffier turn pale, but I think it is much better than many sad attempts at this famous dish that have been concocted. You'll need leftover chicken or turkey. If you dice it, use about 2 cups. And if you use it on the bone, gauge the amount needed by how much meat is left on the bones. If you have a jar of the small white onions on hand, use the liquid for sauce. But regular onions can be used.

QUICK COQ AU VIN

1 jar small white onions or 1 large onion, sliced
3 to 6 tablespoons butter
4 or 5 pieces bacon
3 tablespoons flour
1 cup liquid drained from onions or canned chicken broth
½ cup red wine
2 teaspoons Kitchen Bouquet
2 cups leftover diced chicken

If you are using the bottled onions, drain them, saving the liquid, and brown them lightly in 1 or 2 tablespoons butter. If you are using the sliced onion, steam it in 3 tablespoons butter on low heat, tightly covered, until tender. Meanwhile try out the bacon until cooked through but not crisp. Make a sauce by melting 3 tablespoons butter in a pan, blending in the flour and then mixing in the onion liquid or broth, the wine and the Kitchen Bouquet. Cook, stirring constantly, until thickened. Add the chicken and heat thoroughly. Top with the onions and the bacon strips. Serve with rice or tiny boiled potatoes— if you use the small canned ones, just heat them through—and arrange as a border around the platter of chicken. Serves 4.

Another French dish that can be easily shortcut is jambon à la crème.

QUICK JAMBON A LA CREME

1 small onion, finely chopped
4 tablespoons butter
1 cup white wine
11-ounce can condensed tomato bisque
½ teaspoon Tabasco sauce
¼ cup commercial sour cream
6 to 8 slices precooked boiled or baked ham
Chopped parsley

Sauté the onion in the butter until just limp. Add the wine and condensed soup and blend. Cook, stirring, until it reaches the boiling point. Add the Tabasco and simmer for several minutes. Add the sour cream and blend. Add the ham slices and heat thoroughly in the sauce. Sprinkle with chopped parsley and serve with rice or with noodles. Serves 3 to 4.

Or, if you are feeling in the mood for a spicy Southwestern dish on a cold winter's night, there is nothing better than

QUICK TAMALE PIE

2 one-pound cans chili with beans
1 cup pitted ripe olives
1 package corn bread mix (Aunt Jemima's)
1 egg
½ cup milk or tomato juice

Put the chili in a 9-inch oval baking dish and top with the olives. Combine the egg and the liquid in the plastic bag and mix according to package directions for corn bread mix. Squeeze the contents over the chili and olives and spread smoothly. Bake in a 425° oven until topping is cooked and chili bubbling up around the sides. Serves 4.

If you happen to have some sausage meat and hamburger in the freezer, or need to stretch the ground beef you bought for dinner to feed extra guests, you can make a wonderful spur-of-the-moment lasagna by using refrigerated crescent rolls.

QUICK LASAGNA

1 pound ground beef or ½ pound sausage meat and ½ pound ground beef
¼ cup chopped onion
½ clove garlic, minced
1 tablespoon dehydrated parsley flakes
½ teaspoon basil
½ teaspoon oregano
½ teaspoon salt
Pepper to taste
1 six-ounce can tomato paste
1 cup ricotta cheese or creamed cottage cheese
1 egg
¼ cup grated Parmesan cheese
2 cans refrigerated quick crescent dinner rolls
2 slices (7 by 14 inches) mozzarella cheese
1 tablespoon milk
1 tablespoon sesame seeds

Brown the sausage meat and beef in a large skillet, breaking it up with a fork as it cooks. Drain off fat. Add onion, garlic, seasonings and tomato paste. Simmer, uncovered, for 5 minutes. (The meat mixture may be made ahead and refrigerated.) Combine the ricotta or cottage cheese, egg and Parmesan cheese. Unroll the crescent dough and separate into 8 rectangles. Place dough rectangles together on an ungreased cooky sheet, overlapping the edges so that they form a rectangle about 15 by 13 inches. Press edges and perforations to seal. Spread half the meat mixture down the center half of the rectangle to within an inch of each short end. Top with cheese mixture and spread remaining meat mixture over the cheese. Cover with mozzarella slices. Fold the short ends of the dough over the filling, making a border 1 inch wide, then pull the long sides of the dough over the filling, being careful to overlap the edges only ¼ inch. Pinch overlapped edges to seal. Brush with milk, sprinkle with sesame seeds and bake in a 375° oven for 20 to 25 minutes, or until a deep golden brown. Serves 4 to 6.

Note: The complete dish may be prepared 2 to 3 hours ahead of time and refrigerated, covered with plastic wrap, until ready to bake. Increase baking time to 25 to 30 minutes if dish has been refrigerated.

If you have a few packages of mixes on hand, you can easily turn out all manner of cocktail snacks and hot breads for unexpected guests or family suppers. Hot-roll mix makes quickie versions of the Italian pizza, a teen-age favorite, and its less well-known southern-French cousin, pissaladière.

PIZZA

1 package hot-roll mix
Fresh or canned tomato sauce
Thin slices of mozzarella or Switzerland Gruyère cheese
Thin slices of salami, pepperoni, or any good cured hard sausage
Anchovy fillets
Soft Italian black olives
Tuna fillets
Grated Parmesan or Romano cheese
Hot peppers
Dried or fresh thyme or basil or oregano

Prepare the basic mix by dissolving the yeast in warm water and blending it thoroughly with the dry ingredients. Divide the dough in half. (It provides enough for 2 pizzas; you can set the rest aside and use it for Pissaladière if you prefer.) Roll each half of the dough out to a circle or a rectangle on a floured board and line an oiled 14-inch pizza pan or jelly-roll pan with it. Spoon tomato sauce on the pizzas and top with your choice of any of the remaining ingredients, sprinkling the top with the dried or fresh herbs—oregano is traditional, but try thyme or basil instead. Bake in a 450° oven for 15 to 20 minutes and serve at once.

Note: If you want to make small individual pizzas, cut the dough in rounds varying from 2½ inches to 4 inches in diameter.

PISSALADIERE

½ package hot-roll mix
3 medium onions, thinly sliced
Olive oil
Salt, freshly ground black pepper
Anchovy fillets
1½ cups (approximately) tomato
   sauce
Pitted ripe olives

Prepare the mix according to the directions for pizza, but use only half the dough. Line an oiled jelly-roll pan or pizza pan with it.

Steam the onions gently in about ⅓ cup olive oil until they are soft and lightly colored, then spread them on the dough and season to taste with salt and pepper. Criss-cross with anchovy fillets to make a diamond design, and in the center of each diamond put a spoonful or two of tomato sauce topped by a ripe olive. Bake in a 400° oven for 25 minutes. Serve as a cocktail snack or as a late-supper dish. Serves 6.

VARIATION

Cover onions with tomato sauce and top with paper-thin slices of salami or garlic sausage. Bake as directed.

CURRY-in-a-HURRY

Curries-in-a-hurry are simple and absolutely foolproof. It pays, incidentally, if you have a foreign food store that carries Indian curry powder in your neighborhood, to buy one of the large cans of curry powder. Not only are they better than the supermarket variety, which contains a high percentage of mustard and turmeric, but they are infinitely more economical.

MEAT CURRIES

Combine ½ cup milk or light cream or evaporated milk, 1 can condensed cream of mushroom soup, 1 to 2 tablespoons curry powder and a bit of garlic according to your taste. Simmer this for 4 to 5 minutes, stirring it well. Now combine with one of the following.

1. 2 cups diced chicken, beef, veal, pork or ham.
2. 8 to 12 hard-cooked eggs, quartered or halved.
3. 1 can broiled-in-butter mushroom caps and 4 quartered or halved hard-cooked eggs.

VARIATION

Chicken or Turkey Curry. Use cream of chicken soup and add mushrooms and hard-cooked eggs.

FISH CURRIES

Combine ½ cup liquid (milk, cream, white wine or vermouth), 1 can condensed cream of celery soup and 1 to 2 tablespoons curry powder. Cook until well blended. Mix in any of the following.

1. 1 or 2 cans tuna fish, flaked.
2. 1 one-pound can salmon.
3. 2 cans shrimp.

4. 2 cans whole clams.
5. 2 cans crabmeat or lobster or a mixture of the two.
6. Half fish and half quartered hard-cooked eggs.

Serve any of these curries with quick-cooking rice or noodles, chutney or homemade pickles, and any other additions you may have around—chopped peanuts, toasted almonds, grated coconut, baked bananas, chopped bacon cooked until crisp, thin cucumber slices in French dressing, or sliced raw bananas in French dressing.

CORNED BEEF HASH

In our opinion, a 1-pound can of corned beef hash will serve no more than two good appetites or three medium ones. If you are going to add several other things to the meal, then perhaps you can get four servings from a can, but they will not be hearty. You can try it, of course, and see how your family reacts. If you can get four servings from a can, you can then have an inexpensive meat dish that is flavorful and popular with almost everyone. Here is the simplest way to serve this hash—and one that is especially good for a Sunday breakfast or supper:

BAKED CORNED BEEF
HASH

Mix together 2 one-pound cans of hash, 4 tablespoons chili sauce, 4 tablespoons grated onion—and it must be grated—and 1 teaspoon dry mustard. Arrange the hash in small individual baking dishes or in one large flat casserole. Make indentations in the center into which you can put an egg. Dot the hash with butter or margarine and bake in a 350° oven for 20 minutes. Then break an egg or two into each corned-beef patty and return to the oven just long enough for the egg to set—about 5 minutes.

Sprinkle with chopped parsley and paprika, and serve with thinly sliced onions, tomatoes with French dressing, and hot corn bread made from a mix. This dinner dish will serve up to 6 persons.

CORNED BEEF CREOLE

Melt about 4 tablespoons of fat in a skillet and sauté 1 large onion, finely chopped, and 1 green pepper, seeded and chopped. When these are tender, add 2 one-pound cans of corned beef hash and mix well with the seasonings. When the hash has cooked for about 5 minutes, add ½ cup of tomato juice and a pinch of cayenne. Let it cook down to a crust on the bottom. Carefully fold the hash over, roll it onto a hot platter, and serve with thinly sliced onions and tomatoes with French dressing.

CORNED BEEF AND EGG
TART

Line a 9-inch pie tin with your favorite pastry. Place a layer of corned beef hash in the bottom.

Build it up on the sides and in the center so that there is a trough all around. The center should be built even higher than the sides. Sprinkle the hash with finely chopped onion and chopped parsley. Break 6 eggs into the trough around the tin and sprinkle them with salt and pepper. Next place the top crust on carefully (it is best to chill it well first) so that it rests on the sides and the center mound of corned beef and does not touch the eggs. Cut two gashes in the top crust. Bake in a 450° oven for 10 minutes; then reduce the heat to 350° and continue baking until the crust is nicely browned—about 20 to 25 minutes. Serve hot or cold; when cold, it is good picnic fare.

If you take the trouble to make your own corned beef hash, the results will be remarkably good. We have already told you in Chapter 4 how to make corned beef hash with leftover corned beef. Now here is a method using the canned corned beef. This product, incidentally, is much better and firmer if refrigerated for a few hours before use rather than being taken directly from kitchen shelf to pan.

CANNED CORNED BEEF, HASHED

Use a 1-pound can of corned beef, with potatoes and onions to your taste. (We like 1 pound of corned beef to about ½ pound of potatoes and 1 large onion; you may like more potatoes.) Chop them all to-gether and add nutmeg and a touch of freshly ground black pepper. Cook as for regular Corned Beef Hash.

And finally, a really different dish with a spicy sauce.

DEVILED CORNED BEEF SLICES

2 eight-ounce cans corned beef, well chilled
Flour
1 egg, beaten
Cornflake crumbs
3 tablespoons butter
3 tablespoons oil
1 package brown-gravy mix
1 cup red or white wine
1 teaspoon Dijon or English mustard
1 tablespoon steak sauce
½ teaspoon Tabasco sauce

Open the cans of corned beef and cut the meat into fairly thick slices. Dip in flour and beaten egg and press into cornflake crumbs. Sauté the slices quickly in the butter and oil in a heavy skillet, turning once. The meat should be merely heated through and the crumbs browned. Remove to a hot platter. Blend the gravy mix with the wine and bring to a boil. Add the seasonings and simmer for several minutes. Correct the seasonings. Serve this devil sauce with the corned-beef slices. Serves 6.

FRANKFURTERS

How many times have you had unexpected guests pop in on the

very evening you had planned an economy dinner of franks and beans for the family? You are faced with the problem of dressing up and stretching these humble foods at the same time. We have a number of recipes for these everyday money-savers that have proved so popular they can easily hold their own with far more expensive meals. Except for canned meats, frankfurters are the most readily available and easiest to prepare of meats. They are cheap, nourishing and quickly prepared, and with a little ingenuity you can make a pound of them serve 4.

FRANKFURTERS IN SOUR CREAM

1 pound (about 8) frankfurters
3 tablespoons butter
1 small onion, chopped
1 cup chili sauce or catsup
1 cup heavy cream, sour cream or evaporated milk
Beurre Manié
Salt, freshly ground pepper to taste

Cut the frankfurters into long shreds. Melt the butter in a skillet, add and lightly brown the onion, then add the frankfurter shreds and toss them around until they are heated through. Add the chili sauce or catsup and let it come to a boil. Stir in the cream, sour cream or evaporated milk and blend until smooth. Thicken, if you wish, with Beurre Manié. Simmer until thickened, correct seasoning and serve with rice or noodles or on toast. Serves 4.

SWEET-AND-SOUR FRANKFURTERS

1 pound frankfurters, cut into 2-inch lengths
4 tablespoons oil
1 onion, cut rather coarsely
1 green pepper, seeded and shredded
1 cup pineapple chunks with juice
2 small tomatoes, peeled, seeded and quartered
2 tablespoons cornstarch
¼ cup white wine or dry vermouth
2 tablespoons white-wine vinegar

Steam the frankfurters for 10 minutes in a little salted boiling water. Keep warm.

Meanwhile, heat the oil in a large skillet and add the onion, green pepper, pineapple chunks and juice and tomatoes. Cook just until well blended and heated through. Mix the cornstarch with a little water to make a paste and stir into the skillet with the vinegar and wine. Stir until smooth and thickened. Mix in the drained frankfurters and simmer 5 minutes. Serve with steamed rice. Serves 4.

FRANKFURTER SPAGHETTI SAUCE

This can be made in the time it takes to cook the spaghetti.

1 large onion, chopped
1 clove garlic, chopped
4 tablespoons oil
1 twenty-nine-ounce can (3½ cups) Italian tomatoes
Basil or thyme
1 teaspoon sugar
6 frankfurters, finely ground

Salt, freshly ground black pepper
½ cup chili sauce or catsup

Sauté the onion and garlic in the oil. Add the tomatoes, a pinch ‧of basil or thyme and the sugar. Bring to a boil, reduce heat and simmer uncovered for 25 minutes. After the sauce has cooked for 15 minutes, add the ground frankfurters, salt and pepper to taste and the chili sauce or catsup.

Serve with spaghetti or noodles and grated Parmesan cheese. Serves 4.

TURKISH FRANKFURTERS

1 large onion, coarsely chopped
1 or 2 cloves garlic, chopped
4 or 5 tablespoons oil
1 medium eggplant, peeled, diced and floured
Salt, freshly ground black pepper to taste
Thyme or basil
1 twenty-ounce can (2½ cups) tomatoes
1 pound frankfurters, cut into 1-inch pieces

Sauté the onion and garlic in the oil until golden and limp. Add the eggplant, salt and pepper to taste and a pinch of thyme or basil. Toss lightly until eggplant is browned. Add the tomatoes and allow them to cook down well. Add the frankfurters and simmer 20 minutes. Serve with rice. Serves 4.

BEANS

Whether you usually serve them with frankfurters or not, baked beans and also kidney beans are a must for any well stocked kitchen shelf. They have a multitude of uses. We always try to pick out the brands of baked beans that contain the least sweetening, because we feel that sweet beans have a limited number of uses. Heinz's and Campbell's beans with tomato sauce are both good examples of the more useful brands. We happen to like the combination of beans with almost any meat you can name, and so we have dreamed up quite a collection of quickie dishes for emergencies. All the following recipes are based on 2 large cans of beans with tomato sauce and will serve 4—possibly 6 in a pinch.

BAKED BEANS

1. Combine canned beans with 6 to 8 slices parboiled salt pork, sliced luncheon meat or ham. Put into a casserole, alternating layers of beans and meat. Top with buttered crumbs. Bake in a 375° oven for 20 to 25 minutes, or until thoroughly heated through.

2. Chop and sauté in 4 tablespoons fat 1 onion and 1 clove garlic. Place in a casserole the canned beans with the onion, garlic, any leftover turkey or chicken and some chopped parsley. Pour over this ½ cup red wine or ¼ cup sherry or vermouth. Top with buttered crumbs. Bake in a 350° oven for 20 to 25 minutes.

3. Place in a casserole baked beans, sliced Canadian bacon, a sliced onion, 2 teaspoons dry mus-

tard, 1 tablespoon French mustard, 2 cloves chopped garlic and ¼ cup sherry or vermouth. Bake in a 375° oven for 25 minutes.

4. Combine baked beans in a casserole with 1½ cups diced cold or canned meat (beef, corned beef, pork, salt pork, ham, chicken or an assortment of what you may have at hand). Pour over this ½ cup chili sauce mixed with 1½ tablespoons curry powder. Top with onion slices and dot with butter. Bake in a 375° oven for 30 minutes, or until the onions are tender.

5. Same as No. 4 except that you use chili powder instead of curry powder and serve it with Steamed Rice.

6. Brown 4 pork chops quickly in fat and brush them well with prepared mustard. Place a layer of beans in a casserole, then the pork chops topped with chopped onions, then more beans and buttered crumbs. Sprinkle with ground black pepper and pour over all ½ cup white wine or vermouth. Bake in a 325° oven for 40 minutes. Serve with applesauce.

7. Drain the beans and mash them. Fry them in bacon fat until they are crisp at the corners. Keep mixing and turning them so that the crispness will spread all through the beans. Serve with bacon, sliced raw onions and sliced tomatoes. Toasted tortillas go well with this.

8. The same as No. 7 except that 2 cloves of garlic are sautéed in the pan before the beans are added. Add a little of the liquid from the beans and some chili sauce as they cook.

9. Place a layer of beans in a casserole. Add a layer of sliced frankfurters, a layer of thinly sliced onions and a layer of chili sauce spiked with chili powder, and top with another layer of beans. Sprinkle with crumbs and grated Parmesan cheese. Bake in a 375° oven for 30 minutes.

10. Drain the beans, pour a little vinegar over them, and drain that off. Combine with 2 medium onions finely chopped, any cold or canned meat you have, chopped parsley, chopped eggs, chopped ripe tomato and a French dressing made with oil, lemon juice and prepared mustard. Top with bread croutons fried in oil with garlic.

One of our more successful quick dishes—good for any impromptu meal when you have leftover baked ham—is based on red kidney beans.

KIDNEY BEAN CASSEROLE

1 large onion, chopped
1 clove garlic, chopped
4 tablespoons fat
2 one-pound cans kidney beans, drained
1 tablespoon tomato paste
1½ cups red wine
1½ cups diced cooked ham
Salt, freshly ground pepper

Sauté the onion and garlic in the fat until just tender. Add the beans, tomato paste and red wine. Bring to a boil, reduce heat and simmer 10 minutes. Add ham and simmer until ham is heated through. Taste for seasoning and add a little more wine if necessary. Serve with hot crusty French bread and a salad. Follow with a light dessert, as this is a rather heavy main dish. Serves 4.

KIDNEY BEAN CHILI

2 one-pound cans kidney beans, drained
2 tablespoons chili powder
½ cup red wine, beer or dry vermouth
1 to 2 cups diced leftover meat, fowl, canned meat or any of these: sliced bologna, cut-up frankfurters, meat balls or small hamburgers
Chopped raw onions

Combine the beans, chili powder and wine or beer. Mix in any of the meats mentioned and heat until the chili is hot and the flavors blended. Serve with chopped raw onions. Serves 4.

VARIATION

Mexican Chili: Add more liquid and more chili powder to your basic sauce and serve with rice, shredded lettuce and toasted canned tortillas or fritos. Beer is a natural and necessary accompaniment to this fiery dish. For dessert, have cream cheese and preserves with crackers or bread.

Kidney beans make a wonderful summer salad if the unexpected guest turns up for Sunday lunch.

CANNED FISH AND SEAFOOD

Canned seafood is ideal for making meals in a hurry—and we are not thinking of the tuna-with-a-cup-of-cornflakes type of recipe. Anyone interested in good cooking will avoid such dishes. We have already given you some good recipes for canned tuna, clams and sardines in other chapters. Here are some more recipes that turn canned tuna, shrimp and clams into instant meals. We have included in this section a quick version of quenelles, made with a jar of gefilte fish, a can of the tiny Danish shrimp and a can of frozen soup.

MOCK QUENELLES

16-ounce jar gefilte fish in small pieces
1 can frozen cream of shrimp soup
1 two-and-three-quarter-ounce can Danish shrimp
1 cup sherry or Madeira
¼ cup heavy cream
Toast

Heat the gefilte fish in the top of a double boiler over hot water. Heat the shrimp soup according to directions on the can and add the Danish shrimp, sherry or Madeira, and cream.

Place 2 or 3 pieces of heated fish

on slices of toast. Spoon sauce over all. Serves 4.

TEN-FLAVOR SHRIMP

2 4½- or 5-ounce cans deveined medium shrimp
¼ cup butter
1½ tablespoons minced shallots or scallions
1 medium clove garlic, mashed
2 tablespoons brandy
2 teaspoons soy sauce
1½ teaspoons grated fresh ginger or 1 teaspoon powdered ginger
2 tablespoons minced parsley
4 teaspoons fresh bread crumbs
4 teaspoons grated Parmesan cheese

Drain shrimp. Rinse under cold water and then soak for 10 to 15 minutes in cold water to remove the preserving brine. Drain thoroughly and put on paper towels to dry. Heat butter in an enameled or stainless-steel skillet until it bubbles. Add shallots and garlic and sauté gently until golden. Add shrimp and toss for a minute or two to warm them through. Mix in brandy, soy sauce, ginger and parsley.

Spoon the shrimp mixture into 4 scallop shells or ovenproof glass or china shells, leaving any juices in the pan. Sprinkle each serving with bread crumbs and Parmesan cheese and dribble the pan juices over the top. Heat under the broiler until the mixture is bubbling and the crumbs are browned. Serves 4.

Note: This may be prepared ahead and refrigerated. To serve, heat through in a 350° oven and then brown the crumb topping under the broiler.

SHELLFISH PANCAKES

Mix up your usual pancake batter (either your own or from a prepared mix). Omit sugar, if you generally use it. Add to the batter 1 cup minced, drained clams, or 1 cup canned shrimp chopped fine, or flaked crabmeat. Season well with salt and black pepper. (You can vary the seasoning by adding curry powder or whatever you like with seafood.) Bake on a hot greased griddle as usual. Serve with a dusting of chopped parsley and a good sharp sauce—such as Tartar Sauce.

SPECIAL CURRIED TUNA

1 small onion, chopped
2 tablespoons butter
1 seven-ounce can tuna in oil
2 cups Béchamel Sauce
1½ tablespoons curry powder
¼ cup sherry
6 hard-cooked eggs, halved

Sauté the onion in the butter until just tender. Add the tuna with the oil from the can and toss with the onion. Combine the Béchamel Sauce with the curry powder and sherry, add the tuna mixture and heat thoroughly. Finally add the halved eggs. Serve with Steamed Rice and chutney or homemade pickles. Serves 4.

VARIATIONS

1. Use double the amount of tuna and omit the eggs.
2. Use tuna and a can of shrimp or crabmeat.
3. Use tuna and a can of minced clams.
4. Use tuna and mushrooms— either fresh sautéed mushrooms or broiled-in-butter canned mushrooms.

The next tuna dish is a great money-saver. It serves 4 easily.

TUNA PUDDING

1 cup soft bread crumbs
¾ cup evaporated milk
¼ cup white wine
2 cups flaked white-meat tuna
1 small onion, finely chopped
Salt, freshly ground black pepper
3 eggs, separated

Soak the bread crumbs in the milk for a few minutes, then combine with the wine, tuna, onion, salt and pepper to taste and the egg yolks, beaten. Mix well. Stiffly beat the egg whites and fold in. Pour into a 1-quart mold and set in a pan of warm water. Bake in a 350° oven for 50 minutes. Remove and allow to stand for 5 minutes before unmolding on a platter. I like to serve this with a mushroom or egg sauce.

The following dish is even speedier if you use one of the frozen pie shells that are now sold in supermarkets, instead of making your own. When you bake it, weight it down with a piece of foil and some dry beans or rice to stop it from puffing up in the center.

TUNA TART

1 eight-inch pie shell, baked
1 seven-ounce can white-meat tuna
½ pound shrimp, cooked and shelled (canned may be used)
¾ cup tiny green olives or anchovy-stuffed cocktail olives
¼ cup heavy cream
1 teaspoon paprika
½ teaspoon freshly ground black pepper
¼ teaspoon Tabasco
2 cups rich Béchamel Sauce

Keep pie shell warm until ready to use.

Flake the tuna quite fine. Cut the shrimp into rather small pieces, reserving a few whole shrimp for garnish. Mix the seafood with the olives, reserving a few for garnish. Add the cream and seasonings and enough hot Béchamel Sauce to fill the shell. Heat to the boiling point. Fill the shell with the mixture and decorate with whole shrimp and olives. Serve the remaining Béchamel Sauce separately. Serves 6 to 8.

Canned minced clams are almost as versatile as tuna. If you use packaged hashed-brown potatoes, you don't even have the bother of peeling and cooking potatoes for your clam hash.

CLAM HASH

1 compartment hashed-brown potatoes
¼ pound butter
1 small onion, finely chopped

2 seven-ounce cans minced razor
clams, drained
⅔ cup juice from clams
Salt, freshly ground black pepper
½ cup cream or evaporated milk
¼ cup chopped parsley (frozen
chopped parsley may be used)

Reconstitute the potatoes according to the package directions. Drain
them well. Melt the butter in a
skillet and sauté the onion until
golden brown. Add the potatoes
and cook 4 minutes, pressing the
potato-onion mixture down firmly
with a spatula. Scrape from the
bottom of the skillet and turn some
of the brown crust to the top. Add
the drained clams and the ⅔ cup
juice. Cook the mixture down for a
few minutes and season with salt
and pepper. Add the cream or milk
and parsley. Cook until well heated
and bubbling. Serves 4.

Note: If you have any leftover
cooked potatoes on hand, you can
use these instead of the hashed-
brown potatoes, but they should be
firm. Dice them finely and add to
the onion with the clams. Omit
the clam juice.

VARIATION

Instead of using butter, try out
diced bacon or salt pork in the
skillet and use the fat to cook the
onion and hash. Remove the crisp
bits of bacon or pork and add them
to the hash toward the end of the
cooking.

CLAM FRITTERS

Drain a 7-ounce can minced clams,
strain the juice into a measuring
cup and add enough milk to make
1¾ cups liquid. Blend this with 1
egg, the clams and 1 package po-
tato-pancake mix to make a batter.
Drop by spoonfuls onto a hot buttered griddle. Cook slowly until
brown on the bottom, then turn
and brown the other side. Serves 2.

12

MENUS for Entertaining Economically and Successfully

To entertain well and inexpensively, you need to plan your menus with skill and care. Base your party meals on dishes that are not costly, or offset the price of an expensive food with others that are lower in cost—as we have done in the menu calling for Butterfly Leg of Lamb, for example.

Mere abundance of food is not the secret of successful entertaining. It's true that your guests should feel well fed, but their memory of the party is apt to be more favorable and lasting if there is something distinctive or a bit unusual about the food. The suggested menus given here for dinners and luncheons, buffets and brunches do not follow the traditional pattern of meat and potatoes plus vegetable plus salad, with dessert to follow. Instead they are planned around the idea of achieving palate-pleasing combinations of flavor, texture and color. Appropriate wines and other beverages have been indicated; more information about wines and liquor will be found in the following chapter.

If you are serving cocktails before the meal, it is almost a must to accompany them with hors d'oeuvres, but keep these very simple—nuts, olives, celery and other raw vegetables, savory cocktail crackers or cheese straws. Rich hors d'oeuvres and canapés, especially too many of them, are not a fitting prelude to a carefully planned dinner. On the other hand, if you are giving a cocktail buffet, be sure to have a selection of really substantial foods for the hungry, and raw vegetables for the calorie-conscious.

In the following menus, an asterisk beside the name of a dish indicates that the recipe appears in this book and may be located in the Index.

FALL DINNER FOR 4

Mushrooms with Garlic Butter*
Chicken Vallée d'Auge*
Green Beans with almonds*
Chocolate Soufflé*

With this serve a light, dry white wine, such as a Muscadet or an Alsatian or California Riesling.

SPRING DINNER FOR 6

Anchovy Salad*
Blanquette of Lamb*
Rice
Broccoli with black butter
Suprême of fresh fruits

One of the delightful rosé wines, such as a Tavel or a California Grenache Rosé, chilled, is an ideal accompaniment for this dinner. The Anchovy Salad is both a first course and a salad; the saltiness of the anchovies is an extremely good foil to the suaveness of the main dish.

WINTER DINNER FOR 6

Shrimps Rémoulade*
Crown Roast of Pork
filled with buttered noodles
and sautéed mushrooms*
Horseradish Applesauce*
Brussels Sprouts sauté*
Peach Melba*

Pork goes well with an Alsatian wine such as a Riesling or a Sylvaner, with a Moselle, or with a California Johannisberg Riesling.

FALL DINNER FOR 6

Clams au Gratin*
Daube Aixoise*
Macaroni
Salad of watercress,
cherry tomatoes
and cucumber fingers
Savarin* filled with
cognac-sprinkled strawberries

With the wonderful mixture of flavors in this Provençal main dish, a robust red Rhône wine would be just right. Or try a California Pinot Noir.

SUMMER TERRACE DINNER FOR 6

Blender Gazpacho*
Butterfly Leg of Lamb*
Swiss Onion Quiche*
Broiled Pineapple*

The balance of flavors in this menu is unexpected and delicious. Instead of the usual potato and green vegetable, the Onion Quiche makes an unusual complement to the broiled lamb. With this serve a light red wine—a California Cabernet Sauvignon or a good Beaujolais, such as a Fleurie (better in summer if served very lightly chilled).

BUFFET DINNER FOR 8

Feijoada*
Garden Salad Plate
with French dressing*
French or Italian bread
Gooseberry Fool*

This unusual Brazilian dish calls for a very simple carafe wine; you might offer both white and red California jug wines, en carafe, and let guests make their choice.

BUFFET SUPPER FOR 8

Curried Seafood* with Rice Pilaf*
and accompanying condiments

Sliced tomatoes with fresh basil
*or Tossed Green Salad**
*Icebox Cheesecake**

Beer is the recommended drink with curry; a good imported Dutch brand is particularly appropriate with hot food.

SUMMER SUPPER
OR LUNCHEON FOR 6

*Finnan Haddie Soufflé**
*Green Beans Vinaigrette**
Cheesed Melba Toast (below)
Fresh Peaches
*with raspberry sauce**

This is a light meal, especially good for hot weather. To make the Cheesed Melba Toast, slice bread very thin, brush with butter, sprinkle lightly with Parmesan cheese and dry out in a low oven until lightly browned and crisp.

A delicate white wine, such as an Italian Soave, would go well with the soufflé.

LADIES' LUNCHEON
FOR 4 TO 6

*Macadamia–Chicken Salad**
*Mushrooms à la Grecque**
Tiny brioches
*Melon Surprise**

The best wine to accompany the chicken salad would be a soft, light white—Italian Verdicchio, Alsatian Sylvaner or California Mountain White.

FALL OR WINTER
LUNCHEON FOR 4

*Breast of Lamb**
*with Sauce Soubise**
Garlic bread
*Celery Salad**
*Chocolate Roll**

This light lunch costs little and can be almost completely prepared in advance. You will have enough Chocolate Roll left to serve the family for dessert at dinner. A rosé wine—Tavel, Gamay or Grenache Rosé—would complement the lamb perfectly.

SUMMER SUPPER
OR LUNCHEON FOR 4

*Vichyssoise**
*Chef's Salad**
*Raspberry Soufflé**
Iced tea and coffee

Chef's Salad is an ever popular summer dish, and Vichyssoise is the aristocrat of soups. If you plan a family dinner using some form of poached chicken, you can use the broth for the soup and a little of the white meat for the salad. As the vinegar in French dressing is an enemy of wine, serve iced beverages instead.

Sunday Breakfasts
and Brunches

The weekend brunch is a good way way to entertain informally and inexpensively, as it is possible to invite many more people than to a dinner party. Here are some menus for substantial brunches, simple to prepare and easy on the budget. Drinks are included with each one for those who like an eye-opener before indulging in a hearty meal late in the morning, but you can substitute fruit juice or fresh fruit if you prefer. In menus for four, the recipes may, of course, be doubled or trebled to serve more guests.

SPRING BRUNCH FOR 4

Golden spikes (iced orange juice
spiked with vodka)
Codfish Cakes* and bacon
Hot rolls
Strawberry jam
Tea and coffee

WINTER BRUNCH FOR 4

Bloody Marys
Ham Soufflé*
Pennsylvania-Dutch Tomatoes*
Toasted corn bread
Jam and cream or cottage cheese
Coffee

FALL BRUNCH FOR 6

Whiskey sours
Corned Beef Hash* with
Horseradish Applesauce*
Popovers
Butter
Raspberry jam,
marmalade or honey
Tea and coffee

SUMMER BRUNCH FOR 8

Kir (a few drops
of crème de Cassis
in a glass of
chilled white wine)
Tian Vençois*
Poached Polish Sausages
Melba-Style English Muffins
(below)
Sliced oranges with Cointreau
Tea and coffee

For Melba-Style English Muffins, slice English muffins paper-thin, butter them and dry out slowly in a low oven until crisp, as for melba toast.

Wines and Spirits—and Your Budget

How to Drink Better for Less Money

CHOOSING YOUR WINE AND SPIRITS MERCHANT

We all know that to obtain good meat it is wise to seek out a well-informed butcher whose sense of honesty and professionalism lead him to advise his client the best way possible. He knows that a satisfied customer is the key to economic success and satisfaction in his job. The same is true of the good wine and spirits merchant. There surely must be a trustworthy wine man in your neighborhood or within a half hour's drive of your home.

Once you have established your relationship with the merchant you trust, the probability is that he will deliver to your home without charge if you give him enough notice. And if he is honest and well-informed, the advice he gives you over the telephone is more trustworthy than that given by an uninformed wine and liquor dealer in his shop.

How do you recognize a good wine-and-spirits merchant? The signs are that his shop is maintained neatly and proudly, there is diversity (because no good wine man can resist acquiring a wide range), the wine bottles are lying on their sides to keep the corks wet and tight, and above all he inspires confidence because he knows what he is talking about. You will be able to find this out only by asking him questions. A good wine merchant will enjoy chatting with you about wine, he will not lose patience, and he will give you knowledgeable answers. He should also make available

233

to you mimeographed lists of wines and spirits that he carries, if he cannot afford the expense of a printed catalogue. He will provide you with vintage charts, cocktail recipes and a history of many wines, which he can obtain without cost from his suppliers. (There should be no charge for any of these.) He will take seriously the return of a bottle which you have found bad or disappointing and not give you an argument in place of a sound bottle that you are entitled to receive in exchange. After all, he can return the defective bottle to the supplier.

Those of you who live in more remote areas can always count on finding a reliable wine merchant in the nearest big city—even if it is a hundred miles away—who will deliver to you promptly provided you buy a sufficient quantity to justify the shipping charge involved. It is the responsibility of the wine and spirits dealer not simply to supply the commodity but to inform, to educate and to inspire enthusiasm for the bottles he sells.

THE LABELS CAN BE YOUR GUIDE

Of all commodities sold in the United States, no more exacting information is demanded by the U. S. Government than in the sale of alcoholic beverages. No alcoholic beverage can be sold in the United States unless its label is first approved by the Alcohol Tax Division of the U. S. Treasury Department.

First, there must be a precise statement of net content which can be expressed in fluid ounces or in pints and quarts. This makes it readily clear whether you are buying a 24-ounce, 25.6-ounce (generally referred to as a fifth) or 32-ounce bottle. In some states, the giant economy half-gallon and gallon sizes are available in whiskey, gins and vodkas; and in all states the economy half-gallon and gallon of wine are widely available.

Secondly, the alcoholic content must be clearly stated. It makes a difference to the economy-minded consumer whether a vodka be 100 proof rather than 80 proof (remember, you can always add 25 percent water to the 100-proof liquor and get the same result as with the 80 proof). Whiskeys range from 80 to 100 proof, with Scotch generally falling at 86 or 86.8 proof.

To be an intelligent consumer, you must understand what the proof of distilled spirits means. The proof number is exactly twice the percentage of alcohol in the beverage; e.g., an 80-proof vodka is 40 percent alcohol and a 100-proof bourbon is 50 percent alcohol. Item A may appear cheaper than item B, but perhaps the reason is that its strength is only 80 proof while item B is the more costly 100 proof.

Wine bottles vary in size, although the consumer is usually not aware of it. German wines are generally in 23-ounce bottles, French wines in 24-ounce, French champagnes in 26-ounce, and wicker-encased bottles for

Italian Chiantis reach a generous 32 ounces in contents. A gallon, which is 128 ounces, equals in volume 5 fifths (or 5 times 25.6 ounces). If a gallon of California wine costs you $3.00, this would be the money-saving equivalent of paying 60 cents the bottle (not much more than beer per ounce).

A wine label must show the country of origin. If you are spending over $2.00 the bottle, you have paid for the privilege of knowing whether the wine comes from France, Spain, New York State or California.

Mention of a specific wine-growing area is not mandatory, but this almost always appears on a label (a better origin is something the grower is happy to boast about). Here the French control law is very rigid and can be trusted; growers have been known to go to jail for fraud when they violated this strictly enforced French wine code.

For example, should you be buying the wines of Bordeaux, the most readily available and least specific denomination will read "Bordeaux Rouge," or red wine from anywhere in the area of Bordeaux. Next up the ladder would be the superior soil, more blessed by nature, of an especially choice part of Bordeaux such as Médoc, Graves, St.-Émilion and Pomerol. And even higher, there are the small, excellent wine-growing towns such as Margaux, St.-Julien, etc. Finally, the noblest would be the famed and truly great château-bottled wines from vineyards not much more than 100 acres such as Château Haut-Brion, Château d'Yquem and Château Lafite-Rothschild. Here are the noblemen of the wine world, to be served only at the most special dinner parties.

In Burgundy, the same practice is followed. Here the equivalent of "Bordeaux Rouge" as the most general or widespread denomination would be "Bourgogne Rouge." Then follows the village wine (choicer soil) such as "Gevrey-Chambertin." And finally there is the estate bottling from a small specific vineyard such as Chambertin, Clos Vougeot and Musigny, the Burgundians' answer to the Lafites and Haut-Brions of Bordeaux.

California has learned from Europe and has established a similar hierarchy. It takes the form of a general, over-all phrase such as "California Red Wine" to represent the lowest common denominator. Up the scale, the wine bears the name of a finer wine-growing valley such as Napa, Livermore or Sonoma and, in addition, the name of the noble grape variety, such as Cabernet Sauvignon, Pinot Noir, Pinot Chardonnay. The highest point would be the estate-bottled thoroughbred from a renowned house which grows and bottles its own wine from superior grape varieties, such as L. M. Martini, Wente, Beaulieu and Mondavi.

If you know how to read a wine label, you can find out a great deal about the contents of the bottle, whether it be a vintage champagne, a fine Burgundy, an estate-bottled German Riesling, a premium California table wine or the most unassuming little vin ordinaire. Here are some typical labels and the information they yield to the initiated eye:

BORDEAUX CHATEAU-BOTTLED WINE

The revered name Château Haut-Brion indicates noble soil and one of the greats. The words "*Mis en bouteilles au Château*" guarantee that every drop of the wine was grown in the vineyard and bottled at the property. The year 1964 indicates that the harvest was gathered during a great year for Bordeaux red wines.

A BORDEAUX REGIONAL WINE

Whenever you see the word "Sauternes," you should be dealing with a sweet white wine of Bordeaux. (The most famous is Château d'Yquem, and it is always château-bottled.) However, most Sauternes production is shipped to Bordeaux and bottled by wine merchants. In this instance the wine was shipped to Paris and bottled by the renowned firm of Nicolas. The year 1961 is important, because it is the most long-lived vintage of the decade.

THE MOST POPULAR WINE OF FRANCE—BEAUJOLAIS

Most Beaujolais shipped to the United States is inexpensive and mediocre. Brouilly is one of the outstanding communes in Beaujolais and produces superior wine. This wine was grown and bottled at the château during the 1968 vintage by the proprietor, the Marquis de Roussy de Sales. It proudly boasts of the Gold Award won at the Paris Fair.

A WHITE BURGUNDY REGIONAL WINE

Joseph Drouhin buys his wines from growers in Chablis, blends them and puts his selection under his firm's name. The law requires that Chablis be made exclusively of the noble Pinot Chardonnay grape. The year is excellent—1967. The world reputation of Drouhin must rest upon the quality he puts into his selection.

A NON-VINTAGE CHAMPAGNE

This label describes a world-famous champagne, bottled by Moët et Chandon. It does not bear a vintage date, because it is a blend of more than one year. The word "Brut" means that it is the driest of Champagnes. The word "Imperial" has no descriptive meaning —it is simply a pleasant embellishment.

AN ESTATE-BOTTLED MOSELLE

This German wine is from the town of Piesport, and from a specific vineyard, Goldtröpfchen. "Spätlese" signifies that the grapes were picked late and were richer in flavor than earlier pickings. "Original-Abfüllung" is the equivalent of the French "château-bottled," or bottled on the premises. The vineyard proprietor is the Bischöfliches Konvikt (a Catholic refectory for students), and 1966 is the year the grapes were gathered.

Another valuable piece of information given on a wine label is the name of the shipper. A top name is your assurance that the wine is a good buy of its type and in its price range. Here are some names to look for:

FRENCH WINES

BURGUNDY
Louis Latour
Joseph Drouhin
Bouchard Père et Fils
Eaiveley
Jadot

Piat
Chanson

BORDEAUX
Calvet
Cruse
de Luze
Eschenauer

Barton & Guestier
Ginestet
Nathaniel Johnson
Jouvet
Pierre Cartier
Sichel et Fils Freres

RHÔNE
Chapoutier
Jaboulet
Domaine de Montredon
Rochette
Baron de Boismeaumarié

ALSACE
Hugel
St.-Odile
F. E. Trimbach
Jules Muller
Domaines Dopf

RHINE AND MOSELLE
Sichel
Deinhard
Langenbach
Kendermann
Josef Becker
Valckenberg
Leonard Kreusch

ITALIAN WINES

Bertani
Bolla
Marchesi Corsini
Ruffino
Antinori
Brolio

SPANISH WINES

TABLE WINES
Paternina
Marquis de Murrieta
Marquis de Riscal
Yago
Bodegas Bilbainas

SHERRIES
Bobadilla
Domecq
Duff Gordon
Garvey's
Gonzalez & Byass
Harvey's
Merito
Rivero
Sandeman
Williams & Humbert
Wisdom & Warter

In the case of American wines, the name to look for on the label is that of the grower. Some of the most prominent and reliable are to be found in the following list.

AMERICAN WINES

CALIFORNIA
Almaden Vineyards
Beaulieu Vineyard
Beringer Bros.
Buena Vista
Christian Brothers
Inglenook
F. Korbel & Bros.

Charles Krug
Louis M. Martini
Robert Mondavi
Paul Masson Vineyards
Sebastiani
Wente Bros.

NEW YORK STATE
High Tor Vineyard
Gold Seal

AMERICAN WINES, cont.
Widmer
Great Western
Doctor C. Frank

MARYLAND
Boordy Vineyard

OHIO
Meier

Once you know how to read a wine label, you are launched on a fascinating voyage of discovery. It would be impossible here to cover the history, background and current rating of the many wines of the world, but if you are seriously interested in learning more about this endlessly absorbing subject, we suggest that you read these four top books on the subject, all written by leading authorities:

Wine, by Hugh Johnson, published by Simon and Schuster, $10.00.

Frank Schoonmaker's Encyclopedia of Wine, published by Hastings House, $6.95. (A paperback edition will soon be available.)

Alexis Lichine's Encyclopedia of Wines and Spirits, published by Alfred A. Knopf, $15.00.

Wines and Spirits, by Alec Waugh and the editors of Time-Life Books (Sam Aaron, consultant), published by Time-Life Books, $6.95.

Vintage years, another aspect of wine about which the shrewd and discriminating wine buyer should have at least a working knowledge, is really of concern only when you are buying the wines of France and Germany, where wines can differ considerably from one year to another. The following vintage guide is condensed from the one Sam Aaron prepared for Time-Life's *Wines and Spirits*, with additional material about the 1968 and 1969 vintages. (The information it contains is reproduced here by permission of Time-Life Books, Inc.) As it is becoming increasingly difficult, and expensive, to buy the better wines of the older vintages, we have used 1959 as a cut-off date.

VINTAGE GUIDE

The vintage year of a wine is the year in which its grapes were harvested. Like any crop, grapes may vary in quality from year to year. A great vintage year is one producing wines that can remain at peak quality for a long time in the bottle. A poor vintage year is one in which the crop was inferior to begin with and the wine is poor and doomed to a relatively short life.

The evaluation of wines by vintage year is a relatively recent innovation. It sometimes can prove misleading, because in the very worst of years, when vintage charts rate everything with a contemptuous zero and when most winegrowers are cursing their lot, there are still exceptions favored by some accident of soil or climate.

It is in the château-bottled and estate-bottled wines that vintages have the most meaning (the more commercial regional wines represent blending skill rather than nature's influence). But even in these elevated categories, soil is generally more important than weather. For instance, a Château Haut-Brion of an unfashionable year such as 1960 will prove more of a thoroughbred than a lesser red Bordeaux of a great year like 1959.

Because there is good in every bad year and bad in every good, we have avoided the quick rating system of the movie critic such as "2 star" or "3 star"; this kind of skimpy information can only mislead. What follows is a more discursive rating system that will give a clearer understanding of the complexities and meaning of a "vintage year." It is based on daily wine tastings over three decades, and constant interchange of views with the men who tend the vines. We have rated each vintage from 1 to 20, based on the relative merits of the wines as they stood in the late 1960s, and not by the rating they enjoyed after the harvest. Thus, the superb 1961 red Bordeaux vintage is rated 20, while the 1965s are put at 12.

The ratings are:

Very great—18, 19 and 20.   Fair—12, 13.
Great—16, 17.   Poor—11.
Very good—15.   Very poor—10 and under.
Good—14.

RED BORDEAUX

1969. The drums of exaggerated publicity have been beating a merry tune. In truth, 1969 is simply not in the same league as 1961 or 1966. It is rather a good year, slow to mature in the Médoc and Graves—and on a lower level in St. Émilion and Pomerol. Because of only a 50% normal crop, the prices will be astonishingly high. 17.

1968. Better than '63 or '65. By selection, and reduction of total quantity, the better vineyards have produced a wine at least the equal of 1960. Vineyards such as Latour and Haut-Brion are astonishingly good. 15.

1967. The crop was more beneficial to the wine drinker because it was exceptionally large, about average in quality, and produced a soft, quick-maturing, fruity wine with a fine bouquet. This most useful, satisfying vintage can be consumed joyously while we wait for the maturing '61s and '66s to come to their full fruition. 16.

1966. The château owners were happy as they gathered this great vintage; they were able to obtain the highest prices for claret in Bordeaux wine history. A bit less body than the '64s, but compensated for by unusual bouquet, better balance and a remarkable similarity to the extraordinary '53s, as well as sufficient tannin to provide the backbone for exceptional longevity. Recommended for laying down in private wine cellars. 18.

1965. Some châteaux bottled a small portion of their crops, which will provide light, pleasant wines at bargain prices. *12*.

1964. Rich in fruitiness and charm. Wines from the lesser vineyards are showing attractiveness for present drinking, but more time will be required to bring out the ultimate virtues of the "first growths." Some vineyards of the Médoc fared badly because of the rain during the latter part of the picking season—an ill fortune that spared St.-Emilion, Pomerol and Graves. A year eminently worthy of laying down. *17*.

1963. Bad weather struck and nothing worthwhile was produced in St.-Émilion or Pomerol. Although generally poor in the Médoc, there are exceptions of extraordinary value—specifically, the vineyards that generally produce heavy-bodied wines: Latour (Médoc), Château Haut-Brion and La Mission Haut-Brion (both Graves). *12*.

1962. Quietly, and with a minimum of publicity, the neglected 1962 clarets have finally won deserved recognition among the world's wine lovers. In their own way, they have something to offer us. Uniformly, they are excellent, early-maturing, soft, fruity, of fine bouquet, and can be enjoyed for present drinking. Undoubtedly the best claret values available today. *16*.

1961. One of the best years of this century, the equal of 1945. Unfortunately, the crop was about half the normal size. The grapes were well nourished, resulting in concentrated wines, rich in every quality including color, body, bouquet and fruit. They are the most long-lived wines of our generation—in the classic tradition. *20*.

1960. Sandwiched between two great years, the 1960 vintage has suffered from being unfashionable. In fact, the '60s are better-than-average wines, soft, with a pronounced bouquet—among the best values in good claret on the market today. Buy them for drinking during the next three or four years, not for laying down. *15*.

1959. Acclaimed at the time as the "Vintage of the Century," '59 enjoyed the advantage of early charm and pleasant fruit. Beautiful wines, rich in many elements, but lacking the staying powers of the '61s. They can be enjoyed today; the great vineyards still possess a life expectancy of at least twenty years. *19*.

WHITE BORDEAUX

Here it is important to differentiate between the dry white wine produced in the Graves district and the rich, sweet wine produced in Barsac and Sauternes. The same weather conditions may provide opposite results, because the sweet wines are picked a month later.

1969. Because of the late summer the regional white wine will be relatively poor. The great vineyards, like Yquem, because of rigorous selection will be outstanding. White wine will range from 13 to 17, depending on selection.

1968. A poor year. 11.

1967. In Sauternes, this is the best year since 1962 and can be pronounced great. 18. In Graves, particularly in such wines as Château Haut-Brion Blanc, the whites are fresh, well-balanced, vigorous and dry. 17.

1966. Sauternes and Barsac completely failed here. 10. The dry white wines of Graves fared much better. They are rich in flavor, balance and finesse (defined as a quality of subtle refinement and distinction). 16.

1965. Poor in both Sauternes and Graves. 9.

1964. Excellent in Graves, but somewhat heavy. Lacks finesse. 15. Sauternes performed poorly. 10.

1963. Should be ignored. 8.

1962. The Sauternes, including Château d'Yquem, are glorious. 18. Be careful about the dry whites of Graves—they are getting too old. 15.

1961. Great in Sauternes and Barsac. Will last many more years. 19. Only a few of the dry whites have survived.

1960. Of no interest. 8.

1959. Great heights achieved in Sauternes. Will last for decades. 20. The dry whites are now too old. 8.

RED BURGUNDY

1969. If the Hospices de Beaune auction is an index, 1969 here will go down as the most sought-after and most expensive vintage in history. The crop is half of normal. Some compare it to 1923, the greatest vintage of the century; others compare it with 1961, the best of the decade. Long-lived, well balanced, great depth—at least in the class of 1966. 19.

1968. Gloomy, undoubtedly the worst year since World War II. 9.

1967. Although this was an excellent vintage in southern Burgundy, there was ill fortune along the Côte d'Or. There was frost in the spring, then considerable loss due to summer hail—followed by cold and rainy days just before the harvest. Most '67 Burgundies proved much too light, lacking in balance and color. 10.

1966. Outstanding year. Great fragrance, fruit and superb balance. Will prove to be a better year than '64 or '59. Shows remarkable promise of longevity. 19.

1965. Skip this year completely. 8.

1964. Rich in fruit, well balanced, big and sturdy. Sufficient depth and staying power to indicate many glorious years ahead. A worthy successor to the '61s. *18.*

1963. To be ignored; a dismal failure. *9.*

1962. Following so soon after the great '61s, the '62s did not receive their proper recognition. The wine is not simply good but can be considered great. Red Burgundies ideally suited for present drinking. *17.*

1961. Here we must shout "Bravo!" and salute. The production in 1961 was half of normal and the wines are of exceptional quality and longevity. The better vineyards will still be great twenty years from now. *20.*

1960. A year to forget. *8.*

1959. If you seek great red Burgundy vibrantly alive with fruit and charm, drink the '59s for the next few years. *18.*

BEAUJOLAIS (SOUTHERN BURGUNDY)

The rule is simple: If the label reads "Beaujolais" or "Beaujolais-Villages," choose the youngest possible year, preferably to be consumed within two years of its birth. Beaujolais does not live long. Do not get involved with anything older than 1964. However, the *grands crus*, such as Fleurie, Morgon, Moulin-à-Vent, may be at their best three to six years after the harvest.

1968. Amazingly lucky. Not far below 1967 in quality. *16.*

1967. A small crop, but the best Beaujolais produced in many years. The simpler Beaujolais is fresh, rich in fruit, and with a disarming, arborlike bouquet. The better ones, from the renowned villages, will be well balanced and have six or seven years of good life ahead. *19.*

1966. A record-breaking production of all the fine Beaujolais. Softer and less firm than the '67s. *18.*

1965. Never mind these. *10.*

1964. The simple, less expensive ones are now too old, for the fragrance and flavor of the grape are gone. Any of the nine village appellations (Brouilly, Chénas, Chiroubles, Fleurie, Juliénas, Morgon, Moulin-à-Vent, St.-Amour) will provide joyous drinking for another three years. *16.*

WHITE BURGUNDY

1969. Like the red burgundies, the whites have been produced in limited quantity, are extremely expensive, and are truly great. Be on the lookout for them. They are long-lived. *19.*

1968. Fared better than the red. Good acidity and fresh, but not for laying down. *13.*

1967. A variable year. A May frost destroyed over half of Mâcon's and Pouilly-Fuissé's crop, leaving Chablis untouched; a July hailstorm inflicted added damage to the hopes of many growers, often leaving a next-door neighbor unscathed. The result was that very bad and extraordinarily fine white wines were produced simultaneously. Thus, white Burgundies range from 10 to 19, depending upon nature's kindness or malice.

1966. Better than '64 and in the exalted class of '61, wines of airy lightness and extraordinary bouquet. The wines of Chablis and Pouilly-Fuissé are outstanding. *18.*

1965. Relatively good in Chablis, but generally not acceptable elsewhere. *12.*

1964. Fruity, full-bodied, but somewhat uneven. Similar to 1959 in weight and ripeness. *17.*

1963. Showed early promise, but can be forgotten now. *10.*

1962. Beautifully balanced, relatively light, much finesse, good for present drinking but not for laying down. *16.*

1961. The most long-lived of all white Burgundies since 1952, these are just demonstrating their stature now, and many of the great ones, like Montrachet, Meursault and Corton-Charlemagne, have a decade of glorious life ahead of them. *19.*

Côtes du Rhône

1969. Excellent throughout the valley. Low production, great depth and flavor—the equal of 1966. *19.*

1968. As the region had more sun than Burgundy, many satisfying wines were produced, although not up to 1967. *15.*

1967. The reds are full-bodied and well worth drinking. *16.* The whites and rosés did not fare as well. *12.*

1966. Excellent everywhere. The red Hermitage and Châteauneuf-du-Pape, Hermitage, Condrieu and Château-Grillet are also superb. *18.* The rosés, including Tavel, are the best in many years. *19.*

1965. The reds are fruity but light. *15.*

1964. The reds are big, of great weight, but relatively hard and somewhat unbalanced. *14.*

1963. To be ignored. *8.*

1962. A very good year—followed the pattern of Burgundy. *17.*

1961. Best year in the Rhône since World War II. Great depth, beautiful balance, much fruitiness and great longevity. *19.*

LOIRE VALLEY

1969. A good summer, preceded by satisfactory flowering, happily followed by good weather at the time of the harvest—giving us good quality throughout the Loire Valley. The Muscadet is a delight, and look for good Pouilly-Fumé and Sancerre. *19*.

1968. A bright spot in a generally bad year for France. Some excellent Muscadet and Pouilly-Fumé produced. *15*.

1967. A great year everywhere in the Loire, whether it be Vouvray, Muscadet, Pouilly-Fumé, Sancerre, Anjou or Chinon. All are fresh, glowing with fruit, vigorous, and well balanced. *19*.

1966. On a relatively high level throughout. *16*.

1965. Uniformly poor. *8*.

1964. The reds are still thriving. *17*. The dry whites and rosés are now too old. *10*.

1963. Alas. *8*.

ALSACE

1969. Escaped some of the bad weather which hit the rest of France. The result is normal quantity, high quality, and typical Alsatian wines. *18*.

1968. Not outstanding, but some satisfactory white wines produced. *13*.

1967. Yielded a quantity below the norm, some failures in the lesser wines, but in summation we can consider this the best year in Alsace in the last decade. Rieslings and Gewürztraminers have extraordinary bouquet and balance. *19*.

1966. A great year. It shares neither the failures nor the heights achieved in '67, but the average is superb. *17*.

1965. A failure. *9*.

1964. The distinguishing characteristics of this vintage are great weight and much power, but the wine lacks subtlety and can often be dull. *14*.

1963. Was acceptable when young, now over the hill. *10*.

1961. The good Rieslings and Gewürztraminers are surprisingly excellent and actually taste young. Superb bottles can be found in the United States. *16*.

1960. Over the hill. *8*.

1959. They were always too heavy and rich in alcohol. Now they are completely gone. *10*.

CHAMPAGNE

Champagne shippers declare a vintage only periodically, and most of the wine they sell bears no vintage at all. Unless the storage conditions have been perfect, these declared vintage years are now too old for present drinking: '52, '55 and, in some instances, '59. These years represent excellence for current consumption: '61, '62 and presently '64. As for the future, the vintage years of 1966 and 1967 are reported to be outstanding.

RHINE AND MOSELLE

1969. The world press, shortly after the harvest, compared 1968 German wines to the great '53s. This forced the price up, but not the quality. In truth, the average, less costly wines are on a relatively high level, but no peak of great Auslese quality was achieved anywhere in the Rhine and Moselle valleys. 1969 can be considered a midpoint between 1966 and 1967—a useful but not a great year. 17.

1968. No great wines were achieved, but some pleasant small wines, thanks to sugaring, are available. 13.

1967. Greatness and failures exist side by side. You will find truly great wines from the Rhine and the Moselle—especially among the dramatically rich Auslese, Beerenauslese and Trockenbeerenauslese, the best of our generation. But, alas, some of the lesser wines are poorly balanced. Over-all, the equal of 1964. 17.

1966. Although rain prevented the production of Beerenauslese and Trockenbeerenauslese, all of the Rhines and Moselles below this exalted level achieved outstandingly high quality. Just showing their greatness now, with at least five good years ahead. 18.

1965. Slightly below average. Drinkable but not outstanding. 12.

1964. The Rhines are a bit too fat in body but most pleasant for present drinking. 16. The Moselles turned out fresh, of good constitution. 17.

1963. Should be overlooked. 10.

1962. Relatively dry, fresh, light, but never dramatically big. Still good. 14.

1961. Sound, useful wines without distinction. 12.

1960. Very poor. 8.

1959. The greatest year since 1921. The inexpensive wines either are gone or are too old, but the great Spätlese and Auslese are the best German wines we can possibly drink today or even five years hence. True dramatic glories, they deserve the highest award. If you can acquire them, you are lucky. 20.

DISTILLED SPIRITS

It is important to recognize that distilled spirits can vary tremendously. Those that are distilled at relatively low proof in alcohol, such as bourbon, Scotch, rum and brandy, will show a great range of flavor, bouquet and character and will profit the most with further aging in barrel. Others, like vodka and gin, which are distilled at relatively high proof, do not gain by further aging. The point of all this is that the money-wise drinker should consider a low price a more important factor when he acquires his gin and vodka—and perhaps be willing to spend a bit more for his whiskeys and brandy if the taste, because of aging or uniqueness in flavor, becomes mellower, more rounded and more pleasing to him.

We are not suggesting that you buy the most highly advertised bourbon on the shelf, which can easily approach $10. Nor are we asking that you buy the cheapest bourbon on the shelf simply because its cost is below $4. To extract the maximum enjoyment for the money spent, in most instances, your wisest choice would be somewhat in between; the rule of moderation prevails even here.

Scotch

Almost every Scotch you are likely to run across is a blend of malt whiskeys made in pot stills and grain whiskeys made in patent or continuous stills. The smoky flavor comes from the malt whiskeys which are made entirely of barley. The grain whiskeys are distilled at a high proof, become almost neutral and thus add lightness to the ultimate blend. Usually, twenty different whiskeys are "married" in old sherry casks to give the blend its harmony. The relative proportion of malt to grain determines the character: 50 percent malt gives you a relatively heavy, flavorsome whiskey, and 30 percent malt provides a lighter and more neutral-tasting whiskey. Most Scotches today are lower in malt, following the present trend toward lightness and paleness.

All Scotch whiskeys imported into the United States must be at least four years old, but the age is not usually stated on the label. In fact, the average age of most Scotches runs closer to six years. The premium Scotches that sell for about $9 a bottle, such as Johnnie Walker Black, Bell's, Chivas and Haig Pinch, now arrive with the 12-year age proudly displayed on the label.

Practically all of the Scotches imported in bottle are either 86 or 86.8 proof. Most of the Scotches shipped in barrel and bottled in the United States are 80 proof. The reason for this is that the importer of Scotch in bulk gets a reduction on his duty based on proof and gets a full 20 percent reduction when the proof is moved down from 100 to 80 proof by simply adding distilled water. This is reflected in the lower price at which domestic-bottled Scotch is being offered to the American public. For the large cocktail party, where economy is an important factor, we unhesitatingly recommend that you buy domestic-bottled Scotch whiskey to profit by the important savings involved.

There has been a recent trend in America toward appreciating the unique excellence of the straight all-malt unblended Scotches. These are noble spirits that are comparable to a fine old bourbon and a fine cognac. Among them I can recommend Smith's Glenlivet 12-year-old and Glenfiddich 10-year-old. As an interesting conversation piece after dinner, try serving either of these in a brandy inhaler neat, not filling the glass more than one third of its capacity, so that you can enjoy the bouquet—just as you might with good brandy.

BOURBONS

The most popular whiskey in America is bourbon, a fact borne out by the staggering sales figures of such brands as Old Crow, Jim Beam, Old Grand-dad, Harper, etc.

By law, no whiskey can be called bourbon unless the proportion of the corn in the total mash is at least 51 percent. The higher the percentage of corn, the lighter the taste of the whiskey. Since the Federal Government does not permit bourbon to be distilled at a proof above 160, the result is that it is a relatively full-bodied, rich-in-taste kind of whiskey. However, the U. S. Government will permit a new category called "light whiskey" (starting to be made now but not legally on the market until 1972, when it acquires enough barrel age), distilled above 160 proof. This is consistent with the new trend toward "lightness," regardless of the bouquet and rich taste that will be lost in the process.

Many bourbon distillers proudly talk about "sour mash," and the phrase often appears on the label. In truth, practically all bourbons are made by the sour-mash process. However, some choose to use the phrase and some do not, purely for marketing purposes. It is questionable whether anyone could detect the difference by taste. The important thing to look for is a well-balanced, pleasant bourbon regardless of the process used.

The phrase "bottled in bond" on the label does not guarantee quality. If the whiskey is poor from the start, the fact that it is bottled in bond will not help the ultimate product. All the phrase means is that the whiskey has aged in a U. S. Government warehouse at least four years and has been bottled at the proof of 100, which gives it a stronger, more alcoholic taste than the 86-proof bourbons.

CANADIAN WHISKEYS

The rate of growth and sale of Canadian whiskeys on the American market during the last few years has been astonishing. The two best sellers are

Seagram's VO and Canadian Club. As in the instance of Scotch, many importers are bringing in their Canadian whiskey in bulk, bottling it here, and offering it to the consumer at a considerably lower price.

Canadian whiskey is not a single whiskey, like a bourbon or an all-malt Scotch, but rather a blend of whiskeys made from rye, wheat, corn and malt, with no one grain predominating. Since they are distilled at a higher proof than American whiskeys, the effect is that they are considerably lighter-bodied than their American counterparts. In character, they are similar to best sellers among American whiskeys containing neutral spirits, such as Four Roses, Schenley Reserve and Walker's Imperial.

AMERICAN SPIRIT BLENDS

Spirit blends are generally referred to as rye whiskey, although usually they contain more corn than rye. The names of the more popular blends such as Imperial, Seagram's Seven Crown, Four Roses, Schenley Reserve, Lord Calvert and P. M. have become familiar household words.

These spirit blends usually contain from 30 to 40 percent straight whiskey, the balance of alcoholic content being made up with neutral spirits—a pleasant term for what is practically pure alcohol. They all have in common a minimum of flavor and lightness of body. If made well, they can provide a most pleasant beverage for those who want the effect of whiskey without getting involved in too much taste, and they are excellent for mixed drinks such as sours. Because body and flavor are not the prime ingredients, it is wiser here, as in the instance of vodka and gin, to seek out the lower-priced blends. Provided you find the taste satisfactory to you, why not take advantage of the saving represented by the serving of an obscure name rather than one that is nationally advertised?

BRANDIES

Because there is an aura and a ritual about brandy drinking, the uninformed tend to revere age without relation to quality. Let us not worship age in brandy for age's sake but look for the brandy that genuinely tastes and smells fine.

The United States Government defines "brandy" as a "distillate obtained solely from the fermented juice, mash or wine of fruit." This means there can be grape brandy, pear brandy, apricot brandy, etc. Interestingly enough, America produces a good apple brandy which is worthy of more popularity than it presently enjoys.

The most famous of the grape brandies bears the highly geographic name "cognac." No distillate can be called cognac unless it is distilled from grape wine in the Cognac region of southwest France. All cognacs are grape brandies, but not all grape brandies are cognacs. To understand cognac, let us look to the "stars." These are simply trade designations which go somewhat as follows:

3-Star or *5-Star.* The youngest and basic cognac of the French distilleries.
VSOP or *VSEP.* The first initials stand for "very superior old pale." The
VSOPs are generally darker, older and finer than those that just bear the
stars. VSEP means "very superior extra pale."
Grande Fine Champagne and Fine Champagne. These phrases have important meanings, since they cannot be applied to the label unless the
grapes used come from the best "fine" regions of Cognac known as
Grande Champagne and Petite Champagne. (The word "Champagne"
here bears no relation to the famed sparkling wine produced in the
northeast of France.)
Napoleon. This phrase has no significance whatsoever, but merely creates
an aura of antiquity. It bears no direct relationship to the contents, age
or quality within the bottle.
Unblended Cognac. There are several examples of cognac available, varying
in age from twenty to forty years (the age statement is not permitted on
the label by French or U. S. Federal law). These usually turn out to be
the best examples of fine, untampered cognac available today.

A cousin to cognac is the Armagnac brandy produced in southwest
France. The grape, climatic conditions, soil, distilling process and aging
casks are different. The result is that Armagnacs tend to be fuller-bodied
lacking the delicacy, finesse, bouquet and flavor shown by cognac. The
taste may be earthier, but it has its own validity for those who want depth
of flavor and rich roundness.

Some adequate brandies are produced within the United States, and the
most popular ones are Christian Brothers, Masson Deluxe, Assumption
Abbey and Coronet VSQ. They lack the finesse of cognac, but are reasonably satisfying and acceptable.

For those who want to try imported brandies other than those from
France, the ones most worth considering are:

COUNTRY	NAME	CHARACTERISTIC
Italy	STOCK GRAND RESERVE	Rough, earthy
Germany	ASBACH URALT	Common; lacks finesse
Greece	METAXA 3-STAR	Dark, sweet
Israel	CARMEL 5-STAR	Pleasant; not delicate
Spain	DOMECQ FUNDADOR	Full, sweet; no great distinction

WHITE BRANDIES, OR EAUX-DE-VIE

Some excellent colorless brandies are made from other fruit. The most
esoteric and most sought-after, with the greatest finesse, is the Framboise
of Alsace and the German Black Forest, made of wild raspberries picked at
high altitude. Next is kirsch, distilled from cherries, which finds its best
expression in Switzerland and Alsace. And just below is Mirabelle, which

is made from yellow plums of Alsace. Another favorite is the Eau-de-Vie de Poire distilled from the Williams pear in Switzerland. (I happen to prefer the pear brandy made not far from Avignon on an island in the River Rhône.)

All of these white, bone-dry, colorless fruit brandies are costly to produce, because an amazing quantity of fruit is required to make a single bottle. The cost varies from $8 to $15, but in the long run it may not prove expensive, since a small amount can impart an hour's aroma to your brandy glass, give real meaning to your coffee and work wonders with your fruit dessert. Do not look for American substitutes in this area; an ounce from Alsace or Switzerland has more true flavor than a whole bottle of the domestic variety.

RUMS

Rum, in a sense, started with Christopher Columbus, for he developed sugar-cane plantations in the West Indies. The U. S. Treasury defines rum as any distillate from the fermented juice of sugar cane or sugar cane by-products such as molasses or cane syrup.

All rums are not alike. They vary tremendously, and the final product is affected by soil, climate, the raw material used, method of production, and aging. Anyone can tell the difference between a Puerto Rican rum, with its vodka-like lightness, and a heavy, pungent Jamaican rum. The most popular of the rums are the light-bodied rums, which are produced predominantly in Puerto Rico, with some from the Virgin Islands and the continental United States. The more full-flavored rums come from Jamaica, Barbados, Martinique, Demerara and New England. An intermediary rum called Barbancourt, produced in Haiti, is a distillate of the sugar cane rather than molasses.

Most rum distilleries produce a white or silver label and a gold or amber label. The former are lighter in color and are drier. The gold label is deeper in color and slightly sweeter and often aged for a longer period. The color is generally produced by the simple process of adding caramel. For visual reasons, it is wiser to use the light-colored rum in cocktails and the dark-colored rum in tall drinks. For those who want to save money when they buy their rum and still retain good quality, we recommend rum from the Virgin Islands, which can be obtained under such names as Old St. Croix, Cruzan or Pedro. All three of these can be obtained in most stores below $4 a bottle.

GINS

Gin was invented in the seventeenth century by a physician in Holland. He mixed juniper berries with pure alcohol, redistilled it and offered it as a therapeutic for the ills of his patients. It is still the juniper berry that remains the important flavoring in gin.

Because of the differences in botanical flavorings used, all dry gins are not alike, nor do they taste alike. However, we suspect that few of you could either detect your favorite brand or tell the difference between gins submitted to you for a blind tasting. It is possible to tell a British gin from an American gin, because the British gins are distilled at a slightly lower proof and thus a higher content of flavor remains in the final product. In addition, in London they use English water and not American water—and this makes a difference. The word "dry" in gin simply means absence of sweetness, and this is true of practically every gin you can possibly buy, whether it be the most highly advertised or a liquor dealer's private label. There is no necessity to age gin. However, some producers, such as Seagram's, do keep their gin in wood for a short period of time to impart a golden color.

If you can trust your wine and spirits merchant and if he does have a house brand considerably below the price of a nationally advertised brand, we recommend that you try it. The differences in gin are simply not great enough to justify paying a dollar a bottle more to make your Martini. The effect of the ice and the cold temperature, then the vermouth, are surely enough to obliterate any apparent distinction that may have existed originally between an expensive and a less expensive gin.

VODKA

Since no botanicals are used at all in vodka making, it is the perfect beverage for those who want the effect of alcohol without the element of taste. Vodka can fairly be described as "odorless, colorless and tasteless." Basically, vodka is nothing but alcohol, or, euphemistically, "neutral spirits." It goes with almost anything—orange juice, tomato juice, beef bouillon, vermouth—and even "on the rocks."

The growth in popularity of vodka during the last fifteen years is phenomenal. It started from almost nothing and threatens to outsell gin in the next decade. The most sought-after vodka is made by Smirnoff and is world-famous.

Now we have vodka reaching us from Moscow, Warsaw and London. These imports command from $6 to $8 a bottle, have a bit more flavor than their American counterpart and are excellent when served iced as an accompaniment to smoked salmon or caviar.

As in the instance of gin, trust your merchant, provided you have confidence in him, to select a vodka for you that will save you money and still retain good quality.

LIQUEURS, OR CORDIALS

Basically, cordials and liqueurs are products obtained by mixing neutral spirits or brandy with fruits, plants, flowers or various herbs. This can be done by percolation, maceration or infusion.

The range in variety of liqueurs is endless. Here are some familiar ones:

The anise family. This includes Pernod, Ricard, Ojen, Raki, Pastis and Anise.
The fruits and flowers. The common ones are apricot, blackberry, cherry, coffee, cocoa, cassis, violet, orange curaçao, kummel, maraschino, crème de menthe, triple-sec orange, and peach.
Unique and often secret formulas. B and B, Benedictine, Chartreuse, Cherry Heering, Cointreau, Cordial Médoc, Drambuie, Forbidden Fruit, Grand Marnier, Irish Mist, Galliano, Southern Comfort, Strega and Vieille Curé.

Except for the unique specialties from Europe, I recommend that you buy the liqueurs produced domestically in the United States, because of the dramatic price savings. In my opinion, the best of the European producers is Marie Brizard. For those who want a French product at considerably lower cost, I suggest Cusenier, which is imported in barrel and bottled here for a dramatic saving. Among the domestic producers, I recommend Arrow, Bols, Cointreau, Dekuyper, Garnier, Heublein and Hiram Walker. The American liqueurs should cost between $4 and $4.75 the bottle; their European counterparts range anywhere from $7.50 to $10.

VERMOUTHS—DRY AND SWEET

Dry, or pale, vermouth originated in France but is now produced in many countries. Sweet, or dark, vermouth originated in Italy and is now made almost everywhere on the globe.

The dry, "French" vermouth is a basic ingredient in the Martini and is often served by itself on the rocks with a twist of lemon. The sweet, "Italian" vermouth is a basic ingredient in a Manhattan and is now the most popular apéritif of France and many other countries—generally served with ice and a twist of lemon.

A dry vermouth is a white wine which is infused with several botanicals blended for uniformity and is fortified with brandy to bring it up to 20 percent alcohol. The famed dry vermouths of Europe are Noilly Prat, Martini & Rossi, Cinzano and Boissière—all selling for about $2.50 the bottle. The well-received American dry vermouths are Tribuno, Lejon, G. & D., Heublein, and Christian Brothers—all selling for about $1.50 the bottle.

All of these, whether they be European or American, are quite acceptable. We suggest you start with a low-priced brand and work your way up if you do not find it satisfactory. Some dry vermouths, in their quest for absolute paleness in color, have given up a bit of their flavor in the process.

The sweet, "Italian" vermouth follows the procedure used in making the dry vermouth. It starts with a white wine, to which Muscat wine is added for sweetness and flavor and caramel to deepen the color. The more popular sweet vermouths from Europe are Cinzano, Martini & Rossi, Carpano, Cora, and Boissière, all about $2.50 the bottle. The popular American sweet vermouths are Tribuno, Lejon, Christian Brothers, and G. & D., all about $1.50 the bottle.

THE FORTIFIED WINES

Fortified wines are those to which alcohol has been added either to stop the fermentation, as in port, or to raise the alcoholic content, as in sherry. Nature provides up to about 14 percent alcohol by volume as a maximum. Fortification adds sufficient alcohol or brandy to bring the percentage up to 18 to 20 percent, varying by type and country of origin.

SHERRY

The first of the fortified wines to become popular was sherry, which originated in Spain in a delimited area north of Cádiz in Andalusia. Part of sherry's popularity is due to its wide range, varying from the bone-dry and pale, which can be served as a refreshing apéritif, to the full, dark, rich, sweet sherry that can be served after dinner as a liqueur.

If you like your sherry dry, stick to the Fino family, which includes Manzanilla, Fino (the most famous is Tío Pepe) and Amontillado. These are pale in color, definitely dry, and can be served on the rocks, particularly during warmer weather, as a cool refresher.

If you like your sherry medium or sweet, move on to the Oloroso family. These are heavier and darker and include the medium-dry Amoroso (Dry Sack), the usually sweet Oloroso, the nutty and sweet Cream Sherry (Harvey's Bristol Cream), and the very sweet, full-bodied, very dark, brown sherry.

The sherries produced in California and New York State outsell those that come from Spain, because of nationalism and the lower price levels at which they can be obtained. It is not unusual to be able to obtain a full quart of California sherry for about a dollar. How do they compare? As in the instance of Spanish sherries, U. S. sherries can be obtained in three categories—dry, medium and sweet. However, few domestic wine houses achieve the Solera blending and long aging that prevails in Jerez. Instead of fermenting in the sun and air, California sherries are usually treated in barrel or bulk by various high-temperature techniques. American sherries do have a similarity in taste to their Spanish counterparts but, in general, are inferior. If your wine merchant is an astute buyer and has good taste judgment, he can offer excellent sherries from Spain, ranging from the very dry to the sweet, somewhere between $2 and $3 the bottle.

PORT AND MADEIRA

The sale and popularity in the United States of European port and Madeira is relatively small. We recommend authentic vintage port (a favorite in England) for its unique taste qualities. A good wooded port can be an intriguing after-dinner drink. Most of the port we see does not come from Portugal, but is California-made. "Any port in a storm" is taken fairly literally here.

Madeira, like sherry, can be drunk both as an apéritif and as a dessert wine. It is the longest-lived of any wine, and some of it, still available, dates back to the eighteenth century. Madeiras are named after the grapes that are used, ranging from the dry Sercial to the rich, sweet Malmsey. James Beard considers Madeira perhaps the most useful of all wines as an ingredient in cooking because of its high volatile acidity, which lends increased flavor to the many recipes that call for a fortified wine.

MONEY-SAVING TIPS ON WINES AND SPIRITS

If 100-proof vodka can be obtained for slightly more than 80-proof vodka, buy it, add 20 percent water, and your 100-proof will be identical to the 80-proof.

Do not waste money by buying a big bottle of champagne when there are only two of you. Once opened, it becomes valueless in just a few hours. A half bottle is a better choice when it is "dinner for two."

Buy a gallon jug of Louis Martini or Almadén red wine. Accumulate five empty bottles and five corks. Pour the wine into the bottles and cork them. Magically, the cost of a bottle will average out at only 89 cents. Another reason to do this: If your consumption is not rapid enough, the wine will oxidize and turn sour after a period of time in the large gallon bottle, due to exposure to air.

To serve a superb premium Scotch at low cost, buy six bottles of a low-priced blended Scotch and one bottle of Smith's Glenlivet or Glenfiddich unblended all-malt Scotch. Pour the contents of the seven bottles into a container and mix them. Refill the seven bottles and put on your own label, which might read, "John Smith's Personal Selection." We promise you the result will be as good as any $9 Scotch on the market.

To serve a low-cost apéritif as sophisticated as that in the most elegant Parisian restaurant, buy a bottle of the French white Burgundy Pinot Chardonnay (the cost should be about $1.50) and add one teaspoon of crème de Cassis. Serve cold. The result: the most delightful, beautiful, dry rose-colored apéritif known to man. In France they call it "Kir" in honor of the bishop who was head of the French Resistance and, until recently, mayor of Dijon.

Everybody loves B and B, but it costs almost $10 the bottle. Buy a bottle of Benedictine (not B and B) and a bottle of French cognac priced at about $6 or less. Mix them in equal parts. Your average cost will drop from $10 to $8 per bottle.

Compare the cost of the prepared bottle Martini and the one you mix yourself. Then get a good, low-priced 90-proof American gin and mix it in your favorite ratio with a low-priced American dry vermouth such as Tribuno. Savings—at least 30 percent.

Save money when serving a champagne, Rhine wine or claret punch by simply adding half as much club soda as the basic wine.

When it comes to a flavoring spirit such as kirsch, buy the best. It is much cheaper in the long run. One ounce of good Swiss kirsch will impart more flavor than ten ounces of a substitute.

Use a gallon of good California wine to make claret lemonade or punch. The cost per drink will be less than beer—especially if you add some club soda.

The least expensive drink we know of is called a "spritzer." It consists of half a lemon, two ice cubes, four ounces of white wine and four ounces of club soda. The total cost is not much more than 10 cents.

Look for interesting off-the-beaten-path wines of interesting origin that can be obtained below $2.00 the bottle, such as those of Alsace, Chile, the south of France, the Loire, Portugal, Spain and the Rhône Valley.

HOW TO GIVE GOOD PARTIES FOR LESS MONEY

The cocktail party as a way to entertain guests, especially large groups, has become an American institution, and it is probably one of the easiest ways to entertain because it follows no rigid pattern. It is our belief that the average person can give a cocktail party that will exemplify good living at its best without going to a great deal of expense and trouble.

First, the drinks. Giving a cocktail party does not mean you have to open a complete bar. With a bottle or two of gin, vodka, blended whiskey, Scotch and bourbon and a bottle each of dry and sweet vermouth, you should be able to fill most orders. In summer, you might want to add a bottle of good rum too. If you have friends who prefer to stick to less alcoholic drinks, as many people do now, add a bottle of a good apéritif such as Lillet, Campari or Punt e Mes, and provide tomato juice and Perrier water for the dieters or those who don't drink at all.

Never waste good straight expensive whiskey on cocktails. Save it for those who drink theirs in highballs or on the rocks, and use a less costly blend for Manhattans and Old-Fashioneds. Discuss brands with your liquor dealer. If he suggests something unfamiliar, don't say, "I never heard of it, so it can't be any good." Just because the manufacturer has not spent a lot of money to advertise his brand does not mean it is inferior. Try out your dealer's suggestion in a pint size and buy in larger quantities only if his recommendation pleases you. Remember also that when you find a brand you like you will save money by buying it by the case—no small saving figured on an annual budget.

For drinks on the rocks and for highballs, we contend that the average serving should be a liberal 2 ounces and that the amount of soda, water or ginger ale in a highball should be governed by the taste of the person drinking, not the one who is mixing the drinks. When you are serving liquor this way, count on getting 16 drinks, no more, from a quart bottle.

There are two distinct points of view about who should mix the drinks. Some people like the idea of the host preparing the first round and then letting the guests "ad lib" their own. Others prefer to have someone definitely assigned to the job of bartender. My opinion is that if guests mix their own drinks, some will get good ones and others poor ones, depending on their knowhow and attention to what they are doing. If you want a high standard and uniformity of drinks, the host or his delegate should preside over the bar throughout the party—and the appointee, if he is not a professional bartender hired for the evening, should be someone who is willing to wait until the rush hour is over before serving himself, so that he will have a clear head and an accurate hand for mixing and pouring.

You don't need a whole battery of gadgets in order to make good drinks, nor a cabinetful of glasses to serve them in. Two good-sized types of glass—a double Old-Fashioned glass for on-the-rocks drinks and the versatile long-stemmed all-purpose wineglass (choose a size that holds 10 or 12 ounces) for everything from beer or mineral water to gin and tonic, apéritifs and cocktails—should be quite enough to see you through. It is always better to serve a drink in a glass that is a little too large than in one that is definitely too small; there is not only less chance of spillage but also, because the drink looks a lot more substantial, less rushing for refills when the level begins to drop.

The simpler your equipment, the simpler the whole process of making drinks becomes. Have good jiggers or measuring glasses (those bought at chemical-supply houses are certainly the most accurate and efficient). For stirring drinks, you need a good pitcher with a tight lip—or you may prefer the type of stirring glass and strainer that many professional bartenders use. The glass and its metal companion piece will provide you with a low-cost shaker as well, unless you already have an all-glass shaker you can use. A blender comes in handy for cocktails that need thorough mixing, such as daiquiris and sours. Other essentials are ice buckets, a good sharp bar knife, a bottle opener, a corkscrew, a small board for cutting lemons and a bar spoon for stirring. To this you might add one of those handy little gadgets that strip the peel from the lemon. Plus, of course, a few kitchen towels or washcloths for mopping up.

For large parties, you should also have a big alcohol-proof tray and a really large cooler for ice. If you can order ice cubes in a big insulated container, that is fine, but if you have to make and store them yourself, it pays to invest in the kind of vacuum container that will hold ice before and for the duration of the party.

As for the kind of food that goes best at cocktail parties, turn to our advice in Chapter 2.

How to Give a Wine-Tasting Party

The wine-tasting party is becoming increasingly popular all over the country, especially with the young married group, and with good reason. First, it provides an unusual and interesting way to have a group of friends in for a pleasant and congenial evening at a comparatively low cost. Second, it is an invaluable sociable way for all of you to learn something about wines and to try various bottles from your local merchant before you decide what to buy by the case for your own entertaining. You can also judge the best wines for the kind of food you like to serve, and then lay down your own modest wine supply (of which more later).

For a wine-tasting party, all you need is 8 bottles of different wines (don't try to have more—this is about all a nonprofessional can taste in one evening), cubes of French bread or plain crackers or bread sticks and about a pound of mild cheese, also cut into cubes, to clear the palate between tastings. Also supply a pitcher of water for rinsing glasses (one glass per person) and a large bowl for emptying out the water and any leftover wine, plus a kitchen towel or two for drying glasses. For a simple winetasting, have four bottles of white wine and four of red. You may choose to have all Burgundy or Bordeaux wines, a selection of wines from different California vineyards, a group from one country, such as Spain or Italy, or perhaps, in summer, a tasting of the lighter whites of the Rhine, the Moselle and Alsace. The natural progression is white before red, dry before sweet, light before fuller-bodied wines. Estimate half a bottle of wine, or 12 ounces, for each person; the average amount served at a tasting is about 1½ to 2 ounces from each bottle, so 8 bottles will be adequate for up to 16 people.

Arrange the bottles in groups—white and red, or light and full-bodied—in the order in which they should be tasted; that is, from the least important to the most important wine. Place the glasses in front of them and the cheese and bread at the sides of the table or on a small adjoining table if you don't have room for everything. Chill white or rosé wines for a couple of hours in the refrigerator and uncork the reds about 30 minutes to 1 hour before the party to let them breathe, a process that helps the bouquet and flavor to develop through contact with the air.

The strategy of tasting is quite simple and not at all esoteric. First a little wine is poured into the glass, which is then raised to the light so that you can judge its clarity and color. Then the glass is lowered and slowly rotated so that the wine swirls gently around the inside of the bowl, releasing the bouquet. Then, holding the glass by the base, you put your nose into the glass and take a good deep sniff of the bouquet. It is at this point that you can detect the fragant characteristics of the grape from which the wine was made, be it Cabernet Sauvignon, Pinot Chardonnay, Riesling or any of the other great varieties, and become aware of the aromas that distinguish the different wines. There is a noticeable difference between a Bordeaux and a Burgundy, or between the floweriness of a Moselle and the fullness of a white Burgundy such as a Chablis or a Montrachet.

Finally, take a sip and roll the wine around your mouth, letting it caress your tongue so that your taste buds can sort out and isolate its special qualities—freshness and youngness, floweriness and fruitiness, body and suavity, the degree of acidity or sweetness. When you have extracted the last nuance, swallow the wine. (Professionals, who have to taste many wines at a time, spit their mouthful out, but there is no need to go to this extreme; just let it slide down happily.) Jot down on a pad your impressions and comments, favorable or unfavorable, the name and the year of the wine, the name of the producer and the importer, and any other basic information contained on the label that you may need for future reference. Take a palate-clearing nibble of bread or cheese and go on to the next wine. At the end of the tasting, for half a bottle a head can hardly be considered an alcoholic orgy, you and your friends can relax over coffee and brandy and discuss the wines you have tasted.

Choosing Wines for Dinner Parties

A wine-tasting party or a judicious sampling of half bottles at your own evening meals will give you a pretty good idea of the wines within your price range that you want to lay in for your dinner parties, based on the kind of food you are likely to serve. Whole books have been written on the subject of choosing wines to go with different foods, and it is not our intention here to do more than give you a general guide to the kinds of wine to choose. Wherever possible, throughout this book, we have indicated reasonably priced wines that are appropriate to the menus or the dish.

Although many people now are apt to debunk the whole question of choosing appropriate wines for food, by saying that the wine you like is the best wine to serve with whatever you happen to be eating, there are some time-honored partnerships that deserve to be observed—notably the one about white wine with fish and red wine with hearty red meats or game— simply because they make good culinary sense. There are exceptions, of course. It is perfectly legitimate to serve a light red, such as a young Beaujolais, slightly chilled, with a rich, oily fish cooked in red wine—salmon, for instance. Or to serve an Alsatian white, a Sylvaner or Traminer, with wild boar. Certainly delicate game birds such as dove or quail taste better with the less dominant white wines. However, as a general rule, pair fish with white wines. If you happen to like white wines, you can also serve them with lighter, whiter meats such as veal, pork and ham, and, in the poultry field, with chicken, roast or poached turkey and even goose—a flowery Moselle or the acidity of a Meursault can help to cut its rich fattiness. Duck, on the other hand, seems to need the assertiveness of a red wine. Of course, when you are serving a poultry dish cooked with white or red wine, you would serve a similar wine with it, and the same holds true for meat dishes. Remember that richer foods take more robust wines. A light red would be fine with grilled steak, shish kebab or a simple beef stew, but roast prime ribs or a rack of lamb need a Burgundy or a Bordeaux to do them justice, and heavier, fuller wines are definitely needed when you serve roast meat with a Périgueux or Madeira sauce.

Regional foods and regional wines go hand in hand in every country. The garlic-redolent Bourride with Sauce Aïoli virtually demands a Provençal white wine, such as Cassis. Vitello tonnato is well served by Soave and Verdicchio, pasta with meat sauce and cheese by Chianti or Valpolicella. Paella takes kindly to a Spanish white Rioja, and Quiche Lorraine to an Alsatian wine, while barbecued chicken is happy with a California Zinfandel or a Gamay Beaujolais.

Generally speaking, wines do not belong with the hors-d'oeuvre course, unless you are having something like oysters or other seafood, or perhaps a pâté or quiche with which you could serve an Alsatian or German wine. Nor are table wines served with soup, although you can have a glass of dry Madeira or Amontillado with consommé, turtle or game soup or seafood bisque, if you like. They should definitely be kept away from foods containing vinegar (salads, mint sauce, Vegetables Vinaigrette) because vinegar is the enemy of wine. (If you wish to serve salad, use lemon juice in place of vinegar.) Curries and spicy chilis or hot South American dishes are not designed to partner wine (beer is a better drink for them), and neither are Oriental and sweet-and-sour dishes.

Wines belong with fish, with meat, with poultry, with game, and with cheese when this is served as a course on its own, after the entrée. Always pick a wine of equal stature with the cheese, neither greater nor lesser—a fine red Bordeaux for Brie and Camembert, a more modest red with a Boursault, Crema Dania, cheddar or Taleggio. If you have a maxim, let it be "The better the dish, the better the wine." Food that is a work of art deserves a wine of more consequence; food that is run-of-the-mill merely rates something pleasant to drink. You really can't improve mediocre food with glorious wine, and it would be a crime to try.

Few people nowadays, apart from the great wine connoisseurs, serve wine with the dessert course. They prefer to spend their money on the dry table wines, where it is more effective and necessary. If you wish to, the traditional and acceptable choices with sweet dishes are champagne (the extra dry harmonizes better than the austere brut), cream sherry, dessert port and Madeira, and the sweet white dessert wines—Sauternes, the German *Spätlese* and *Auslese*, or a California dessert wine. With fruit, fresh or poached, there are other choices. A light red wine or a sweet white wine can be very pleasant with fresh strawberries, raspberries, peaches and pears, and the spicy floweriness of Gewürztraminer is surprisingly good with apples.

If you are serving more than one wine with a meal, the progression is the same as at a wine tasting—white before red, dry before sweet, young before old, light before full-bodied, modest before great.

You may notice that we haven't touched on brut champagne or rosé wines as companions to food. The theory that champagne can be served with any course throughout a meal is a fallacy, in our opinion. In any case, if you are going to all that expense, champagne belongs on its own or with something as grand as fresh caviar or a marvelous foie gras, so it hardly concerns anyone interested in eating and drinking better for less money.

Rosés have a place, limited but acceptable, on a menu. You can serve them with certain lamb dishes, such as shish kebab, occasionally with pork or ham. They are really at their best with cold food or simple summer food, but they should certainly never be served with dishes of any consequence. If you do serve a rosé, be sure it is one with some character—a French Tavel or a California Grenache Rosé—not just a pink insipid liquid. But if you have only a limited amount of money to spend on wines, it is our advice to stick mainly with the reds and whites. With their wider, more interesting range to choose from—the wines of the world, in fact—you can make some felicitous discoveries and some very wise investments. Which brings us to the next step in wine buying and wine serving—the laying down of wines for future pleasure and profit.

LAYING DOWN WINE: THE WHYS AND WHEREFORES

Fifty dollars invested in wine will grow in value much faster than the same sum will yield in the bank, even at 6 percent interest—and, in addition to the financial advantages, you will get emotional dividends that cannot be measured by the Dow-Jones index but are equally valid.

By having your own wine cellar, you can buy the wines you like at the strategic moment when they are on sale, and often you can obtain a 10 percent discount because you are buying in a quantity of 12 or more bottles at a time.

The arguments for developing your own basic cellar (perhaps a better name would be "a library of wines") are many and varied. Here are some of the advantages:

You will have the personal pleasure of watching the bottles reach their maturity under your own loving guidance, reinforced by the knowledge that the wine becomes more valuable with each passing year.

You will no longer need to go to your wine merchant at the last moment and serve a wine that has been badly shaken en route from the store to the dinner table.

You will enjoy the happy privilege of making a leisurely selection based on your mood and that of your guests, and in harmony with your menu.

Like the book-lover, you will have the fun of lingering lovingly over your own labels and bottles. This will lead you into a new world of reading books on wine and thus expand your knowledge.

Before we guide you into how to select your wines wisely, we should comment briefly on the surroundings for wine which often scares people off unnecessarily.

As far as temperature is concerned, we obviously do not recommend that you store your wines next to a roaring furnace ar expose them to wintry weather. Not even the strongest among us would like such extreme conditions. As a rule of thumb, the temperature should not be much below 50 nor soar much above 75. These limits are adequate for the average household.

Wines do not require specially built shelves or elaborate wine racks. We have seen noble collections happily stored in their original wooden cases and on do-it-yourself shelves. Provided the wines lie on their sides so that the liquid remains in contact with the cork and prevents it from drying out, and the storage area is away from light and free from vibration—two factors that affect wine adversely—the setting has almost nothing to do with what happens in the bottle. The appearance of your wine-storage area depends entirely on your budget and your taste in decoration. Most people can afford to give up part of a closet or cabinet, and that alone is sufficient to start you off with a respectable number of bottles—say one or two mixed cases—that will supply you with a wine for just about every dish you want to serve. If your storage area is a closet, arrange the bottles so that the whites, which need to keep cool, are near the floor, then the rosés and champagne, and finally the reds, which can take a higher temperature. Have some method of identification so that you disturb the bottles as little as possible, and use the youngest, most ephemeral wines (those of Beaujolais, Alsace, the Loire) first. Try to keep the reds that need time to mature, such as the Bordeaux wines, some Burgundies and California Cabernet Sauvignons, until they reach their peak, and drink first the reds that do not need bottle age. For everyday drinking, keep on hand a couple of gallon or half-gallon jugs of California Mountain Red and Mountain White. For $50 to $75 you can amass a fairly respectable wine library, if you select from the suggestions below.

CHOICES FOR A $50 WINE CELLAR

(By expanding your selections or doubling the quantities, you can arrive at a $100 cellar if you want to start in a more ambitious fashion.)

Red Bordeaux: Four bottles from the vintages '61, '62, '64 and '66. Choose from the districts of the Médoc, St.-Émilion, Graves and Pomerol to get maximum variety of taste. Stick to château bottling.

Great medium-priced vineyards:

Beychevelle	Lascombes
Bouscaut	Lynch-Bages
Cos d'Estournel	Léoville Lascases
Dassault	Palmer
Gruaud-Larose	Pichon Lalande

White Bordeaux: Two bottles of '62, '64 or '66 château bottlings.
Graves—dry

Bouscaut	Haut-Brion Blanc
Domaine de Chevalier	Olivier

Sauternes or Barsac—sweet

Climens	Rayne-Vigneau
Latour Blanche	Yquem

Red Burgundies: Four bottles of '61, '62, '64 or '66 from any of the following vineyard areas of Burgundy.

Beaune	Pommard
Gevrey-Chambertin	Volnay
Nuits-St.-Georges	Vosne Romanée

White Burgundies: Two bottles from '62, '64 or '66. Choose estate bottlings from villages such as

Aloxe-Corton	Meursault
Chablis	Pouilly-Fuissé
Chassagne-Montrachet	Puligny-Montrachet

Vin Rosé: Two bottles for everyday drinking (the younger the better) from the vineyards of

Anjou	Provence
Tavel	Bourgogne

Also include some of the excellent California pink wines, made from the Grenache and Gamay varietals.

Vin du pays: Four bottles from '66 or '67. Trust a good wine merchant here to get young, fresh, charming wines. They should not be expensive and they should not remain in your cellar, generally speaking, for more than two years, else their freshness will go.

FRENCH RED	FRENCH WHITE
Beaujolais	Alsace
Châteauneuf-du-Pape	Muscadet
Côtes-de-Provence	Pouilly-Fumé
Côtes-du-Rhône	Sancerre
Crozes-Hermitage	Vouvray
Hermitage	Montlouis

OTHER REDS	OTHER WHITES
Italian Chianti or	Austrian Gumpoldskirchner
Valpolicella	Italian Verdicchio, Soave or
Portuguese Dão	Orvieto
Spanish Rioja	Swiss Fendant or Neuchâtel

American Reds: Don't overlook these. Some superb wines are produced in America, but unfortunately they are consumed too young. Two years in your cellar will make them taste dramatically better. Stick to the well-known growers of northern California and insist on varietal grape types, which are listed below in order of merit. Two bottles are recommended.

Cabernet Sauvignon   Gamay
Pinot Noir

American Whites: Two bottles of varietals from the following types in order of merit.

Pinot Chardonnay	Sauvignon Blanc
Johannisberg Riesling	Chenin Blanc
Semillon	Traminer

Rhines and Moselles: Estate bottlings here; avoid regionals. Two bottles— some glorious '59s plus mostly '66 and '67.

RHINES	MOSELLES
Eltville	Berncastel
Johannisberg	Brauneberg
Nierstein	Graach
Oppenheim	Piesport
Rauenthal	Urzig
Rudesheim	Wehlen

Champagnes: These are not included in a basic cellar, but you may want to acquire some. You will do well if you limit your selection to the following world-renowned firms.

FRENCH

Ayala	Moët et Chandon
Bollinger	Mumm
Charles Heidsieck	Piper-Heidsieck
Clicquot	Pommery
Heidsieck Monopole	Roederer
Krug	St.-Marceaux
Lanson	Taittinger

AMERICAN: CALIFORNIA	AMERICAN: NEW YORK STATE
Korbel	Charles Fournier Brut
Kornell	Gold Seal
Almadén	Great Western

The selections above have been limited to wines that nature has produced without further alcoholic embellishment by man, but most households cannot afford to ignore such fond, familiar creatures as sherry, port, Madeira, apéritifs and the basic brandies, gin, vodka, whiskeys, and liqueurs. As a useful checklist, below are other possible areas you should at least consider in order to achieve a well-rounded and quite complete bar.

Fortified Wines and Apértifs:

Byrrh	Madeira
Campari	Marsala
Dubonnet	Port
Dry vermouth	Punt e Mes
Kina Rok	Sherry
Lillet	Sweet vermouth

Spirits:

Aquavit	Gin
Armagnac	Irish whiskey
Blended whiskey	Rum
Canadian whiskey	Rye
Bourbon	Scotch whiskey
Cognac	Vodka

Liqueurs and Eaux-de-Vie:

Benedictine	Crème de Cassis
Chartreuse	Crème de menthe
Cherry Heering	Drambuie
Cointreau	Framboise

Grand Marnier   Pernod or Ricard
Kahlúa   Poire
Kirsch   Strega
Mirabelle

SERVING WINE

There is very little to the mystique of serving wine, whatever you may
have been led to believe. Apart from a good wine, your main needs are an
efficient corkscrew and wineglasses of a sensible shape and of a size that
will hold an average serving of wine (about 4 ounces) without the glass
being more than one-third to one-half full.

Choose the corkscrew that suits you best, preferably one that works by
leverage or draws the cork up smoothly so that the bottle is not jerked
while it is being opened.

We have long been convinced that one large (10- to 12-ounce), clear,
stemmed glass is ideal for white, red, and sparkling wines. As a matter of
fact, there is no more elegant way to present any number of liquids—
brandy, iced coffee or tea, fresh orange juice, Bloody Marys, highballs,
martinis on the rocks or even chilled summer soups. Our choice is the
tulip shape, free of any decoration and tapered inward at the rim to
capture the bouquet of the wine. Baccarat makes beautiful wineglasses
of this type, but for a more economical choice we particularly recommend
the Frank Schoonmaker "Magnum," a 10½-ounce size available in leading
department stores throughout the country. Good glasses represent a worthwhile investment; when you are serving wine it is false economy to settle
for the inferior dime-store variety.

Unless you are serving an old wine that has thrown a heavy sediment,
there is really no need to decant a wine. Standing the bottle upright for
from two to eight hours before dinner will give any trace of sediment time
to sink to the bottom. However, there are advantages to having a beautiful
decanter—mainly that it enables you to serve white or red jug wines at
table with a little more finesse. Also, the flavor and bouquet of a young
wine are often improved by the slight aeration afforded by the action of
pouring wine from a bottle into a decanter. (Except for jug wines, there
is no reason to decant a white wine. Simply refrigerate it for a couple of
hours or put it into a bucket of ice and water to chill naturally.)

The simplest, handsomest and most useful decanter we own is yet another product of Baccarat, but, surprisingly, it costs only $16.50. It is car-
ried by stores that sell Baccarat's fine glass. Look on a decanter like this
as yet another good investment. It will give you a lifetime of service and
pleasure. Not only wine, but also bourbon, Scotch or brandy poured from
it will give your entertaining an air of elegance, even though the contents
may be nothing more than the weekend special from your local liquor merchant. As with so many things in life, presentation is half the art of
good living.

INDEX